D1179808

WHEN THE ROAD ENDS

Dylan Samarawickrama
Martina Zuercher

Translated from
German by
Susanne Wagner.

Zürcher
PUBLISHING

Original version published in German by Zürcher Publishing, February 2015
"Am Ende der Strasse" ISBN: 978-3-9524448-0-1

First Edition in English published by Zürcher Publishing, December 2015

ISBN: 978-3-9524448-5-6
www.zuercher-publishing.ch

Text: Dylan Samarawickrama, Martina Zuercher
Translated from German: Susanne Wagner
Editing: Katherine L Ryan, Casey Cheuvront, Stephen Baker
Layout and Design: Martina Zuercher
Photography: Dylan Samarawickrama
Printed by: EUROPRINT a.s., Prague, Czech Republic.

Coverphoto: Anchored in Brujas, Panama.

To adventurers & dreamers.

A new motor for the *Courage of Bridget*: *El Mecánico* carries the second-hand motor to my raft.

Travelling brings out the essence of life: Bruce and I are overwhelmed by the beauty of our planet. Here in Salar de Uyuni, Bolivia.

PROLOGUE

~

I spend the day on the lookout for other boats.

Again and again I scan the horizon in all directions ...

Nothing!

Nothing but water ... water and then sky, converging at the very edge of my vision.

Shortly after noon I see dense, white clouds accumulating. My sail, which has been hanging listlessly for days begins to dance in the air, gently at first, then more energetically.

The surface of the water begins to change as well; only moments before it had a benign, mirror-like surface, but now friendly little waves have begun to roll towards my raft.

Minute by minute I feel the breeze become a decent wind. Is this my chance?

I get busy setting the sail but at that very moment the fishing line jerks – was that just the waves?

Sceptically I reach for the line that is tied to the bamboo mast; this replaced the fishing rod I lost a week earlier in the ocean.

I have never caught a fish before; maybe today is my lucky day?

I check the thin line between two fingers and feel an unequivocal twitch.

There definitely is a fish there!

Carefully I draw in the line and haul in my catch. It's a big one!

My first fish tries to free itself with wild jumps and I struggle to subdue it as the wind increases in strength. Typical!

For the last 48 hours I have been drifting aimlessly with nothing to do and now everything is happening all at once.

I work fast but it still takes a few minutes to free the thrashing fish from the hook and stun its head against the mast. It stops moving.

Celebrations must wait – the wind forces me to act immediately.

I set sail and hope that the wind is blowing in the right direction, against the treacherous current and towards the mainland.

I feel the motion straight away as the sail catches the wind.

Onwards! Finally!

I am elated but apprehensive. I do not know where the wind is taking me – further out into the ocean perhaps? I hope not and wait with bated breath, staring at the tiny display of my GPS. For a long time nothing happens, just slowly moving through a blue expanse, then finally I see the first dot … I bite my lip and wait for the second … There! And another one and another one until a line has formed: my route. I am headed for the mainland! What a relief! The wind is carrying me back towards civilisation.

I can feel the frustration of recent days falling off me, like shedding a rock from my shoulders.

"Yeah! Bruce, all will be well!

We're going back to Las Perlas!

All will be well! Yeehaw!"

The wind gets even stronger and blows into my sail. We are not going particularly fast though: only one mile per hour. I do not switch the motor on yet, hoping to take advantage of the wind to carry us within sight of the coast. All I want is to see a familiar sight, land and hopefully people. I catch myself thinking wistfully of life in Panama City, of the harbour, the *Kiosko*. I think of giving up, playing it safe, going back to where I had started. A change of wind distracts me: it increases in strength and so does our speed. Soon we are going at two, even three miles per hour. The more the gusts of wind whip up the water, the higher the waves grow. When I take my eyes off the GPS, I see that something has changed, on the horizon a thick, pitch-black wall of cloud is building up.

My joy disappears and is replaced with fear.

It is not just the clouds that make my hair stand on end but also the lightning that illuminates the squall line. My eyes cannot even register all of it, so frequently does it strike.

The clouds slide over the sky in thick ribbons. The storm is only a few miles away from me. The waves swell and the water's surface becomes choppy. White crests flash up for a moment before the wind tears them apart. The waves by now are about ten feet high. My horizon has shrunk – now all I can see are walls of water.

I freeze with fear for a minute or two, but then spring back into action. I roll the sail away so that we will not capsize. The wind and the waves make this task almost impossible as again and again I lose my hold on the canvas and the wind rips it from my hands and blows it in a frenzy of directions. The control line which is attached to a corner of the sail becomes a whip and I have to twist and turn like a boxer to avoid being hit, at the same time I try hard to catch it and bring the sail back under control. The raft is thrown every-which-way and I have to be careful not to lose my balance and get thrown overboard. So I brace against one of the bamboo masts, with my legs wide apart on the deck to gain stability.

Slowly, inch by inch I manage to turn the boom so the sail will wrap around it. It's an enormously difficult job. Everything I touch seems to slip away, as if my hands are smeared with grease. The constant exposure to salt water has made my skin soft and smooth and every grip requires three times as much energy as usual. But I am glad about one thing; that is to see that Bruce – my motorcycle – holds his position on the raft effortlessly. He stoically absorbs each jerk and jump of the raft without moving. As calm as you like, he defies the waves as if he were born for it. When I finally manage to wrap the sail around the I lay it down and tie it to the deck.

I think I can hear Jacques' voice, "Turn the bow against the waves, so you won't capsize."

For that I have to throw out my sea anchor. My version comprises of two old tyres, I had tied one end of a thick rope on to one tyre and the other end tied to the bow of the raft. A sea anchor creates a resistance underwater that acts as a brake. When wind pushes the raft in one direction it automatically turns the bow against both the waves and the wind, stabilizing the raft and keeping it from capsizing.

Slowly, I make my way to the bow of the raft and throw the tyre into the water. The tyre moves away from the raft. Then I see to my dismay that the rope comes undone and the tyre sinks and slowly disappears into the deep blue water.

"Dylan, you are an idiot! You are such an idiot!"

At this moment I remember that I untied the rope the day before, to use it for something else. I never bothered to tie it properly afterwards but just coiled it around the tyre in a slapdash fashion. "Argh! Idiot!"

There is no time to berate myself any further, the left side of the raft is exposed to the waves – and the next big one might cause a calamity. Hurriedly, I tie the rope to the second tyre, and double checking it is properly attached I throw it out into the water.

I begin to breathe easier when the raft begins to turn slowly against the wind and the waves. Now the raft seems to be more stable, however the worst is yet to come. The black clouds have caught up with us and the lightning strikes in ever shorter intervals. The chances of surviving a lightning strike out here are zero. In my mind's eye, I already see myself being struck and falling overboard, unconscious. The only comfort is that it would be a painless death.

There is a deafening sound. A lightning bolt strikes the foaming water only a few hundred yards away from the raft. If only I had a metal cabin in which I could hide.

Michael Faraday.

Michael Faraday! In the middle of this storm I remember the name of the scientist who showed that a closed metal cage protects from lightning … but what is the point of this knowledge when I can't apply it?!

I have never felt so helpless in my life.

The waves are enormous. I try not to look, focussing instead on my hands and on my feet and on what I can do to protect myself. I check once more if all my electrical appliances are switched off and secure everything that is loosely stored on the deck with ropes. Then I stretch a tarpaulin over Bruce, fix it tightly to the deck and creep underneath it.

The wind whips the tarp wildly and the sound mixes with the thunder. The noise is deafening. Even from under the tarpaulin and with closed eyes I can still see the bright flashes of lightning. Raindrops and splashing sea water mix with cold sweat. The raft lurches on the water like a roller-coaster. Left, right, up and down, all at breakneck speed. I hold on to Bruce with all my might, push my feet against the deck and hope to make it out alive. I just want it to be over, to go to sleep and wake up when the storm has gone. What the hell am I doing out here anyway?

Why am I all alone on a small raft and with a motorcycle lost in the Pacific?

The skyline of Panama City: It is in stark contrast with the rest of the country.

CHAPTER ONE

"Some people forget that they were mere dreams and chase after them until dreams become reality."

The first time I met László I noticed that he would always turn his head to the right to look at something. I suppose he was in his late thirties, tall, slim and tanned, the colour of his short hair as faded as his clothes, a washed-out and threadbare T-shirt and a pair of dirty shorts. Unlike his ramshackle appearance, his handshake was firm and strong. It reminded me of something my Mother used to say, "You can tell a lot about a man by his handshake."

With his head turned to the side he eyed first me and then the copper sheet that I had given to him with regards from Ron.

"Ron has told me so much about you! I have to say I'm looking forward to hearing more about that crazy idea of yours," he said, slapping my back approvingly as if he were talking to an old friend who he had not seen for a very long time – and somehow, that was exactly how it felt.

"I don't know that my crazy will measure up to yours, judging by what Ron has told me about you," I replied. He grinned at me like a schoolboy and began to ask about my plans.

We were standing on the marina dock. The flags of the ships were flapping in the wind and with each new breeze the steel cables were clanking against the masts, as if the boats were calling for their masters. As in every port the seagulls were shrieking reproachfully. Before us in the water the yachts were gently swaying. Further away the historic part of the city, the *Casco Viejo*, rose over the water, behind it towering the glassy skyline of Panama City, the skyscrapers tickling the underbelly of the clouds. László turned his head and followed my gaze.

"The view from here is impressive, but what's out there, ..." he gestured towards the open sea, "is more impressive than anything you have ever seen." You could hear the passion of a true sailor in his voice and his words wakened me from a reverie. My thoughts had no longer been with László but had drifted to another place and another time – long ago and far away …

On the beach of Colombo, Sri Lanka, there stood a boy whose naked toes were playing in the sand. He was wearing shorts that were much too loose, held up by only a thin nylon cord. His eyes were fixed on the horizon, dreaming of distant places and being far away. He felt a yearning for adventure, for a life without worries. What he wanted, more than anything else in the world, was to travel over the waves and discover the world beyond his island. I began to feel a deep happiness that crept from my heart into my limbs. My fingertips were tingling and I could not wait for my trip to begin. I whispered to the boy from the past, "Now it is time for your dream to come true."

I felt a warm breeze enveloping me. There was a rich aroma in the thick air, of pungent seaweed, fish and brine. I licked the salt off my lips, floating on a cloud of happiness. The adventure was finally here!

Ron, an American expat who I had met by chance a week previously in Rio Sereno, a small town near the border of Costa Rica, invited me to stay with him and his wife Christina for a few days. When I told them about my plan for building a raft, Ron was insistent that I should meet his friend László. He would be, 'My man in Panama City', just the right guy to help me make my dream a reality.

"He's quite a character. He has a ton of experience out on the sea. A real-life Jack Sparrow, just what you need. Can't those damn dogs shut up?" Ron got up abruptly and opened the front door. Only when he appeared, loudly cursing, would the four dogs retreat to the other side of the house, with their tails between their legs. As soon as the next car drove past however the dogs forgot all about Ron's fury and jumped against the fence with renewed vigour, barking vociferously. Once the dogs had quietened down,

Ron told me that László used to ferry backpackers between Panama and Colombia and had weathered a few 'damn difficult' sailing trips.

"He is the right man for you – just as crazy as you are. He tried to sail to Antarctica once, all by himself."

I was intrigued, – "Oh wow! How did that go?"

But Ron wouldn't be drawn in. "That story you'll have to hear from him in person – I wouldn't be able to do it justice," he said, and got up again to shout at the dogs.

Ron wasn't sure if elusive László could still be found in Panama but hoped to be able to reach him by phone.

"Panama may seem like a nice place to you, but if you want to get somewhere, build your raft, well, I tell you, you'll need someone with the right connections. Someone who knows people … I'm speaking from experience. The people here are different. If László can help you find your way in Panama City, it will make your life much easier."

"Oh, it can't be that bad," I said. Up until now I had managed quite well on my own. "I have seen many things over the last two and half years and learnt a thing or two."

"Well, yeah, but don't be fooled by the western mask of the city. Despite all the skyscrapers, we're still in Central America. Weapons, crime, dubious business, that's a normal day here! In this place, a trustworthy face is as rare as rubies. Seriously, don't be fooled by the façade of Panama. Don't be fooled."

He lifted his index finger as a warning. At the time I thought he was exaggerating, but the next few weeks would show me just how right he was.

Ron and Christina were staying at the house of an affluent Panamanian family who had gone abroad. They were renting the place while their own house was being built, and it was surrounded by lush nature but secreted behind a high fence. Ron had lived in Panama for two years already and had set up a small organic coffee plantation. Now that Christina had come down from the US, they had decided to become part of the undulating townscape of Rio Sereno, in the middle of coffee country, enclosed by gently rolling hills.

Ron is one of those people who are a little crazy, albeit in a likeable way. He is a conspiracy theorist. His theories start with 9/11 and end with the Illuminati and those "god-damn extra-terrestrials." He curses as often and as passionately as he speaks about his theories. In those few days that I spent with him, I was informed, in great detail, about how the American government manipulates its citizens and how the Internet was invented specifically to monitor everyone. Ron is convinced that the White House will switch off the Internet at some point – "And then we'll see where you'll be!" Christina often agreed with him, but when it came to the Internet she just rolled her eyes. Unlike Ron, she would have liked to have an internet connection at home. I answered Christina's look with a grin. Ironically, Ron and I had first met at an internet café.

Ron had many stories. Every evening we would sit until late at the oval wooden table, while Christina put out home-made chocolate chip cookies. My interest in Ron's theories ignited fireworks in his head. The sky above Rio Sereno was illuminated with ideas, each one more fantastical than the next, and once their glow faded in the night, some left more smoke than others.

Ron is convinced that nothing is the way the 'gullible citizen' thinks it is. His reason for leaving America is his growing mistrust of the government and his conviction that the US economy will inevitably collapse entirely. You may not share Ron's beliefs but he is still a very interesting and thought-provoking person.

It was these unexpected encounters, all over the world, with strangers who opened their homes and their hearts that made my life as a traveller so interesting and rewarding. I took something with me from every single person I met on my journey. An imaginary suitcase full of dreams, fates and experiences from each encounter, travelled with me wherever I went. If it had actually existed, instead of a raft I would have needed a cargo ship.

When Ron and Christina went to sleep late at night, I would return to the plans of my raft. Over the last couple of months I had become obsessed with them. I would constantly turn its construction over in my head. Over and over I searched for technical flaws in my plans, or sketched details, visualising how to construct the rudder, pondering the transmission or recalculating the buoyancy volume of the raft. Sleep was often impossible.

On the third day with Ron and Christina I was woken by the barking dogs. The sunrays penetrating the mosquito net had me sweating already. A quick glance at the clock confirmed that I had overslept. It was already nine o'clock. When I entered the kitchen, the two of them were already having breakfast. Ron took a bite of a sausage and proclaimed the good news, "I was able to reach László just now. He is in Panama City and wants to meet you. He's happy to help you. Also, he'll be pleased to receive the copper sheet over there." Ron pointed to a thick shiny sheet that was leaning against the door. "I brought it from the US for László, months ago. It's high time he got it."

The news that László was lying at anchor in Panama woke me up much faster than Christina's strong coffee. I would be happy to play the courier.

"Sure, I'll take the sheet. No problem – I'll be able to store it in one of my boxes. But what does László need it for? I mean … can't he get something like that in Panama City?" I was thinking of the material I would need for the raft.

"The copper plate is for making an engine head gasket for his boat. In Panama, you would never be able to get your hands on something like that. Impossible!" said Ron between a sip of coffee and the next sausage.

I was amazed. "But that place is a metropolis! With an enormous harbour and the Panama Canal!"

"Well, yes. But this is still a developing country. Don't be fooled by the skyscrapers!"

Again, there was that warning finger. Ron's answer rattled me: would I even be able to find the material I needed for my raft here?

Christina poured me coffee and filled a plate with eggs, sausage and fried plantain. I was still standing by the door but in my thoughts I had already travelled on.

Christina seemed to feel my impatience "Come and sit, eat your breakfast." I sat down but then got straight back up again to look for my GPS device, which was stored in one of my three boxes. Once I found it, I punched in the coordinates for Panama City and received the result with a beep. Two hundred and twenty six miles linear distance, to László, the man who would help me build my raft!

Despite my impatience to reach Panama City, I decided to get to know the country and its people on the way. I split the route into several days of travel to give me more time to explore.

One day I got caught up in a festival in a city called La Concepcion. There were horses as far as the eye could see, flank to flank; never have I seen so many horses' legs all at once. It was a wild bustle of pounding and trampling and dancing hoofs.

The horsemen were wearing boots and cowboy hats, denim and leather; and for this special day, the horses were sporting their most beautiful headgear, the red bridles gleaming against their shiny coats. Children, women and men – everybody was cheerful and on horseback. I even spied someone pulling a saddled cow behind him.

The horsemen were cantering along the street. There was no method to the madness that I could see, maybe there was none? Among the horses there were pick-up trucks, forcing their way through the chaos, and on their flat backs bands played trumpets, saxophones and trombones – loudly and out of tune – while people in the front handed out free alcohol to the horsemen and pedestrians. I was amazed that the horses did not try to escape among all the commotion. The gauchos were three sheets to the wind but seemed to have everything under control.

In a small makeshift wooden arena they were holding a small rodeo. Bullfighters, dressed up as women were provoking a dazed bull with lassos and red flags. Visitors, mostly young men, jumped off the stands into the arena, running towards the other side in wild leaps and climbing up the pavilion. The bull was not overly keen to charge at them.

I had found a space in the cheap viewing stand, where the shoes of the spectators sitting in the upper level hung down in my face. On the plus side, the sweet-sellers were at eye-level. Whenever they completed a transaction, they would leap away, to save themselves from the charging bull.

I did not stay long; I felt sorry for the animal and I did not want to watch him being tormented to the point of exhaustion. Even though no blood seemed to flow, I did not like what was going on: the inebriation seemed to be increasing and the mood of the whole festival became more and more anarchic.

During a detour towards the north coast I came across a small village where I had planned to take a short break, but I had hardly passed the first few houses when I began to feel uncomfortable. The houses along the narrow street were smudged and worn out like an old dress. I encountered only grim and unapproachable men. "What do you want?" they seemed to be asking, sitting in front of closed shop fronts as I rode past them slowly. I noticed that not only the shops were closed but also the windows and doors of many of the houses were nailed shut with wooden planks. A little further up, on a side street, cars had gathered and I could see a group of men standing close together. Short sharp calls could be heard. My curiosity overcame the apprehension I felt, and I rode as close as possible to the crowd. The street ended at a dock, shut off with a thick metal chain across it. A couple of yards further along, two men were standing face to face in a hostile pose, and with rags wrapped around their hands they threw punches at each other furiously. Blood flowed from their noses and mouths onto their naked torsos. With murderous intent on their faces, the men were constantly ready, waiting to deal out the next blow. At some point, blood began to ooze out of their heads, smearing all over their hair. These were not trained athletes, rather they were thrashing each other like clumsy boys during a school fight, but their punches were serious and more aggressive.

The crowd was watching the fight dispassionately and I did not understand the purpose behind this distasteful scene. Was this a bar fight? But where was the bar? And why did no one step in to put an end to this? Was Panama as brutal as the Wild West?

The scene bothered me so much and it just didn't gel with the picture I had made of Panama. So far I had met so many kind and generous people who had welcomed me, a stranger, to their country.

Once, I stopped at a tiny little shop right by the side of the road. Besides a few cans of coke, they sold what grew in their garden. A bunch of bananas, some melons and papayas were piled up on an ancient table, its indigo paint peeling off in many places. Behind it, there sat an old couple, he with his nose buried in a newspaper, she smiling warmly with her eyes full of curiosity. She poked the old man, and the paper went down to his knees as a wrinkled but gentle face emerged. They called for their grandson, who spoke English, to find out more about the stranger. With the grandson as an interpreter, we chatted for a while. The old woman refused to take any money for the coke that I consumed and even gave me a papaya and some bananas to eat on my way.

Another day I was buying breakfast in a bakery. An elderly lady was waiting behind me in line. I only noticed her when she interjected into my conversation with the cashier. I had just ordered a coffee and something sweet and she was insisting on paying my bill in order to welcome a foreigner to her country. A chat, a smile, a friendly face, another happy memory. More valuable than any souvenir.

However, the savage fight that I had just witnessed left a bad taste. Despite my many fortuitous encounters, I knew that Panamanians were not people who spent their days hugging each other, always sweet, always amiable. But I also knew that most people were not as barbarous and vicious as those fighters. The hospitality that I had experienced made for a strange contrast with the brutality that I had just witnessed. Perhaps this was what could be found behind the high fences and barred windows with which many here protected their homes. I had just had my first glimpse of the face of Panama that Ron had warned me about.

László was to meet me later that afternoon at the *Kiosko*, a bar which was supposed to be the meeting place for the sailors' community here in Amador.

Amador can be found at the south end of a man-made causeway, constructed with rock excavated during the building of the Panama Canal. Its purpose is to keep the ocean currents from blocking the entrance of the canal with mud. When the canal was still controlled by the US, the Amador peninsula was a US Army fort. Since the canal was handed over to Panama on December 31st, 1999, the former *Fort Grant* became the *Calzada de Amador*, a promenade where today the large marina can be found. The boats, lying at anchor there, look as if someone has shredded a white sheet of paper and scattered it over the blue water, littered as it is with boats of all shapes, sizes and classes.

Imagine a dimly lit dive, right by the water. The space is cramped, the walls are darkened by smoke, and the air smells of stale booze and tobacco. Tattooed, rough-looking, weather-beaten men are sitting at the bar. They're being served by scantily dressed girls, who they hassle and sing shanties to as soon as someone throws a coin into the jukebox. That's how one thinks a dockland bar should look like anyway. In reality, the *Kiosko* is the exact opposite; situated in the last lot of a covered shopping promenade for tourists, it is really more of a small supermarket than anything else. Out front there are a few wooden tables where the sailors can be found in the evenings, lit by glaring neon tubes. They exchange weather info and stories and enjoy each other's company, sipping beer after long voyages. The clientele is allowed to use the internet for hours, with a minimum spend of only three dollars. Everything here is kept very simple. This place is where one meets sailors with small private boats, the majority of whom speak Spanish only as a foreign language. Immigrants, emigrants and escapees – whether they've escaped from the law, or from themselves – they all rub elbows here.

Ever since that first afternoon, it wasn't just László and I hunched over the hand-sketched plans for my raft, other sailors would join the conversation too, getting caught up in our enthusiasm and offering their help and their knowledge. My idea to travel from Panama to Colombia on a homemade raft rekindled their sense of adventure. Others would just shake their head but give me advice nonetheless and tell me of their own experiences.

At the end of that first day in Panama City, a helpful trio had formed around me: László, the Hungarian Jack Sparrow, who had been travelling the sea around Panama for the last year or two and two of his friends, both Frenchmen and passionate sailors. After many years abroad, they felt more at home in Panama than in their native country. Jacques was a sail-maker in his mid-forties, living on a boat in the harbour of Amador. He had bags under his eyes as if he had not slept for days. Lionel, the oldest of the group, was around about fifty. He was rather gaunt, with sinewy arms poking out of his T-shirt. He was a carpenter and worked somewhere on the embankment of the Panama Canal, where he was building the interior of a banker's luxury yacht. Three rough, but good-natured men, whom I began to like more and more.

I had planned to travel from Colón, the second largest city in Panama, on the Caribbean coast, to Turbo, in Colombia. Discussing how to make this plan a reality, the three repeated what Ron and Christina had already warned me of: Colón is 'a shithole', nothing but bandits and crooks. Murder, drugs and kidnapping were the order of the day.
"You only go to Colón to get rid of all your things, including your life, if you're very unlucky. Not a chance of meeting anyone reliable enough to help you there," said Lionel, as he lit another cigarette. He inhaled the smoke and looked out towards the harbour. His thoughts seemed to be streaming past us. Then suddenly he grasped one of them, "Build the raft here! We'll help you and you can transport it over to Colón."
This suggestion was met with agreement from Jacques and László. The sailor on the next table got involved, "In Colón, there were

thirty murders in the first forty days of the new year. That's what it said in the paper yesterday."

Again I saw Ron's warning finger in my mind's eye. It helped make my decision. I would build my raft in Panama City and transport it to the other end of the canal. I knew that I would be taking enough risks out on the ocean over the next few weeks; taking further risks building the raft just seemed unnecessary. Plus it would definitely be possible to take the raft across Panama on a pick-up truck, since the distance from coast to coast was only 50 miles.

"But," interjected Jacques, "about this time of year the weather on the Caribbean side could get wild. There are storms and the wind will be coming from the east. Wrong direction for you."

"Huh, that's true," muttered Lionel.

Another cigarette was lit, this time by László.

"If you left now you'd be fighting from Colón to Turbo against high waves, currents and headwind. An impossible task, especially with such a small raft."

László knew what he was talking about. As a ferryman, he had transported tourists between Panama and Colombia in just these waters. "Wait a couple of months here for better weather. We'll make sure you won't get bored."

"I have a better idea." An American with a bushy grey beard who had been sitting quietly at the table next to us joined the conversation. He took his baseball cap off and fanned himself. Even late in the day it was stuffy and damp, you could have strung up water beads like a pearl necklace if you stabbed a needle through the air. He cleared his throat, "Why don't you sail on the Pacific side? The waves ain't much smaller but the weather is much more stable than in the Caribbean."

Curious about the man hiding behind that beard, I asked, "Are you a sailor too?"

"Yes, sir. I'm waiting for the north wind. I'm going to the Galapagos."

He reached out his free hand. "The name's John," he said, while still waving the cap in front of his face with the other hand. "I might already be gone by tomorrow evening."

John's voice sounded hopeful and he gestured towards the screen of his laptop. "The weather forecast for the next few days is looking good."

Something that is completely normal to every sailor only now became clear to me, the biker – out on the ocean; I would be at the mercy of the elements. I would not be able to decide the course of the wind and the waves but would have to wait patiently and humbly until Nature went my way, as a beggar waits for a dime. If the weather was in my favour, I would have to take that opportunity and use it to the best of my ability.

"Have you ever sailed on the Pacific side to Colombia?" I asked John.

He shook his head. "No. I came here from the US and am now sailing for the first time to the Galapagos."

"What about you, Jacques, have you ever sailed on the Pacific to Colombia?"

"Yes … well, almost. I travelled far out on the ocean to the south, not along the coast," said Jacques, whose face was weather-beaten and coarse from long exposure to the elements.

"Me neither," said László, before I could ask him the same question.

Jacques recommended that I speak to Edward, an Englishman who had recently sailed in his fishing boat from Buenaventura to Panama City. Edward had originally planned to set up a travel agency in Buenaventura but the local drug gangs suspected that he was a CIA agent who had come to spy on them. After several death threats Edward had had no other choice but to flee on his boat one night towards the north. He had to leave behind practically everything that he owned, and with no money and almost no fuel. Luckily for him, the ocean currents took him straight to Panama.

The three of us were sitting before my laptop, studying the coast with Google Earth. László traced the map on the screen with his finger.

"Look, you have to go to Buenaventura. Before that, there is no settlement that's connected to the road network."

"Oh … so the journey on the Pacific will be twice as long as on the Caribbean side?!"

We measured, a linear distance of 450 miles.

"Can I do that?"

Without expecting an answer, I buried my head in my hands and stared at the map. It was either blue or green, ocean or jungle. There were almost no villages and no bays where I would be able to stop, or find refuge in case of bad weather. However, on the Caribbean side, there were islands, bays and villages and the route was only 250 miles long.

"The weather in the Pacific is supposed to be stable for another few weeks. I think you could, without major problems, weather-wise. But …" Lionel stopped and eyed me up.

We had only met three hours ago. He did not know what I was capable of. Hell, even I didn't know what I was capable of!

Meanwhile John had moved his chair to our table and they were all regaling their tales of adventures on the high seas. Whether the beer, my plan, or even the truth inspired them, it was not always clear. They were telling me about the jungle and precipitous cliffs, about indigenous villages and no villages at all, about how very rarely boats travel along that route, and of course about the giant swells of the Pacific.

And the waves. Again and again they would come back to the dangerous surging billows along that coast, because of those waves, the drug smugglers and the possibility of being kidnapped by rebels, László and Jacques advised me to travel as far away from the coast as possible.

"The best thing to do is to stay in deep water and only steer towards the coast once you're near Buenaventura."

"No," said Lionel. "That is nonsense, and dangerous. The weather won't be stable out there for long enough. When you're too far out you'll not stand a chance on your little raft if there is a storm. You'd be better off staying within sight of the coast, so you can seek shelter if necessary. And storms… they can strike anytime out there!"

The drug smugglers would not be interested in me as long as I was not interested in them, argued Lionel and John.

"With a little bit of luck you won't even cross their path," said Lionel.

"With a little bit of luck there won't be a storm!" Jacques quipped. This discussion continued whilst I considered, whether I would prefer to be kidnapped or to be caught in a storm on the open sea. Meanwhile, the others delved deeply into their rich treasure chests of adventures, the stories becoming more colourful with each beer. I was only listening with one ear and staring at the map, weighing the adventure against the danger, my impatience against waiting for the right weather, my gut feeling challenging my common sense. And then I made a decision.

"Right! I will travel over the Pacific. Double the distance means double the adventure!"

The stories about the rugged Pacific coast had tipped the scales in favour of the route across the Pacific, and waiting was not an option anyway. I am an impatient person and when I want something, I want it now. When I decided to travel the world I arranged for the storage of my furniture, vacated my flat and sold my business in the picturesque Swiss village of Ennenda within just two months. Then I crossed the Swiss border with a sense of liberation. Over the coming months and years I would cross the borders of my comfort zone many times. It was time to raise the bar once more.

Lionel, who by now had drunk a few more beers than the rest, whistled and looked at me with admiration.

"For real?"

Before I could answer he hugged me and planted a kiss on my cheek.

"You, my friend, are a champion!"

I pulled a face and wiped my cheek, and the others laughed.

"Enjoy! You're his latest victim," joked Jacques.

László lit another cigarette, while I wished Lionel was a pretty young French girl, without beer on her breath. But since that wouldn't happen, I gently pushed Lionel away from me and asked if he would get another beer for himself and one for me too, to celebrate.

I was surprised by how quickly everything was happening. To-morrow László would take me to a workshop where I would begin building my raft.

Once again I recalled that little boy on the beach of Colombo, jumping for joy.

I had honed the construction plan for my raft over many weeks and I just knew that it would work. What I felt less confident about was the official paperwork I would surely need. This issue had been on my mind for longer than the matter of which route to take.

"What about official stamps? Safety regulations? The exit permit for a makeshift raft and a captain without a sailing certificate?" I asked the group.

I had no doubts about the construction of a seaworthy raft, nor my willpower to see this thing through, but I was worried that the authorities might confiscate my raft and put an end to my dream, before it had even begun.

While Jacques and John were unsure, László was optimistic.

"Not a problem, *amigo*! I will take care of that. You just need to have the right connections in Panama, then everything is possible! And hey, you know me!" he said, beaming a boyish rascally smile.

Jacques asked where I had learnt to sail.

"Nowhere," I grinned, "I'm a natural talent," and at that the men roared with laughter and said that I was a nutcase.

"Eet is what eet is," said Lionel with his strong French accent, then he shook his head and pulled me into his arms once more and showered me with kisses. 'Eet' was time to go.

Sri Lanka: I was born here and it will always be a special place. But I feel at home everywhere.

CHAPTER TWO

"Your present is best measured by your past."

~

A question I was asked many times on my journey was, "Why?"
Why had I decided to travel the world alone on a motorcycle?
I found this question hard to answer. When I first started out, there were many different factors that played a role in my decision and often I gave different answers.
"The world is so beautiful and I want to discover it."
Or, "I want to find myself on this journey."
In retrospect, the answer is simple, I'm an adventurer, and therefore the question of how I became an adventurer becomes more relevant, than the question of why.

I was born in Sri Lanka in 1970. As a little boy, I always had my nose buried in a book, especially those full of action and adventure. When I was thirteen years old, I discovered a book which made a deep impression on me: *Madol-Doova* by Martin Wickramasinghe. In Sri Lanka, it is a classic of children's fiction. It tells the story of two teenagers who run away from home and travel to the south of Sri Lanka, to start a new life on a small uninhabited island called Madol-Doova. That was exactly what I wanted to do too … to run away and leave everything behind.

When I look back on my childhood today I remember it as a happy one, but it was not always easy. When I was six years old, my Father was killed by two robbers. A life ended just for the contents of a wallet. His death changed my family's life dramatically.
My Father and his two partners had a business selling spare parts for agricultural vehicles. Trade was good and my still-young parents were planning to build a house. I remember that wherever we went,

we always took a cab, or our own car. "We don't walk through the dust," my Father used to say, not without pride. At that time, cars in Colombo were a rarity. If you owned one, you had it made. We were the only family in our neighbourhood with a car.

My Mother was 27 when my Father died. She was a housewife, as are most women in Sri Lanka to this day. She left school after her compulsory studies, married young and soon gave birth to her first child – me. Three more sons followed in the next five years and she dedicated her life to us. In those days in Sri Lanka, money and business were not a housewife's concern and my Mum did not know the first thing about savings, nor about my Father's business. When he was still alive, my Father gave her a generous household allowance once a week. We lived in a five bedroom house and he also supported my aunt and my grandmother, who lived with us.

After my Father's death, it turned out that his business partners had no intention of involving my Mother in the business or of supporting us in any way. Of all the money that my Father had earned, we never saw a single rupee. Neighbours and relatives told stories of what a generous man he had been, and how he had always helped the less privileged people in the area; but all that was left, after he died, were a few spare tractor parts in storage at our home. These we sold one by one.

I remember little from the time after his death, but that first morning is etched into my memory.
The neighbour's rooster crows and the light of the new day filters through the window as I awake. I hear my sleeping brothers breathing steadily. And then, instead of the familiar noises from the kitchen – I hear the clattering of cups and my Mother sobbing.
I hear her crying. I freeze and pretend that I am still asleep – a tactic that I developed to cope with my parents' fighting. My Father was a generous man but he had a terrible temper and as a result quarrelling wasn't a rare occurrence in our house. I lie on the bed rigidly, waiting for my Dad to leave the house and for calm to return. It takes a while for me to realise that I cannot hear my Father's voice,

only agitated women and my Mother's loud sobbing. Finally I get up and go to my Mother, who is sat surrounded by my aunts, and yet seems very lonely. To this day, I can still see her face, wet from tears.

"Daddy is dead," she says to me and I start to cry, even though it will take a few days for me to understand what her words mean.

All other memories of this day have faded, slowly but surely, like the ink on an old letter that eventually disappears into the yellowed paper.

Life went on – it had to. My Mother took on work as a seamstress. She was not properly trained and her employer paid her badly. At the end of a long working day, she often did not have enough money to buy food for us all. As the eldest son, I took on some of the responsibility. I looked after my brothers and even began working in a factory after school, once I was old enough. There I made small rubber parts and was able to support my family with a few additional rupees, but we struggled from meal to meal, day to day.

After my Father's death, my aunt soon got married and moved in with her husband, while our grandmother moved with us, from one rented house to the next. These houses got progressively smaller and cheaper, until we stayed in a small room without electricity. Rent swallowed up most of our money and our plates were often empty. Hunger became normal.

No wonder that my thirteen year old self dreamt of running away from home and having adventures, just like those boys in *Madol-Doova*. But it was not yet to be. At that point in time, I had already become a father figure to my brothers and my sense of responsibility and love for my Mother made me postpone my grand plan for later. I became a day dreamer and lived adventures in my head, and through them I escaped the hardships of my life.

I remember that I owned only two pairs of shorts and two shirts. Underwear was a luxury that we could not afford – and I was bullied at school because of that – but my Mother did everything to ensure that her sons could go to school. She would never have allowed me to skip school, let alone leave school to get a job – but boys will be boys and we would run away from school now and again, not to work, but because we wanted to experience little adventures.

To me, the eldest son, these small detours from my daily routine were the only hours I had without the worries of a grown-up carried on my shoulders.

We had no toys, other than those that we made ourselves. We produced cricket balls by bundling up bits of fabric that were leftover from our Mother's needlework. The cricket bats were carved from the thick, sturdy stalks, of palm leaves. The rough palm fronds were trimmed along the stalk and what remained would be worked on, until a passable cricket bat emerged. This improvisation did not keep us from having passionate cricket matches. Even today, emotions get high when all four of us are on the field. For us, there is no such thing as a friendly match ... brotherly love only returns afterwards.

We had no formal playground. On our way to school there was a church, and its backyard had become a dumping ground for a company that produced coconut ropes. During the processing of the coconut fibre, the soft and unusable fibres are separated from good ones. The fluffy, dusty waste, soft as sponge, was thrown into a huge pile. Every day, the heap grew bigger and bigger, until finally it turned into an irresistible trampoline. We jumped around on it like little imps, turning somersaults and becoming smothered in the fine brown dust, so that after a wild playing session only our white teeth betrayed that we were human children.

The river near our house, with its large rocks, was ideal for climbing. We often played there and dared each other to perform small feats of strength and bravery. Among my favourite memories are the days when a mahout came by to bathe a baby elephant. It was just as playful as we were, but of course much stronger. I can still feel its rough skin pressed against my palm, as if the little elephant were still pressing his forehead against it. When we stood before him, holding still, his trunk would start exploring, winding itself around our skinny legs and gently pulling on our shorts, tickling us until we could hold still no longer. The little elephant chased us, we chased him, and we jumped into the water with him, or were pushed by him.

Water and me, there was a close connection, even then. I loved the river and the ocean. Both were forbidden as too dangerous by my Mother, but I loved to dive into the waves and roll around in the roaring white foam. Once the first teacher had checked for attendance, I often slipped away from class to run to the beach and play in the waves until the position of the Sun indicated that the school bell had already rung and I should be on my way home. Often I asked my brothers to come along. Sometimes we forgot the time and got home late. The sand in the pockets of our school uniform betrayed where we had been and my Mother was merciless. We all got a good walloping but that did not deter us from skipping school again, just a few days later.

Like most Sri Lankans, my Mother cannot swim and was therefore always afraid when we went into the water. Sri Lankan parents in general are overly cautious when it comes to their children and anything that might result in even a little scratch is strictly forbidden.

Books were just like underpants – too expensive for us. Whatever I read, I borrowed from the school library. That was why I was particularly excited when my Mother bought me a newspaper when I was nine years old – the Sinhalese children's weekly newspaper *Mihira*. Because I had never held a newspaper in my hands before, I read from top left to bottom right, one line after the other. As a newspaper is written in columns the text made no sense whatsoever, but this made no difference to my sense of pride and the joy I felt at having a newspaper, all to myself.

After I had gobbled up *Madol-Doova*, I continued with *The Adventures of Tin Tin* and Roald Dahl's autobiography *Going Solo*, which fuelled my desire for adventures and travel to far-away places; stoking a fire that still burns to this day. In my dreams, I often drifted on a raft that carried me safely across the sea, to the island *Madol-Doova* and beyond.

Thirty years later, as a grown man with his own business and a daily routine in Switzerland, everything was different, except for one thing; I still had that lust for adventure and discovery. During the last twenty years, I had travelled often, but the idea of a trip around the world was still hiding in a dark corner of my brain, like a seed buried under the soil waiting for spring. Sometimes that idea almost got lost in the routine of my daily life. As most people do, I tried to find happiness in material things and only realised once I owned them that even expensive sport cars kindled only short term delights.

On one cold, dark winter's evening, this idea of a trip around the world crept back into my thoughts, but this time it stayed and sprouted in the fertile soil of my wanderlust.

It was winter 2010. I had enough money and a comfortable life, but I was restless and looking for something – for myself, for true happiness, for the meaning of life.

Compared to my childhood, I was well-off. My business was going well, but it no longer made me happy. My long-term relationship was failing and my sense of humour and positive attitude were faltering. I questioned everything, my faith in God and religion as a whole, myself and the reason for my supposedly happy life. The working days were long and exhausting; I had depressive episodes and little energy. I felt cold, inside and out. Where was that man I used to be? I felt as if I had lost myself in the jungle of civilization. That was when that little seed that I had stored away germinated and began to grow roots. I knew that I would only be able to find myself out there, in the wide-world.

My name is Dylan Samarawickrama. For someone not used to Sri Lankan names, this tongue twister is hard to pronounce and remember. For a long time, I struggled to accept my name, especially in Switzerland where people are called Müller or Reber. Samarawickrama is not only a mouthful; it sometimes also attracts negative attention. Well, for these reasons I did not like my name for the longest time, until someone asked me about its meaning and then I realised, Samarawickrama means, 'the one who celebrates adventure'! So, it is not just my past that turned me into an adventurer but I carried that destiny with me from birth. Now I fully identify with that name. And I am grateful to that little boy from Sri Lanka who I still carry around in me and whose dreams gave me back my zest for life and inspired me to venture forth and explore the world.

If you take a trip around the world, you cannot possibly take a guidebook for every country, especially when you travel on a motorcycle and carry your plunder in just 3 aluminium boxes. I also preferred travelling cluelessly. I wanted to discover my new surroundings through the eyes of the people who I met on the road. This style of travelling requires courage and openness to new experiences, but it also allows you to meet new people and creates many interesting opportunities to explore a new country. I procure maps and information when I need them and I used my GPS device without road maps for direction, like a compass. That way, at least I always knew where I was lost. On this journey, there was no wrong way and no plan, nor schedule. To me, 'to get lost' means 'to discover something new'. It means discovering a little village that is not mentioned in any guidebook, living each day, each moment, just as it comes. Not knowing in the morning where you will rest your weary head at night. That's one of the charms of adventures.

In this haphazard fashion, Bruce and I travelled from Switzerland to Scandinavia and Russia. From there to Eastern Europe, Turkey, Syria and Jordan, to Egypt and the east coast of Africa down to Kenya, to the Arabian Peninsula and then to Dubai, where I shipped Bruce to India. After two months on the Indian subcontinent, I loaded Bruce onto a ship once more to Sri Lanka. I stayed at home for six weeks and rarely slept in my tent. My Mother and my many aunts were thrilled to have me there and I ate like a king during that time – I must have gained a fair bit of weight, but is there anything better than your Mother's home cooking? No matter how old you are, eating is home.

Next stop for Bruce and me was South East Asia. After the indulgence of my Mother's cooking, indigenous dishes such as snake stew garnished with deep-fried maggots and grasshoppers, in such places as Laos, ensured that any extra pounds I had gained were soon lost. During that stage of my trip I often resorted to cooking simple noodle soups on my gas stove.

After many thousand miles in continental Asia, Bruce and I travelled across the many Indonesian islands and approached Australia. From Dili in East Timor, Bruce and I reached Darwin, but not before a three-day long very wearisome and very intensive cleaning: Australian authorities are uncompromising about keeping germs out of the red continent. I had to take Bruce apart to clean every nook and cranny and then put him back together again. This was a tedious and protracted chore, especially because Bruce had only been washed once during the last two years of my journey. The same was expected of the clothing too. Riding gear, shoes, boots and the tent, everything had to be immaculately clean. Up until then, the cleanliness of my motorbike clothing had not had much of my attention. But thanks to Australian customs, it was high time to get those things cleaned too. After I had soaked the riding trousers in the bathtub, the water became as black as tar ...

As I sat on the edge of the bath, staring into the heavily discoloured water, my mind drifted to Fatima, Abdul, Amin and their family, who I had met a year ago in Syria.

Shortly after leaving Aleppo, I asked a family of farmers for their consent to pitch my tent on their property. Instead, the farmer invited me into his house and offered me a room, even though we had no common language. As soon as the family sat down on the floor to have dinner, the visitors began to arrive. Neighbours came on bikes, in cars and tractors to catch a glimpse of the foreigner. For hours I sat on the floor amongst scores of smiling people who spoke a mix of Arabic and sign language with me. My host kept refilling my cup with strong coffee. Despite thirty cups of the thick, dark and bitter liquid, I got tired eventually. It had been a long day and all I had in my mind was to just lie down and drift away, but people kept coming, even long past midnight, shaking my hand and staring at me in fascination. Everyone who left seemed to tell their neighbours about me and it seemed as if the news of my arrival had made the rounds of half of Syria. The simple living room of the farmhouse was buzzing with guests. The farmer sat next to me and never got tired of telling them what he knew about me – which was very little. My presence in his house seemed to elevate the status that he normally held in the rural community. Suddenly, he was a celebrity! I did not begrudge him all the attention he got but eventually I could hardly keep my eyes open. When my head sank onto my chest, the last visitors finally took their leave.

The next morning I awoke early. Breakfast was more coffee, and homemade flatbread. Then Amin, the eldest son, and I took a trip on Bruce through the village. Whenever I caught his eye in the mirror, he would laugh cheerfully. I was introduced to the village and each time I was served with more coffee and sweets. Amin took advantage of the situation and enjoyed the attention while the mothers offered me their daughters' hands in marriage. After many hours, we went back home, but not until we had visited every single house and I had dodged many marriage proposals.

Here I learnt that hospitality and cordiality can be communicated without a shared language. The seven children of that family, aged between five and fifteen years, had lost their hearts to the foreigner who played with them and showed them things they had never seen before, and who was always up for mischief.

When I got ready to leave two days later, I found my panniers to be empty. All I had were the clothes on my back. Where had they gone, my clothes and my motorcycle riding gear that I had thrown into a corner? I looked all over the house and did not find them. I asked the family but they did not understand what I was looking for. Then the eldest of the two daughters seemed to grasp what I was seeking. She took me by the hand and guided me behind the house, and there it was, all that I possessed, hanging neatly on a washing line, soaking wet. The thick fabric of my riding clothes in particular must have been impossible to wring out for those little hands. I laughed and so did the children, who had looked rather frightened until then for washing my clothes, unauthorized. I had no other choice but to wait for the clothes to dry. When I finally left, the children were standing on the road, crying and waving until I could no longer see them in the swirling dust created by my wheels. The smell of soap that hung in my clothes followed me around for weeks, and whenever I opened the panniers I was reminded of their adorable gesture.

Since I visited Syria in 2010, the country has lived through unimaginable hardships. It must be changed beyond recognition. Aleppo, especially, was hit very hard by the war. Often I think about 'my' family and wonder what happened to those wonderful people. How is little Abdul? And Fatima, with her gorgeous, shy eyes? Does Amin's laughter still rise above everyone else's? Do they have enough to eat and drink? Do they still have that glimmer in their eyes? Are they even still alive? It is likely that I will never find answers to these questions, but I shall not forget the days I spent in their home and I wish for them and for everybody else in Syria, that these evil times will soon be over. I can only hope that their future will not be as black as the water in that bath tub. Before washing the jacket, I held it to my nose, hoping to catch a last whiff of that Syrian soap, but to no avail.

After three days washing Bruce and my gear, I entered Australia without a problem. Travelling through this large, dry and flat country seemed to take forever. We had circled it once and then traversed it in line with Ayers Rock and already half a year had passed. After the koalas and kangaroos, the wild coasts and wide fields, Bruce was stored in a shipping container and sent straight to Vancouver, Canada. Meanwhile, I flew to New Zealand and Fiji to pass the time until his arrival, and then I took a plane via Korea, for our reunion in Vancouver.

Whenever he was stuck inside a container ship, it always felt strange to be without Bruce, as if I had lost a limb. When I heard, five weeks later, that the ship with Bruce on board had arrived in Vancouver and that he was ready to be collected, I was elated.

However, I had lost my old passport and my bike's papers at the airport in Seoul. The documents had to be reissued by the Swiss traffic authorities and then sent to me. Losing the old passport as means of identification was not an issue because the Swiss embassy in New Zealand had issued me a new one upon running out of pages, but that passport was also one of the best souvenirs of my travels – in the end, not a single space was left that was big enough for a rubber stamp and whenever I leafed through it, I remembered the story hidden behind each entry.

Crossing a border is always special. Crossings give me butterflies in my stomach. Behind each border post awaits a new language, a new culture, and so many new things to be discovered and understood. The food smells different and so do the banknotes. The petrol is more expensive, or cheaper, and the political mood may be completely different. One's senses have to become accustomed to whatever is waiting beyond the border. From Cambodia to Thailand, from Thailand to Laos, the traffic changed sides. From Sudan to South Sudan, the roads deteriorated immediately after the border crossing. In South Sudan, there were only six miles of paved roads in the entire country, the rest is an accumulation of holes, stones and mud filled irrigation canals.

At other border posts I had to wait hours at counters, before being told to queue at another counter for more stamps and documents. It felt like being stuck inside a Kafka novel. And then there was that border crossing between Egypt and Sudan …

The border from Egypt to Sudan can only be crossed by ferry. The two countries are in conflict so the only open border stretches over Lake Nasser. There is something a little unique about Lake Nasser, the reservoir looks like a Fata Morgana in the dry desert and the landscape along the shore looks like the dry skin of an elephant, caked with mud.

The Nile, the longest river in the world, was staunched for the first time in 1902 at Aswan. The water was regulated in order to prevent flooding and irrigate the land. The original dam was raised twice over the next 32 years and was considered to be the highest construction of its kind. However, the rapidly increasing population of Egypt meant that the dam soon did not hold enough water for dry spells. Therefore Aswan Dam was built in the Sixties, an enormous structure over 12,500 feet long and 364 feet high. Behind the dam, the water of the Nile accumulated and became Lake Nasser. It reaches across the border more than 200 miles in length and on the Sudanese side the lake's name changes to Lake Nubia.

In October 2010, I reached Aswan on a Monday morning and learnt that the ferry to Wadi Halfa in Sudan sails just once a week, on Monday afternoons. I rushed to the Sudanese consulate in Asuwan to get a visa. Even on a trip around the world, Monday mornings can still turn out to be stressful! Upon filling out the application form and handing it in to the consular staff I could do nothing but wait. The minutes passed excruciatingly slowly and turned into hours, until finally, by the time I received the visa, the ferry had long gone.

At least now I had a week to prepare for the crossing. I bought a ticket for the next ferry and started exploring the area by visiting many archaeological sites around Aswan including the temple complex of Abu Simbel. It had been built between 1290 and 1224 BC during the reign of Rameses II when the stones were quarried from a single piece of rock. The entire complex was relocated in 1968 to keep it from sinking into the lake. At a cost of 40 million dollars, UNESCO shifted it, cutting it into pieces and rebuilding it 65 yards higher up on the banks of Lake Nasser. Looking up at the massive temple complex, it seems unbelievable that it has not always been where it is now.

The following Monday I made my way to the ferry port, which lies on the eastern side of the mighty dam. The route to Wadi Halfa would take between eighteen and twenty-four hours. Here Bruce and I were separated for the crossing. Along with all the other vehicles and crates, Bruce was loaded onto a barge. I, together with a crush of other passengers, crossed the unsteady wooden planks to board the ferry. Before and behind me were men in long white robes, veiled women clutched their children's hands, so that they would not be lost in the river of people. More men were pushing and bumping and shoving each other. I became part of this massive surge forward, which eventually ended with us spilling all over the ferry. I was carried along amongst a sea of hands and sweat, unable to control the direction in which I was going.

The barge looked terribly overloaded and the ferry was much the same, every inch was occupied by passengers and their luggage and everywhere crates and bags were piled high; some passengers had even made themselves comfortable in the lifeboats. It was hard to find a place to sit, so I squeezed myself into a little space between some crates on the upper deck and tried to find the best position that was least painful. Only those who had booked a private cabin were lucky enough to have a license to stretch.

Travellers with their own vehicles were required to attend the offices of the customs authorities at 9 a.m. on the morning of departure. There were fifteen of us, ten bikers who were in a hurry, travelling from the north of Finland to South Africa in 25 days, a Swedish couple, about as old as their VW bus, on their way to Ethiopia, a Belgian father and son travelling in a Land Rover down to the Cape of Good Hope, and me. We all had to comply with the formalities which involved a lot of red tape. We had to fill in about fifty different forms and it had to be done in Arabic. We then had to get them stamped by fifty different clerks, in the right order, and only then could we return the local licence plates which every vehicle had received upon entry into the country. Then, finally, we could obtain a certificate from a judge stating that we had not been in conflict with the law during our stay in Egypt.

We tourists were treated as a group and all had to wait until the last one of us had completed our formalities. Five hours later, we were escorted down to the harbour by policemen and the vehicles were loaded onto the barge, one by one. The long waiting and the endless formalities made us bond. After five hours at the customs office, you stop being strangers. We passed the time telling stories from our travels and on the ferry we continued to get to know one another even better.

The only other way of passing the time, besides chatting to fellow passengers, was to take a little walk to the other end of the ferry to stretch your legs. This quickly turned into a steeplechase.

The majority of the passengers that used the ferry were traders of Sudanese origin. They had flown from Khartoum to Aswan to buy trading items in bulk and then travelled by ferry back to Sudan, as it was cheaper than by air. Hardly had the ferry left the harbour when all the merchants began to unpack their goods and repack them shrewdly. Two packs of light bulbs became one. Three packets of spices were stuffed into a single packet and so on and so forth. The merchants were old hands at decreasing the numbers of their goods, thus reducing the import duties. Although there were customs officers on board the ferry, nobody seemed bothered about it. The volume of noise climbed as high as the soaring thermometer. The roaring ship engines continued their never ending baseline as a contrast to the stillness of the desert. In fact I wished I was somewhere far away out there in the sands, so that I could enjoy the desert silence. But since I knew that this was just a onetime hassle, I gladly endured it.

Shortly before sunset, the Sudanese immigration officers began collecting everyone's passports. All formalities had to be completed before our arrival in Wadi Halfa. I reached into my shirt pocket. Empty! I opened the bag where I had stored all my documents in a folder. Everything was there except the passport! Then I searched the backpack. Nothing! The last place to check was the camera bag, but my passport was not there either. Frantically I racked my brain ... where had I left the stupid thing? And then it dawned on me, it was safely tucked away in one of Bruce's panniers and Bruce was travelling on the barge and was already out of sight, as the barge was much slower.

The officials were none too pleased about my missing passport and told me that I would be unable to disembark without it. I would have to wait until the barge reached Wadi Halfa. Not a problem I thought, I need to wait for Bruce either way. A few passengers who were familiar with the route told me that the ferry remained in the harbour in Wadi Halfa for one whole day before returning to Egypt. "By then, the cargo ship will have reached the harbour. Don't worry!" I was reassured, but still spent the night sleeping uncomfortably among the crates and luggage turning and twisting every thirty seconds.

When we reached the harbour of Wadi Halfa the next day, the Sun was at its highest point.

The word 'harbour' is perhaps a little exaggerated to describe the dock and the few bollards that were used to moor the ferry, with the vast Sudanese desert landscape stretching out behind it and without any hint of civilization. I watched as the noisy crowd disembarked. Some were welcomed by relatives; others haggled with a taxi driver to take them into town. Whilst my friends tried to explain my situation to the officials to get me off of the ferry, the rest of the passengers took off in taxis and overcrowded minibuses. Emptied of people, the dock became quiet and my fourteen friends called out to me from the pier that I had to remain on the ferry for now. I thanked them and yelled that I would "See you tomorrow!" when they returned to collect their vehicles. They clambered into the last minibus and drove off.

Without the passengers on the ferry, it suddenly felt much larger. For want of anything better to do, I stared at the horizon for hours, hoping to see the cargo barge carrying Bruce. Finally, the crew invited me to share a meal with them. They even gave me a private cabin where I could sleep and shower.

When I stepped on deck the next day, I was refreshed. I scoured the lake for the barge but there was no sign of it. I scanned the horizon, nothing. There were still five hours left before the ferry was due to depart. I was certain the barge would arrive at any moment. After breakfast, I resumed my position at the railing and kept watch until my eyes began to water. Nothing happened. The lake was quiet and there was no sign of anything and the crew informed me that they had no means to communicate with the cargo vessel. Even though the officials had been very clear that they would not let me leave the ship without a passport, I tried my luck once more when they came back aboard to accompany the next batch of passengers across the border. As soon as they saw me, they put on grim faces. They felt no pity for me. If they had a heart, then they were hiding it behind their faded, light blue uniforms very effectively. The crew got involved, tried to appease the officials and cheer me up. Apparently, nobody could remember the ferry leaving for Egypt before the barge had arrived in Wadi Halfa. Surely everything would work itself out. If necessary, they would be able to delay the departure of the ferry a little … or at least I kept telling myself that.

The planned time of departure came and went and still there was no sign of the barge. Still more luggage continued to be loaded and more passengers embarked. My optimism was replaced by an increasing nervousness. After two more hours, the cargo vessel had still not shown up. This time there were fewer passengers – this crossing would be more comfortable than the last – but I really couldn't bear the thought of going back to Aswan! I did not feel like spending another week in that place and crossing that damn lake two more times! And besides, what would happen to Bruce in this godforsaken place, if he was not collected for a week?

As the hours of uneventful waiting passed, my edginess increased accordingly.

I had to take action!

I would simply stay here! If necessary, I would jump off the ferry and swim ashore. The ferry was only about fifteen feet high – no problem. I was fed up with this ferry and angry at the obstinate officials but mostly just annoyed with myself for forgetting the passport.

My situation soon became known among the few passengers who were travelling to Aswan that day. While we were waiting in the harbour, I chatted to an Englishman and a Sudanese gentleman. I asked them if they would throw my luggage on to the pier if I jumped off the ferry just as it was leaving, without the knowledge of the crew. My idea was to jump into the water sneakily and then swim ashore, so that by the time the officials discovered me, the ferry would already be gone. The Englishman and the Sudanese man looked at each other, and then both lifted their eyebrows and began to counsel me as if we were standing on the Golden Gate Bridge and I was about to put an end to it all. But once I convinced them that it wasn't an attempted suicide, they agreed to help me out.

When the ferry was about four hours behind schedule, the captain could wait no longer. He started the engine, the ropes were taken off the bollards and the ferry began to move. Brown dirty water churned beneath us, until it was pulled into the maelstrom of the ship's propeller. Looking down into the tumultuous waters, I contemplated my plan, but the ugly broth, combined with the words of the Sudanese and the Englishman who had pointed out that such a stunt could create the opportunity for the officials to refuse my entry even with a passport, convinced me that my plan was futile. I resigned myself to my fate.

We had not been moving for five minutes when in the horizon the outline of a dark object appeared. I could have screamed! Just five minutes earlier I had longed for this to happen, but now I was cursing. Why had that stupid thing not shown up a little sooner!

I ran up to the captain, who by now I knew personally, and tried to convince him to go as closely as possible to the barge so that I would be able to jump over. A crew member translated my words into Arabic. The captain, who looked more like Allah's messenger in his long white robe, discussed this with his men. They hesitated, and did not seem too keen on my plan.

In my urgency their discussion seemed to take forever. In truth, it can't have been more than a minute before the guy who spoke English announced the result, "Yes, the captain will try, but it is difficult. We have not done this before."

Their words did not sound as confident as I would have liked them to be.

Another hour passed until we came closer to the barge with its, for me at least, precious cargo – Bruce and my passport. But the ferry captain was not trying hard enough to get close to the barge. In fact, it passed us by a mile and I could just about see Bruce through the zoom lens of my camera. That far, even I had to admit, nobody would be able to jump and swim across in a crocodile infested lake. The Sudanese man and the Englishman were noticeably relieved when they saw that I had given up my plan. But my eyes followed the barge for as long as I could see it.

We continued through the hot desert landscape, the stifling air was cooled by the water making it bearable, but it was still hot enough to feel uncomfortable. I was glad that the ferry was half empty. Everyone found a little spot in the shade where they could stretch their legs and doze. In the dead of the night we passed by the illuminated temple complex of Abu Simbel. While the other passengers marvelled at its beauty, it held no charm for me. I had seen the temple three times already and would go past it again for a fourth time soon.

The accent of another passenger revealed that she came from Switzerland, like me. Her name was Karin and she had worked as a project volunteer for a year in Tanzania, but was now homeward bound. She had already heard about my situation and said that she might be able to help. Whilst waiting for the ferry in Wadi Halfa, she had made friends with the family of the customs clearing agent. Karin reached for her mobile and called the agent. She didn't waste any time, got straight to the point and told the man at the other end that he would have to take care of my motorcycle and that under no circumstances was it to be sent back, as this would mean – and I shuddered when I imagined it – that Bruce and I would cross each other's paths again next week. She also told the agent that the motorcycle would need to be covered by a plastic sheet, so that the desert dust would not damage it. I shook my head. Bruce would cope just fine, he is an adventurer just like me and to coddle him like that was almost an insult, but Karin was adamant. The agent promised to keep Bruce and to keep him safely covered until my return to Wadi Halfa.

A few hours later, the Egyptian border guards began to collect the passports. That game again! "Without a passport, you cannot go ashore," they told me.
"Till next week? Until we go back?"
"That's right. If your passport is in Wadi Halfa, you will have to remain on board."
This possibility had not even occurred to me until now. I had to restrain myself from getting into an argument and making the officers angry. The ferry did not seem to want to let me go.
The young Swiss woman came to my rescue for a second time. A year in Africa had apparently taught her how to deal with obstinate officials. Without missing a beat, she said to me, "Just wait, we'll get you out of the tight corner."
I watched in fascination as she began a charm offensive which

would have been irresistible for even the Pope to withstand. Karin was pretty and she knew it. She paid the officers compliments; she laughed at their silly jokes, played with her blonde hair, and smiled at one and then winked at the next. She asked questions, showed interest and it even seemed to me that her neckline sat a little bit lower than before.

Karin's flirting seemed to be working. Once she had charmed the men sufficiently, she brought my miserable situation to their attention.

"How unkind it would be to make him stay on the boat for a whole week" she said with a pitiful face.

Suddenly, the uniformed men were much friendlier than before. After some vacillation and deliberation, they concluded that I would be able to leave the ferry with a special permit. But only on one condition, I had to pay 15 dollars for a new visa. 15 dollars for my freedom for a week? I would have gladly paid them double! They gave me a small piece of cardboard on which they glued my picture. It was stamped and my name was hand written onto it in Arabic, phonetically. Karin beamed, "What did I tell you?"

It goes without saying that her dinner was on me that night.

Monday soon came round and I went to the ferry port – again. The director of the Aswan Ferry even gave me a free ticket and food vouchers for the next crossing. They had told me that I was the first person ever to be refused permission to leave the ferry in Wadi Halfa and sent back to Aswan, and that everybody on the Egyptian side were apologetic for what I had to endure at the hands of the harsh Sudanese.

Back on the ferry, there was the same hustle and bustle as the week before. Apart from the passengers, everybody knew me by my name and I was almost part of the crew. The pungent smells, the noise and the stuffiness of the quay embraced me, the oily ferry engines greeted me noisily and from the galley, the smell of boiled beans wafted up as I prepared myself for the crossing, much more relaxed than the last time. Two Germans who I had met at the hostel in Aswan offered me the floor in their private cabin to spend the night. It was rather cramped but better than sharing the deck with hundreds of other passengers.

At night, the passports were collected. Ha! I already knew this game, but I still couldn't play along. The Sudanese duty officials were as unfriendly as ever and they clearly did not like me much. My passport was waiting for me at the port, I explained as amiably as possible, something which they already knew. But they were unimpressed. They repeated the same message as before – they would not let me get off the ferry in Wadi Halfa without a passport. Somebody was clearly enjoying their power. I smiled, told them in German what I thought of them and decided to let them play their game.

Many hours later, the engines quietened down, indicating that we had reached Wadi Halfa. I was tense but the clearing agent stood at the quay, as punctual as a Swiss watch. As soon as we got close enough, I threw him the motorbike keys and told him where to find my passport. He ran towards Bruce who was indeed hidden beneath a plastic sheet and returned a few minutes later, waving the red passport in the midday heat. What a relief!

Before the officials could devise further difficulties, the agent was on board and I was once again the proud owner of a passport. The officials begrudgingly stamped it and Bruce and I resumed our journey.

More than two years after that adventure, I was in Vancouver and faced with similar problems. It was just as stupid to lose Bruce's original documents as it was to not have one's own passport. While I waited for my brother to send me a new vehicle registration from Switzerland, I heard that Bruce had arrived. Even though all I had was just a printed email, I tried my luck and found that Canadian officials are much more easy going. Just a single form later and without having to show any documentation, I collected Bruce from the customs warehouse. I was relieved and pleasantly surprised, but also a little concerned; could someone else, anyone else, have collected Bruce? But nothing else mattered, at last I was reunited with my companion.

If you travel with a motorcycle for such a long time and in the same manner as I did, it becomes your best friend, your home and your conversation partner. No wonder I was looking forward so much to seeing him again – and he was just as excited to see me.

Our last picture together: Clicked as I visited Thushari on my around the world tour. She always had a winning smile.

CHAPTER THREE

"Positivity trumps even the most careful plan."

~

A new continent and new challenges were awaiting me.

Having spent so much time in Australia, I could not get over how green and lush Canada was in comparison. The long distances, however, were familiar to me. My plan was to discover the west coast first and then travel south, eventually reaching Argentina. Since my bank account had been much depleted by the last two and half years of travel, I had decided to only pass through the west of the North American continent in order to reach Central America all the quicker, where life and travel are more affordable. Before leaving Vancouver, I checked my emails. There was a short, but sad, message from a cousin whom I had not heard from for a while. He wrote that our cousin, Thushari, had been diagnosed with lung cancer. She was being treated with chemotherapy, but her chances did not look good. Nonetheless, she was incredibly brave and she was doing well, all things considered.

There I was, at the other end of the world, with a cup of coffee, a chocolate muffin and my laptop in front of me. Bruce was waiting outside, ready for new adventures. I had been so happy and carefree just a moment ago, happy with how things were, with myself and that finally I could start my road adventure after Bruce and I had been separated for so long. Now I was in shock. I read and reread the message a few times, hoping that the words would change into something happier, such as, Thushari had finally fallen in love again and was getting married, but no matter how many times I reread the message, the letters would not change their meaning. Minutes passed before I was able to gather that this wasn't some kind of bad joke. Thushari had been one of my best friends during our school days. We were almost the same age and spent a lot of time together as teenagers. Even though we did not see each other often once I moved away to England and then Switzerland, we always had that special bond that you only have with someone who has known you since childhood. Friends like these never have to ask about your family, because they are simply a part of it. When I last saw her in Sri Lanka, I had noticed how young and pretty she still looked, unchanged in almost ten years. Whenever I saw her, she was that same school girl I knew from long ago, always cheerful. I remembered her strong dark hair, her gleaming eyes and winning smile. Thushari laughed a lot and, when she spoke, her voice was as gentle as the rustling of the leaves of a Bo-Tree in a summer's breeze.

As soon as she saw me outside her house on my last visit to Sri Lanka, she came running pulled me into a big hug and held my hand for the next two hours, as if she never wanted to let me go. On some level, I wonder if she knew that this would be the last time we would meet.

The lump in my throat got bigger while the merry bustle in the café continued unabated. Life went on regardless. Just a moment ago, I was just as happy and content as the strangers around me. Now everything had changed and nothing was as it should be. While Thushari was being robbed of her time, I was enjoying all the liberties of life and my freedom. Was it wrong to be travelling while one of my family members fought for her life? I felt guilty. But was it not also right for me to follow my dreams, to do what made me happy? My cousin's fate only proved how quickly things can change. Everyone runs out of time, sooner or later. I took a deep breath and, instead of the coffee, I smelt the tea and freshly picked cloves of Thushari's home in the highlands of Sri Lanka. I thought of the house she had lived in all her life, together with her parents. She never married and therefore never left her parents' home. At college she had fallen in love. The two of them had been a happy couple until her parents disapproved of their relationship, which was pretty common in Sri Lanka in those days. To please her family, she stopped the relationship but Thushari was heartbroken and I believe that she was always true to her first love. She was never with anyone else again, preferring to be on her own. I buried my head in my hands and closed my eyes – and her face appeared and reappeared before me with a beautiful smile.

When I had regained my equilibrium, I called her. As soon as I heard her voice my composure was lost. Thushari remained upbeat, raised my spirits and told me that all would be well. It sounded as if she had struck a deal with her fate: if she only held her head high, her diagnosis would be erased. I was overwhelmed by her positive attitude but glad that she could not see my face. Probably my faltering voice gave away my emotions, but I tried hard to hide them. It was ironic, I had called to cheer her up, but it was Thushari who comforted me. I wanted to hear more about her illness, but she wanted tales from my travels, one after another.

"I am in Vancouver and will travel around Canada for the next few weeks. I thought about going to Alaska but …"

"Alaska! I have always dreamed about going there and seeing the bears and the wilderness." She had seen documentaries and pictures. She spoke so enthusiastically about green hillsides, icy blue rivers and shaggy bears, as if she had only just returned from there. "What luck," she sighed, "now I can still travel to Alaska before I die thanks to you. You have to send me pictures! I want to hear everything!" She sounded so excited and happy about my supposed journey to Alaska that I did not have the heart to explain the misunderstanding.

It was hard for both of us to end the call. She promised to show courage and I realised once more how fragile life is. There is a thin line between happiness and sadness, and they may just be an email, or a phone call, or just seconds apart.

I started Bruce. Instead of heading south I started riding north …
North to Alaska.

A few days after speaking to Thushari, I was riding through a wooded area north of Kelowna in British Columbia. The afternoon was changing shifts with the evening and I was looking for an ideal place to pitch my tent somewhere along the road. Ideal means that I cannot be seen from the road and the ground is dry and even, preferably covered with grass. In that respect, my instincts had been sharpened in the last two years and I never settled for the next best option. Not that I am particularly demanding (to camp in the wild is, to this day, the greatest luxury in the world to me) but I knew all too well that if you feel safe, you will sleep well. However, I was not yet quite at ease in the Canadian wilderness. Bears, moose and mountain lions were at home here: wherever I pitched my tent, it would be in their territory. Moose can be just as dangerous as bears. In North America, there are twice as many deadly attacks on humans by moose, as there are by black bears and grizzlies combined. That I had so far not seen any of these creatures did nothing to lessen my discomfort. I decided that the next day I would take myself to a town where I would educate myself on Canadian camping rules.

While I was riding through the woods looking for a suitable place to pitch my tent, I came across three bikers by the road-side, standing around one of their bikes, trying to fix a fault. I slowed down and stopped.

The area was uninhabited and I had come across maybe two cars in the last hour. I did not have to think twice about lending them a hand.

"You guys look like you need a mechanic." At first they thought I was joking, but then they were relieved when they realised that I actually was one.

With my help, the bike was fixed in fifteen minutes. Father and son duo, John and Kevin, German Canadians who lived just a few miles further away, invited me to spend the night at their place. I accepted gladly. Tarayn, the guy with the faulty bike, thanked me for my help and took off. He lived where I had left from that morning and still had a long way to go.

Later, that same evening, I saw my first bear. Kevin, John and I were sitting in their living room and exchanging stories when something large and black darkened the window.

"What's that?" I asked and John answered, as if it were the most normal thing in the world, "Oh, that's just a bear paying us a visit. We see them most days."

While I got my camera out and took pictures of the bear through the open window, John continued, "You should be here a few weeks from now. During the salmon run. By the river, at the end of our property, you can see ten, twenty bears every day."

"Wow, for real?"

I slowly began to get an idea of what it is like to live alongside bears. They are part of everyday life here. John also told me how you ought to behave out in the Canadian wilderness. "You always have to make as much noise as possible. We're all in the habit of talking to ourselves when out and about, or carry a bell. The one thing you don't want to do is surprise a bear. A surprised bear can be a dangerous bear."

I was intrigued to learn that bears like toothpaste, deodorant and soap. Better to gently stink than to smell of the bear's next meal, I concluded. But the most important rule was, and they could not emphasise this enough, "Never, EVER, run away. That will trigger their hunting instinct and then you're done!" Not even Usain Bolt can outrun a bear. "And you, with your short legs, wouldn't stand a chance."

The next day I was travelling on my own again. My destination for that day was Jasper National Park, the largest national park in the Canadian Rockies. Ice fields and hot springs, where snow-capped mountains and acres and acres of stunning landscape beckoned me. When I took the first break of that day, by a waterfall, a large vehicle stopped next to me and someone called out, "Hey, Dylan! Good to see you!"

Surprised, I turned around. Tarayn was grinning at me from a red pick-up truck. Together with his friend, Greg, they were on their way north to Fort McMurray, one of the largest mining regions in Canada. They were both carpenters and often got work there, and well paid it was too. A trailer attached to their pick-up served as their workshop. They told me that Fort McMurray had grown from nothing into a -town in the space of just a few years. The enormous oil sand deposits of the Athabasca County attracted more and more people and they were building one house after another.

"That's one of the few places where you can still get work easily. You can earn a thousand bucks in a day."

"One thousand dollars? Per day?" I thought I had misheard, but the two of them nodded.

"Yep, a thousand bucks a day. Time is money!"

"Fort McMurray is by now more expensive than Vancouver, or Toronto. The town has too much money and not enough houses, which is good for us," added Greg.

"Come along and I'll give you work for a few days," offered Tarayn.

A tempting offer – some extra money would hardly go amiss. I hesitated, but decided that quick money might lead to more problems than it was worth. I did not have a work permit for Canada. It seemed to be more sensible to continue my simple life rather than risk being thrown out of the country by the Canadian authorities. And I wanted to travel on to Alaska; Thushari's time was short and I had promised to send her pictures.

Tarayn reached for his wallet and gave me fifty dollars. "Then take this at least. As a thank you for your help yesterday. I don't know how I would have gotten home without you."

I declined. "No way! Your money isn't necessary. To help someone on the road is a given."

But he insisted, "Come on. You haven't earned anything for a while and you will need quite a few tank loads to get to Alaska. And you know how much money we make," he said, with a wink. He left a fifty dollar note on Bruce's saddle and I had no other choice but to thank him for his gift.

Tarayn's friend, Greg, also an enthusiastic and well-travelled biker, invited me to stay at his place on my way back from Alaska.

"I want to hear more about your journey. Just stop by! By the time you're back we'll be home as well."

He gave me his address and phone number. "*Mi casa es su casa*," he said, gave a wave and then off they went. The humming of the truck was added to the roaring of the waterfall and eventually got lost in the wilderness.

Many Americans dream of visiting their northernmost state, and for good reason. As if through Thushari's eyes, I was awestruck by the beauty of Alaska. That close to the polar circle, everything seemed dramatic. Clouds reflected in the crystal clear mountain lakes, ice-blue glaciers, carpets of violet flowers gently swaying in the wind. Foaming rivers and waterfalls, the veil of the bride Alaska, flowing into the valley. The truly awesome beauty of the craggy mountain ridges, behind them the peaceful tundra, warmed by a Sun that had forgotten to set – it was all simply magical.

Those never-ending summer days robbed me of all sense of time. Often, by the time Bruce and I stopped to rest for a few hours, it was long after midnight. I often ended up picking berries, or taking pictures instead of resting. My average speed decreased from day to day. Not because the roads would not have allowed a faster speed but rather because I had to stop after every curve of the road, at every hill, and at every little lake to take more pictures. My eyes were happy and so was my soul. I only wished Thushari could have been here to see everything for herself.

If there is one place in this world to see before you die, it is Alaska. Even the salmon knew this. In many rivers, I could see that the salmon gave their all on this – for them a once in a lifetime journey. They travelled upstream and fought with all their strength on shallow parts to move forward and reach the place where they would spawn and then die.

I encountered moose and caribou grazing peacefully and saw bears fishing for salmon with their mighty paws, or dexterously plucking berries from the shrubs. All creatures seemed to enjoy this short but intense summer. It is a carefree time, a time of abundance before winter returns. I was elated by this magnificence and I will always be grateful to Thushari for taking me to this corner of the world.

☙

I had gladly accepted Greg's invitation to stop at his house on my way south. Greg is a passionate traveller himself and he did everything he could to make me feel comfortable. After a month of canned food and noodle soups and icy cold glacial lakes to wash in, I felt as spoilt as a prince in Greg's house – it was bliss to have a hot shower, a proper bed and dinner at a set table.

It wasn't long ago that someone asked me if I was a loner. I had to think about this for a few days before deciding that I would describe myself as a part time loner. As much as I enjoy travelling on my own, I do like good company. Those days with Greg were great, and when he asked if I would like to go on a motorcycle tour of the area, I didn't have to think twice about it.

Greg is a tall muscular guy, with a strong faith in God and a well-functioning single person's household, whose wanderlust is as strong as mine. A few years ago, he rode his bike from Canada to Argentina – just the route that I was planning to take. He was also looking into a bike trip to Asia, a part of the world that I already knew. Our conversations therefore never flagged, and if it did, then we both enjoyed the silence, lost in memories or kneading the dough of plans for future adventures.

We had just set up camp for the night somewhere in the great woods of Canada. Greg brewed us some coffee and told me about driving on the Pan-American Highway. "The Pan-Americana is more a network of interconnected roads than a continuous highway. The condition and the width of the road changes all the time, depending on where you are at any given moment." He handed me my cup and we huddled as close to the fire as possible.

Because I prefer side roads, dirt roads or even just mere tracks, I had not been particularly interested in the famed Pan-Americana, but now I was intrigued, "From where to where does it go?"

"From Prudhoe Bay, Alaska, to Ushuaia in the south of Argentina. About 30,000 miles but the numbers vary depending on who you talk to. The longest continuous road in the world!"

A cold breeze rippled through the undergrowth. We both listened to make sure that it was only the rustling leaves that we had heard and nothing else. The silence returned and left us to it. Greg sighed, deep in thought.

"So you rode every mile of it?"

"Not quite. I started from home, not all the way from Alaska, but from here all the way down south. I liked Mexico and Guatemala especially. Oh, and you have to be sure to book a place on a sailboat. I can give you the contact details."

I listened up, surprised.

"A sailboat?"

"Well, yes, didn't you know? In Panama, the Pan-Americana is interrupted for about a hundred miles. The border region between Panama and Colombia is nothing but jungle."

"But didn't you just say the Pan-Americana is the longest continuous road in the world?"

"Well yes, it's true. Just except for those hundred miles, the Darién Gap, where there is just undeveloped swamp-land and jungle. Not a single road connects the two countries."

"You're kidding!"

I live in the here and now, on the road even more so than in everyday life, and so far I had not wasted a single thought on the road situation of Central America. Greg told me that several attempts at building a connecting road had failed – the resistance had been too fierce. The destruction of the ecosystem and the habitat of the native tribes were as much a part of the discussion as the fact that, without a road, infectious diseases and drug smugglers have a much harder time travelling from one country to the other. That is why, even today, there is no road connecting Panama and Colombia.

Greg kept talking about the highway, but I was not listening as attentively as before. My thoughts kept returning to the Darién Gap. I do love a challenge. Maybe there is a challenge in store for me ... in the Darién?

That night, I slept badly, not because of the cold which covered our tents with frost, but because my brain was buzzing. A few weeks ago, I had hit upon the idea of turning Bruce into a raft in order to travel the length of the Amazon River. Now I had learnt that the road ended in Panama, so I would not be able to travel on land anyway. Is this a sign from above?

Between sleep and sleeplessness, I began to dream of the little boy. He was on the beach of Colombo, building a raft. He was working busily, his hands raw from the chafing of the coconut rope. He lashed the ropes tightly around the bamboo and made a deck. When he pushed his creation into the sea, the saltwater burned in his wounds but he was elated: The boy had made a raft!

When I climbed out of my tent the next morning, the decision had been made. I would sail on a raft across the sea.

"Greg, I will travel around the Darién Gap on a raft that I will build myself," was how I greeted my bleary-eyed, just awake, travel companion. A grin stole across his sleepy face. He yawned and pulled on a warm jumper.

"Do you always come up with crap like that so early in the morning?" It took him a while to understand that I was deadly serious.

"But that's the ocean! And if I remember correctly, the people in the region are not said to be particularly friendly. Just think of what I told you yesterday, they deliberately don't build roads so that drug smugglers and FARC rebels have a harder time getting into Panama!"

"But that's just it! That's why I want to go over the ocean, so that I can avoid all those filthy bastards," I grinned.

"But an ocean isn't a river. It's the OCEAN!" Greg was seemingly irritated.

"That's what makes this so exciting! A proper adventure!" I was wide awake.

Greg shook his sleepy head and retired behind a tree. He shouted from behind the trunk, "You're nuts! You're completely nuts!"

I grinned. I couldn't argue with that.

Greg would not be the only person to look at me aghast when my plan came up in conversation. Since I did not want anyone to think I had a death wish, I often stuck to the official version of crossing the Amazon River, which of course some still found reckless enough – but to board a chartered ship along with all the other travellers seemed dull in comparison to my new plan.

When I left Greg's house to continue south, I knew once more why I never planned my life, or my journey. Originally, the idea had been to travel south from Canada. Instead, I had gone to Alaska for Thushari. On my way, I had met John, Kevin and Tarayn. And by chance, I met Tarayn's friend, Greg. And he was the one to tell me about the Darién Gap and sowed the seed for my greatest adventure yet!

Mexican generosity at its best: Marco (left) and his men worked a full day on my transmission modification for free.

CHAPTER FOUR

"Recipe for one adventure:
Take a large dollop of passion
and a pinch of recklessness.
Mix well."

~

Would László really come and take me to that workshop today, to build my raft?

From the moment I opened my eyes, I sensed excitement and tension building inside me. I am finally here, where my big adventure kicks off. Excitement and tension had been crawling around in my subconscious all night. In fact I had not been sleeping well over the last few weeks. Ever since Greg had told me about the Darién Gap on our trip in Canada, I had dreamt about building my own raft. And today that dream would finally start becoming a reality. I took a deep breath, got up and had a good breakfast before I went on my way to Amador.

László had not forgotten me. Right on time he was standing on the marina dock, with a wet face of sea spray from his dinghy ride. He lived on a boat which was anchored in the marina of Amador. He earned his living by repairing boat engines, until he saved up enough money for another sailing adventure.

I passed him the second motorcycle helmet, but László's head didn't fit in. He motioned nonchalantly and said, "Never mind – in Panama, nobody gives a rat's ass about rules and regulations. You'll see that for yourself. You'll profit from this at some point too, I'm sure. *¡Vamos!* Let's go!"

He directed me over the causeway and back to the city. The traffic was heavy, and the buildings that we passed on the outskirts of town were dilapidated. It was shortly after 10 a.m. and the Sun was already beating down on the line of cars creeping towards the city centre. It was only eight miles from the pier to the workshop, but progress was painstakingly slow on the congested roads of Panama City. Construction work for the new overhead metro line only added to the chaos.

For once, Bruce was travelling without panniers, so we were able to slip past the waiting cars, squeezing through small gaps between them. László did not hide his smugness from the drivers, who were stuck, jammed behind a thousand other cars. He waved to people left and right whenever we overtook them. He shouted words at open car windows that the wind took before I was able to understand them – probably for the best. He directed me towards gaps in the traffic. We rode past the neighbourhood of *El Chorrillo*, heading towards *Santa Ana*. Although it was a dreary looking area the brightly painted houses lent it a thin veneer of cheerfulness.

László pointed across to the neighbourhood and shouted into my ear, "Over there is *El Chorrillo* – never go there by yourself! Not even during the day! Unless you want to be shot! Not even the police go there!"

"I thought it's just Colón that is so dangerous?" I shouted across my shoulder. In the mirror, I could see László shaking his head.

Run down houses with broken glass in the windows seem to guard many unshared secrets. Here and there, I thought I could even see bullet holes in walls, but perhaps that was just my imagination after László's warning. We went on, past the misery. On to meet Antonio.

I would soon see that László had not exaggerated. Once I was walking to a store close-by to Antonio's workshop, just to buy some nuts and bolts. As usual, I was wearing my scuffed motorcycle trousers, a T-shirt that was dirty from the workshop and a beard. Two policemen patrolling the area stopped me and I was ordered to stand against a house wall with my arms held high and my legs spread apart. Then I was searched for weapons. They checked my papers, but only once they had made sure that I was not carrying anything dangerous. When they saw my passport, they asked what I was doing there by myself and escorted me to the store and then back to the workshop. They were both armed to the teeth and wearing bulletproof vests. When I asked in my pidgin Spanish about their reason for escorting me, they replied, *"Es peligroso aquí, amigo. ¡Muy peligroso!"* It's dangerous around here, mate. Very dangerous!

Later I learnt that whilst there are fewer violent crimes in Panama City than in Colón, nevertheless shootings and robberies take place on a daily basis. The Panamanians go all out and use guns for nearly every criminal activity. A life does not count for much here. At one point, there were so many illegal weapons in circulation that the government set up a programme called *Programa de Armas y Municiones por Comida y Medicinas* ("Weapons and ammunition for food and medicine"). Illegal weapons can be swapped for food stamps and medication, without the owner having to answer any questions. The programme was a success and repeats every year. In the first three years alone, 1,514 weapons and more than 109,000 pieces of ammunition were withdrawn from circulation. Nonetheless, the suburban areas are still controlled by gangs who specialise in violent robberies and drug trafficking. They draw in unemployed, disaffected youths by giving them a sense of belonging, and when one gets killed or put behind bars, there is no shortage of new blood ready to take his place.

The shabby neighbourhoods that huddle around the historic town centre of Panama City, the *Casco Viejo*, are in stark contrast to the polished glass of the skyscrapers of *Punta Paitilla* in the eastern part of the city. There, the picture changes from dreary to dreamy, with fancy cars driven by money launderers, bankers and politicians, through fancy boulevards and between high rises that would make you think you were in Miami.

László is an electrical engineer who used to work for a large automobile manufacturer in Germany. In Panama, he earns the money for his next adventure by fixing boat engines. Every morning at 8 o'clock, all the sailors gathered around their radio network systems. If someone needs something fixed, they ask for help over the wireless, "This is the *Nenufar* speaking. Our boat's engine isn't running properly. Can anyone recommend a mechanic? We're on channel 13. *Gracias*. Thank you."

If László had time and saw that it was a big enough and lucrative enough job, he would answer. I learnt later that the wireless was not only for exchanging general information for sailors but also a kind of market place. It was not just odd jobs that were on offer but also hammocks, chairs and life vests and of course now and then you would hear that someone had something to give away.

László's repair jobs meant he was a good customer of Antonio, who owned a workshop near the *Casco Viejo*. Any mechanical jobs such as milling, lathing, or welding that he couldn't do himself were passed on to Antonio. They were well acquainted and László was convinced that Antonio would be able to help me with building the raft.

The walls of lined colonial buildings on the *Calle Ramón Valdez*, showed hardly a trace of their original colour, and were discoloured as if they were constantly blasted by exhaust fumes. The street was unevenly sloping on one side, and a trickle of water made its way between the pavement and the street, watering the blades of grass that struggled to sprout between the slabs of concrete. There was a strong smell of fish in the air, since the famous fish market *'Mercado de Mariscos'* stood only 100 yards away.

Antonio's workshop was a dark, noisy hole gaping in a row of houses lining the *Calle Ramón Valdes*. We were greeted by a blast of heat, smoke and the smell of sweat, as we entered through the wide gate. The concrete floor had cracks in many places which over time had clogged with iron filings, metal shards and broken screws. In the middle of the workshop there stood an enormous drive shaft from a small ship. Its heavy weight seemed to be more than the floor could possibly bear in the long term. I imagined that at some point it would sink and take the entire workshop with it. The thing was about 12 feet long, almost a foot in diameter and, being positioned as it was, stood in everybody's way. Two workers hammered and sawed on a propeller, while two others stood around and gave advice. Further back was another man welding something, without wearing a welding mask. Seeing him made me wince with the memory of the pain I had endured for days after trying to weld something without eye protection. The bright arc stung my eyes so badly, that for days after I was unable to open or close them without a ghastly and unbearable pain. The worker narrowed his eyes to focus on the piece of work. As calmly as he worked, he must have moved past the threshold of perception a long time ago and his eyes had got accustomed to the bright light. The sparks went flying left and right past his head, brushing the tips of his moustache, before spreading like a swarm of glow worms in the workshop. The welding mask was sitting on a bench nearby, untouched.

Everywhere there were bits of metal, half-finished jobs and forgotten spare parts. I saw lathes and milling machines. The mechanic in me rejoiced. The machines were probably from the Sixties and blackened from many jobs and oily hands but they were exactly the machines and tools that I needed to build a seaworthy raft.

László looked at me inquiringly, his head cocked, "Happy?"

I grinned and nodded, whilst checking out the workshop. Mostly, it was a big mess, but that did not bother me. As a born anarchist, I actually felt quite at home in all that chaos – it unleashed my creativity. I work better in a messy environment than in an orderly one, and every little part that I saw lying around inspired me with new ideas. Inhaling the metal oily smell, I began to feel – This is it!

The workmen stopped when they noticed us and László was greeted with open arms. He was always welcome here because he related to the guys there and often arrived with a new job as well, and today he had brought them a very special assignment indeed.

He told them about my raft and I thought I could hear pride in his voice. The workmen raised their eyebrows. There was one line in particular that stood out from their conversation that I heard many times, *"Loco. ¡El está loco!"* "Crazy! That man is completely crazy!"

"Is Antonio around?" asked László, nodding towards the office. A few seconds later a bald head appeared from a simple partitioned area. Antonio didn't just walk, he glided towards us, greeted László with a hug and me with a friendly handshake. The two spoke, nodded, pointed towards me and nodded some more.

It would be a shameless exaggeration to claim that I speak Spanish – I understand a few words and I can just about muddle my way through with gesticulation and perhaps with the help of a dictionary.

While the two were talking, I adopted a serious expression and pretended to understand what they were saying. Finally, László translated the conversation with a single sentence, but it was all I needed to hear, "You can build your raft according to your plans here and they will help you," he said, grinning from ear to ear. The first step was taken.

Once that was sorted, we began to look for the material. László took me to the next street corner where a man was selling dark blue plastic barrels in all sizes.

"But what I need are oil barrels," I said to László.

He gestured for me to wait. A few words were exchanged and then the vendor walked with us back to Antonio's workshop.

"He has oil barrels stored in the back," I was told, and indeed, in the darkness at the back, there were piles of them.

"I need ten. Five today and the other five later," I told the vendor, who then clambered up the barrels as agile as a monkey, and threw down the first one, accompanied by much cursing. I stopped him and explained that I needed the barrels undamaged. Dents in the material would diminish the raft's ability to glide through the water and it would take more effort to move it. The man had trouble understanding what I wanted, but then he cursed some more and the following barrels landed on the floor more gently. We haggled and finally struck a deal, eight dollars apiece – a good price!

László then took me to the enormous hardware store nearby, and left me alone with my construction plans and shopping lists. I felt like a kid in a sweetshop and spent the next few hours roaming around the store until I had acquired most of the things on my list. I was very pleased to have been able to find almost all the stuff that I needed just a stone's throw from the workshop.

Ever since deciding to build a raft, it had been clear to me that I would not have unlimited resources, but, once I arrived in Colombia, I should, at the very least, be able to buy a plane ticket back to Switzerland.

Even though I had spent a lot of nights under the open sky and lived frugally, I had spent money travelling over the last two years and my bank account was almost empty. Not that I want to complain about money issues or about how much this journey has cost me, not in the least, each rappen, penny, peso or cent was well-spent on this adventure. I also do not want to give the impression that travelling is only possible with a beefed up bank account – quite the opposite. When someone in the western world says he or she does not have enough money to travel, they probably just have different priorities – children, a career, expensive cars or other interests and obligations. Then there is also a fear of material loss which holds many people back. However, once you make a move, you will realise that it does not matter if you wear the same pair of jeans practically every day for three years. Travelling light means it enables you to have all you need in just three aluminium boxes. Less luggage allows more space for more experiences, for spontaneity and improvisation. I learnt that being happy is related to my own personal attitude towards life, rather than a question of wealth.

Planning the raft sometimes made me feel like the director of a low-budget film. When the budget doesn't allow for special effects one simply improvises, or even rewrites the script. From that first conversation with Greg up in Canada, until my arrival in Panama, the construction plans had always been on my mind, constantly evolving. I spent hours, entire days even, optimising that raft. Often I would sit absent-mindedly on a park bench, unaware of my surroundings, completely absorbed in a world of virtual reality, where the raft was being assembled piece by piece. Whenever I saw the ocean – which happened often along the American West Coast – I would spend hours watching the waves. In my mind, all kinds of scenarios took place. How could I construct a raft stable enough to master high waves? How would I make it durable enough to last through the journey? How to efficiently use Bruce's motor to power the raft? How much fuel would I need? How big should the rudder be? How hard would it be to navigate out in the open sea? How strong would the currents be? And what would I do in case of an emergency?

My mind was always busy trying to find answers to these questions. I knew that the answer to all of these questions lay in building a 'sturdy' raft. To reach my destination safely, I had to know exactly what I could demand of my raft. That was why I had to plan it and build it myself. This was a challenge that demanded my full attention. I loved it.

The most important thing was choosing the right material. What would give me and Bruce sufficient buoyancy to glide over the waves? What material would be robust enough to withstand the salty water and the forces of nature?

At first, I thought of large plastic canisters; for a few days, I even considered PET bottles. Then it occurred to me that those large dark blue plastic barrels that are frequently used in the chemical industry might be an option. Plastics and salt water, that was a combination that would work, but how could I process plastic to turn it into a robust, load-bearing construction? I would need to be able to bolt and weld things to it. The load-bearing material would need to be mounted without gaps, otherwise the water resistance would be too strong and the raft would be too slow. To be able to move with as little resistance as possible also meant using less fuel. This was essential, as I had no idea how much fuel Bruce would need on the water and I would hardly come across a fuel station along the way.

I was still considering wood for the base of the raft when I drove by an abandoned warehouse somewhere on the west coast of the USA. I remember how humid the air was, and that dark thunderclouds were brewing over the landscape. I took a break until the rain clouds had passed by. Behind the warehouse, old oil barrels had been stacked up. I felt as if I had been hit by lightning, even though the storm had not even begun.

That was it!

Oil barrels!

They would be easy to obtain anywhere. I could bolt and weld them to my heart's content, and they should be able to hold up to saltwater for long enough.

Once the decision was made, I had to calculate the buoyant force, in other words, figure out how many barrels the raft would require to float. In order to do that, I had to calculate the total weight. Bruce and his boxes weigh in at about 660 pounds. Then I would take 32 (imperial) gallons of water and 32 gallons of fuel, about 45 pounds of food and an anchor, two rudders, rope and various other bits and pieces, all of which would add up to another 180 pounds. Add my own weight of about 135 pounds, and I had a total weight of 1,630 pounds. Then of course there is the material of the raft itself. I researched online and learnt that an empty oil barrel weighs around 45 pounds. If I used ten such barrels, that would add another 450 pounds. For the deck, I planned to use galvanised metal tubes and bamboo poles, weighing another 330 pounds. A total weight of 2,410 pounds.

Would the buoyant force of ten barrels be enough to keep me above water? Archimedes had to help. A simplified formula enabled me to calculate the buoyant force of my raft; one barrel has a volume of 43 gallons, therefore my ten barrels would have a combined volume of 430 gallons. This equals a buoyant force of almost 4,600 pounds. My raft, about half that weight, should be able to ride the waves with ease. *Eureka!*

My plan was to make two hulls with two rows of five barrels on each side and then build a robust platform between them. To reduce the water resistance, I would construct pointed hulls.

For the propulsion of the raft, I had two options; I could install a propeller, or, construct a paddle wheel similar to those of the old paddle steamers on the Mississippi. A paddle wheel is quite easy to build, even though it is made from many individual parts and I would be able to attach it to Bruce's rear wheel. This conjured up a romantic image; a large red paddle wheel at the stern of my raft propelling me and Bruce forward into the sunset. But the image was flawed – as at every turn of the wheel it would pull up half the ocean with it and spray sea water all over us. The constant drizzle of salt water would be harmful to Bruce and all my material and provisions. Also, paddle wheels work best when they turn slowly, while the opposite holds true for a motorcycle motor. So I figured it would be best to install a propeller, even though this would not be easy to engineer.

A final drive passes the propulsion energy of the motor on to the wheel, which then turns and causes a forward motion. So, theoretically, all I had to do was build in a propeller where the wheel was mounted; in reality this is a little less straightforward. After much deliberation and sketching, I bought a second final drive for modification. That way, I could keep the original drive as it was and build it back in, after ending the raft adventure.

In the meantime, I had reached the south of the United States and decided to buy the propeller before entering Mexico. I had learnt the hard way, in places such as rural India, Laos and Sudan, how difficult it can be to find certain spare parts. In developing countries, even if you do find what you need, you will end up compromising on quality most of the time, which I wanted to avoid.

So of all places, I began looking for a propeller in Phoenix, Arizona. There is an urban myth that claims that Arizona, that arid state, has more boats per capita than any other US state – but you try finding a boat shop in a desert city!

What I mainly knew most about the propeller where the details that I did not know. I had no idea what diameter it should have, how many blades would be ideal, which pitch and which angle of attack would be needed in order to mount it onto a motorcycle engine. All I knew was the rotation speed of the transmission in relation to the engine speed and that the output shaft turned left.

The shop was stuffed to the rafters with propellers of all sizes, but also with fishing rods, anchors, life vests, binoculars, ropes and board computers. The shop assistants were not much help but I couldn't blame them, it probably wasn't every day that they were asked for a propeller for a motorcycle.

They told me that they did not have any left-handed propellers in store but would be able to order one for me. A fat catalogue was slammed down onto the counter and the many options and price ranges made my head spin. I decided to take a look around first. They really had heaps of propellers there, aluminium, chrome, bronze or plastic, small and large. They came in all shapes and sizes; some would not have looked out of place in a sci-fi movie. There was every kind of propeller that you could possibly imagine, but they were all right-handed.

I had almost resigned myself to the fact that I would have to keep looking elsewhere, when I saw it – right under my nose. The only left-handed propeller in the shop.

An old relic, it was hanging on the wall behind the counter. It had a golden gleam but had clearly been retired a long time ago. The three blades that I could see were left-handed; and it had a diameter of about ten inches and looked extremely sturdy. I just knew: that was my propeller!

73

Angle of attack, pitch – whatever, I didn't care that much. I would build the raft in such a way that it would all work out in the end. I asked about the propeller in question, which caused much consternation among the employees, until someone said that it was not for sale. It was from the fifties and its only use was as an ornament, the new models were all much better and they really would not mind ordering one for me. I shook my head without giving them a chance to reopen the catalogue.

"That's the one I want. Who decides if it is for sale or not?"

"Ed! Could you come over here a sec?" The young man behind the counter called towards an office door and a moment later the boss appeared. I told him about my raft. He shook his head disbelievingly and said, "You want to propel a raft with a motorcycle?"

"That's right – my motorcycle and your propeller."

After much equivocating, Ed finally agreed to sell me the thing. The price he named corresponded to my enthusiasm.

"Well, if you really want that old thing, you can have it for 150 dollars."

Finally! But wait – how much?!

"150 dollars? Are you sure? If I don't buy it it'll just hang on that wall and be of no use to anybody. I'm giving it a new lease of life. But, 150 dollars. I can't afford that."

The grey-haired man nodded. "Yes, 150. Alright, fine. Maybe I'll accept 130." He thought about it, whilst rubbing an oil stain on the counter with the sleeve of his shirt. The clean blue-red flannel shirt soaked up the oil.

While I haggled, he got a ladder, climbed up and reached for the propeller and handed it to me. The bronze mass felt just as robust as I had hoped. Michigan SMC650 was punched into the hub in small letters. While I was already excited about my new propeller, Ed remained sceptical about my plan of travelling along the Amazon River ... If he only knew!

We kept bargaining and finally I said, "If I survive this adventure, then you can be proud that the propeller came from your shop. If I don't, you won't tell anybody that I was here."

He grinned. My enthusiasm began to infect Ed. "That's the best argument I've ever heard." He laughed and tapped on the propeller. "Well, give me fifty dollars and promise that you won't get yourself killed out there!"

So the raft would be built from empty oil barrels. Bruce would be at a safe distance from the water surface, which was good. On the other hand, the distance between deck and water posed a particular technical challenge, I had to connect the propeller to the motorcycle in such a way that the propeller would be immersed in the water at the right depth, at the right angle, to propel us forward as efficiently as possible. If it wasn't immersed deeply enough in the water, it would swallow air, which would cost energy and slow us down. That was Problem Number One.

Problem Number Two was that the final drive of a motorcycle is built in such a way that it cannot easily be converted into a ship engine.

It took a few more days and nights until I had worked out a solution, but I would not be able to do this with my own tools. I needed milling machines and a welding unit. I figured that this would cost me a pretty penny in the US, so, I decided to wait and look for a suitable workshop once I got to Mexico, where the living is cheaper.

The first settlement behind the border was Hermosillo, where I made a stop. The city greeted me in typical Mexican fashion, heat … and also, rather luckily, with a large hardware store. Once more I went shopping for parts that would turn Bruce into a maritime vessel. When I left the store, a few hours later, with security keeping a close watch over me, I saw that someone was standing next to Bruce admiring him.

The overloaded motorcycle, dusty and dirty, with its many dents and scars collected on our travels, had intrigued him. After the obligatory small talk Hector asked what on earth a motorcycle traveller was doing in a DIY store, when there were many more beautiful places I could visit? I explained my plan and mentioned that I was looking for a workshop with reliable workmen. Hector happened to speak more English than all the gauchos in Central America put together and immediately understood what I was looking for. His neighbour had a small workshop and before I could blink we were on our way. Serendipity. Hector explained to the team in the workshop what I wanted. The workers nodded and were ready to help. I should come back *mañana*, the next morning, and they would do everything that I needed in one day. When I asked about the price, Marco, the boss and owner of the workshop, said, "Don't worry, it won't be much. We'll give you a good deal," and sent me away without any concrete information. I had no other choice but to trust him. *¡Mañana!* Tomorrow I would know more.

The next day, I was greeted with enthusiasm by the workmen. They flocked around me and asked many intelligent questions, so that I could tell that these boys knew what they were doing.

Our goal was to modify the final drive of the motorcycle in such a way that we would be able to connect it to the propeller. The final drive would have to be completely sealed so that no oil could get out and no water would get in. Everything had to be well-made to ensure that it would weather the trip over the ocean. We understood each other in some sort of international mechanics' language. Whenever necessary I would look up a few words in the dictionary. Otherwise we managed with our hands and feet. The entire team was involved in the propeller job, they all experimented, sawed things, welded and filed. All other clients were put off until the next day. This made me a little uneasy; I would have to pay for a whole day's work for all of them. On the other hand, I was really grateful to have met such helpful and capable workers, who put so much effort and passion into the job and were happy to try things out until I was satisfied with the end result. At noon, Marco ordered pizza for me and the workmen, who normally went home to eat. We all had lunch in the small garden behind the workshop. Then we went back to work, and the men skipped their siesta without a word, even though the temperature had risen considerably and left everyone dripping with sweat.

Finally, with closing time long past, the mechanism seemed to be working as I had hoped. We did a last test and indeed the propeller rotated without imbalance, the shaft connection between final drive and propeller was robust and the final drive was as sealed as I needed it to be.

I was a happy man!

The most important and complicated job was done. Impressed by the precision and dedication that these strangers had shown, I asked how much I owed them.

"¡Nada!" said Marco, the boss.

"Nothing?" I shook my head and told him in Spanglish we had agreed that he should name a decent price for the work done that day. Cheap does not mean free and the excellent work of his mechanics had an enormous value to me, for which I did not mind paying. In the end, he was more obstinate than I and all that was left for me to do was to thank him and the team.

In order to at least pay them in appreciation, Hector and I organised a slideshow that evening. Everybody brought some food and a few friends, and I, with Hector as my interpreter, told them about my adventures. None of the mechanics had ever crossed the Mexican border into another country. They did not have more than a week or two of holidays a year and most of their hard-earned pesos were spent on their children and the family. To be able to choose not to work, for as long as I did, was something that they could not imagine. For these reasons they absorbed the stories that I had brought from all over the World all the more eagerly. I was touched to see their wonder and interest and innocence, and was glad that my tales allowed them to experience a different world.

And I, for my part, had been immersed in a new world, where I had been accepted unquestioningly. I had met new people and made friends, who had helped me to come closer to my dream becoming a reality.

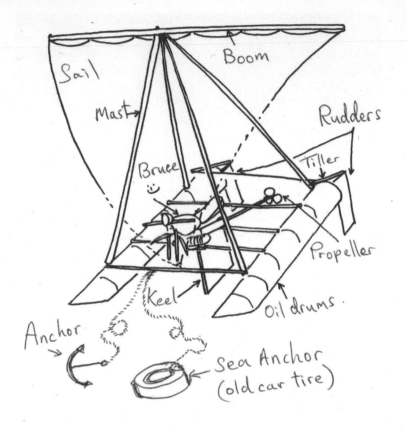

Sail

Boom

Mast

Rudders

Bruce

Tiller

Propeller

Keel

Oil drums.

Anchor

Sea Anchor
(old car tire)

In Antonio's workshop: things were done at leisurely pace.

CHAPTER FIVE

"Patience can only be learnt with patience."

∼

In Antonio's workshop I learnt my next lesson, just when everything seems to be going right, that's when everything will start to go really wrong, and there is always a fly in the ointment. I soon noticed that the five employees only worked when and how they pleased. Antonio may have nominally been the boss but he gave off the aura of a loser. He was much too nice a guy and the workmen were frankly walking all over him. I liked him nonetheless. He was reserved, softly-spoken and guileless. He had taken over the workshop and the building it was in after his father's death. He had sold the building and now paid rent to the new owner, but he was certain that he would have to give up the workshop soon as well. The buildings and the rent near the historical city centre had grown sky high over the last few years; Panama City needed more space and the modern buildings crept ever closer towards the *Casco Viejo*.

We had decided that I would tell the workers how my raft was to be constructed and that I would supervise their work, however I would have preferred to do it all by myself quite frankly. Out on the ocean I would be left to my own devices and I had to be certain that the raft was well-constructed and safe. I wanted to be 100% responsible for my own safety but instead, I had to rely on the capabilities of Antonio's workmen.
The work began on a Monday.
For our first task we were going to construct the two rows of barrels. Three of the workers began welding these together, but they

had hardly got started when I had to bite my tongue as I did not like how they were going about it. It was a delicate situation – we had only just begun and I did not want to affront anybody. At the same time I could not bear that Carlos was welding the barrels without cleaning off the rust beforehand. I chose my words carefully:

"You know, out there on the water I'll be risking my life. If you could clean off the rust first and make the welding seams on a clean surface that would be really great."

Carlos, the head mechanic, nodded agreeably and then just kept going. When I repeated my concerns, he nodded again and then just kept welding. I repeated myself two more times, a little more urgently, until finally Carlos stopped, looked up and said, "Yes, I get that. But this is also about OUR life."

He held up the welding helmet in front of his face and kept on welding, without worrying about the rust at all. The sparks that flew illuminated the workshop but not me.

The lion's share of the time in the workshop was spent waiting. Antonio had told me that the workshop opened at 9 a.m. Excitedly I showed up the next day at 9 a.m. on the dot. The shutters were still closed and nothing stirred. The workmen were there, sitting in a line in front of the workshop, but Antonio was the only one who had a key, they told me. They offered me a chair, smoked their cigarettes and waited. I sat down and watched the bustle in the street as everywhere else people went about their business. All the other shops were already open and customers came and went. From a balcony, a woman called down to her husband. Or was it her lover? An older woman in a red dress with braided grey hair was hanging out her washing. The colourful clothes were flapping in the wind like the sails of the boats down on the water. When Antonio finally showed up, I knew by heart how many flowerpots were standing on each balcony and where each piece of clothing hung on the washing line. This was how it would be every morning from now on.

Panamanians must have a special patience gene – a gene which

I am missing. There is no other explanation as to how Antonio's workshop was run. Each morning we began by working on the raft. Then – maybe ten minutes later – the first customer would show up. He had brought an old kerosene cooker, and apparently the container was leaking and had to be welded, so everyone stopped working on the raft and began to tinker with the cooker. Another ten minutes later an old grandmother arrived, she lived two doors down and the handle of her frying pan had come loose, so now of course customer number one would have to wait until the frying pan was mended. But before this could be done, Pedro turned up with a broken wooden leg that belonged to his uncle – and so the grandmother joined the queue. The wooden leg was now worked upon until Valentino turned up. Valentino had a large boat propeller in tow. It was so badly knocked-about that it was as if the man had run his boat up against a rock, at full speed. It was so battered and torn up that I was flabbergasted that he wanted to get it fixed. I was even more flabbergasted when Antonio accepted the job without batting an eye lid. "Of course we can. No worries. We'll get started right away." And they did get started, only to leave the job half-finished fifteen minutes later when Alicia entered the workshop with a broken ventilator. Alicia's cleavage was so inviting that just one of the men worked on the ventilator whilst the others stood around her as apparently they had to discuss something of the upmost importance with her … And so we waited, the guy with the kerosene cooker, the grandmother with her frying pan, Pedro with his uncle's wooden leg, Valentino with his battered propeller and me, we all waited for Alicia's ventilator to be fixed. And we waited. And waited.

With a team of five workers, it should have been possible to attend to five customers at the same time, I thought, but that was not how things were done around here. Antonio's men always worked together. One opened the gas bottle, another one held the work-piece while the third welded whilst telling the fourth man to fetch this, or that, as the fifth man chatted outside with one of the waiting customers.

None of the customers showed any signs of impatience. No one looked pointedly at their watch, no one complained or made a fuss, or paced up and down. And so, just like everybody else I waited patiently until the mechanics had completed the jobs of Alicia, Valentino, Pedro, the grandmother and the guy with the cooker and then returned to my raft. There was one difference though ... I waited every single day!

With all these people waiting, the workshop was a regular meeting place. The men gossiped more than the housewives outside and only interrupted themselves when a young woman went past. Then one of them would shout something like, "Oi, sexy! Nice arse!" and the others would join in. The women of course were thoroughly unimpressed and just went on their way. This sexist way of treating women was completely normal here and the men would have been horrified to learn that their behaviour would, elsewhere, be considered extremely offensive.

At some point, the bell of the food van sounded. You could hear it coming down the street, until it stopped in front of the workshop. Everyone had some fried chicken and coffee, which made the time pass by a little quicker.

One morning a fisherman showed up, he brought a few fish that were wrapped in newspaper, probably, in order to pay a bill. And of course, all the workers stopped what they were doing and had a little chat with the man, while the fish on the workbench were stinking out the place. If you could turn a smell into money, that man would have paid far too much, but the workers were not bothered by this. In the mess of the workshop they found a knife, wiped it with a dirty rag and proceeded to gut the fish right there and then. This took all five of them, of course, one of them gutted the fish and the other four watched, pointed now and then to the fish and gave advice. The smell attracted stray cats that slipped through the open gate to lick the blood from the floor and eat the guts.

Me and my raft, which was not yet a raft, watched and waited patiently. I celebrated every tiny bit of progress on the inside, while the days passed, painfully slowly.

I had to suppress the impatience I felt, whether I wanted to or not: to show it to the men would have been counterproductive. By the end of the first week my restlessness had increased tenfold. In six days we had only managed to finish the first of the two rows of barrels. The work that had been done by five men in seven days, I could have done on my own in two.

The following Saturday evening I met up with László, Jacques and Lionel at the *Kiosko*. I complained about how slowly the job was going and was met with the conviction that Antonio had, "the best work crew in all of Panama."

"But they weld the seams before cleaning off the rust! It's dangerous! The raft could fall apart in the middle of the ocean!"

"Eet is, what eet is!" said Lionel philosophically and told me that by Panamanian standards, Antonio's men were, "excellent" workers.

"Antonio can't tell them to work quicker, or better, because they'd just leave. Whether they do a good job or a bad one in your eyes, is irrelevant. Antonio has to accept it all, otherwise they'll go off to work for the competition and he can close the workshop."

"What, close it? If they leave he is bound to find five new guys. They couldn't be much worse than the ones he has now!"

"You've got no idea. His men have at least a few years' experience. They're a good team; they know what they're doing. No mechanic here has proper training! Anybody coming in to replace the men Antonio employs now, will be much, much, worse. You should be grateful they know a welding machine from their own arse!" Lionel was not joking. He blew smoke rings into the evening air, which vanished slowly and patiently.

Slowly and patiently, that was something that did not come naturally to me.

"Jacques, would you mind if I moved into the boat this weekend?

85

Does the offer still stand?"

When Jacques had first offered me lodging on his boat, I had just taken up lodgings with a Swiss expat family, but now I didn't want them to think that I was taking advantage of their hospitality. I had stayed with them for a week and it was time to move on. Besides, their youngest son would surely be keen to have his room back, I thought. Hospitality is a wonderful thing, but, it requires a compromise between your own feelings and those of the host.

There was no hesitation from Jacques. "Of course. You can come over whenever you like. Just call me when you get to the marina and I'll pick you up."

I enjoyed one more night in a proper bed, before moving in with Jacques. On board the *Red Princess* I would get the chance to get used to the constant movement of the waves. From a fenced-in high security family home, with air conditioning and a housekeeper, I basically moved aboard a pirate ship.

So lovingly did Jacques speak about his boat that you might have thought she was his lover. Maybe the ship filled a void created by his absent family. His son was in France. Sometimes Jacques felt nostalgic and one evening he told me about his wife. The two of them had stolen yachts and sailed across the seas, before selling them on somewhere else. This worked because Jacques used to get rid of old boats on an assignment basis. The boats he would sink as agreed with his employers, but their papers he would keep and pass them off as the papers of the boats he had stolen.

"For real? You guys used to steal yachts worth millions?"

"Oh yes."

"And you never got caught? Never got arrested?"

"Nope." His eyes sparkled. "Sometimes it was a close call. But we always had the right answers ready and we were a great team." Once, after a few weeks, they had returned to a stolen yacht that they had left in a harbour, in Cuba. Meanwhile, the police had figured out that the boat had been reported as stolen and were waiting for the thieves to come back. Jacques and his wife returned to the boat, unaware, and were promptly arrested and interrogated.

"So they asked me, 'Did you know this ship was stolen?', I said, 'Of course not! I'd have never accepted the job'. The cop asks, 'What job?' I say, 'We were contacted, by someone named Jerry, who asked if we could take the ship from here to the Dominican Republic. And that's what we were just about to do. That's why we're here'."

Jacques told this story with gusto. He imitated the cop's voice and changed his position according to whose lines he was speaking.

"Who is Jerry?" he asked with a deep, serious voice, and then he moved to the other side of the bench.

"Well, that's what I would like to know. Who the fuck is Jerry?" He laughed. "The police ended up looking for this Jerry guy and we got off the hook."

Another time, somewhere in the Caribbean, Jacques and his wife were having wild sex on a stolen ship and didn't hear the US coast guard dropping anchor next to them. When the officers came aboard and 'caught them in the act', they were so embarrassed that they settled for the explanation that Jacques fed them, 'he and his wife were on their honeymoon and would like to continue enjoying it if the officers would kindly leave them to it'. The officers retreated, glad to escape that embarrassing situation as quickly as possible, and forgot to ask any more questions about the stolen boat. Jacques laughed out loud at the memory of it, "Those prude Americans! All of them fled with bright red faces."

Jacques was equally proud of and amused by his escapades.

I imagined him and his wife as a kind of Bonnie and Clyde. Even as a young man, Jacques, rebellious, charismatic and intelligent, had always felt the need to overstep boundaries. He was a leader, someone who drove change. As a student in France in the early eighties, he was the leader of several youth movements and a bit of a revolutionary. He had organised endless protests and strikes, but soon he reached his limits as a politician and became a sailor instead. Ever since his first sailing trip he was hooked. He bought his own boat as soon as he could afford to and enjoyed the freedom of the nomadic life at sea. The ocean was the perfect way out of standardised society. Being always on the move allowed Jacques to gauge his limits and then overstep them. If it got too much, he could always leave. But Jacques is not just a rebel. He has charm and charisma and many stories to tell. He is also conscientious and exact. He gets angry when someone throws rubbish into the sea. He has all the patience in the world when teaching László's girlfriend Isabella how to sew and patch a sail. His stitches are as neat and straight as the wooden planking on his *Princess*.

When it came to food, he seemed more in need of food for thought, than for his stomach. The ship was stuffed to the rafters with books. Wherever there was no canvas to be fixed, there were books. Whenever he had time, he would put on his reading glasses, adjust them with his index finger and read. There was always a book lying around somewhere, a dog-eared page indicating where he had left off the last time.

Jacques, in his bright Hawaiian shirts, is a person who does not want to conform and who has found his own way of being. In Panama, among the sailing community, he has made himself a name as a sail-maker, but, at some point, he will haul in the anchor and leave it up to the winds where he will end up next.

The second week in the workshop began with an exhausting commute. As a lodger on Jacques' sailboat, I unrolled my mat under the canvas each night, slipped into my sleeping bag and listened to the waves until my eyes closed. I loved waking up there, out on the sea, being teased awake by the morning Sun, and the gentle swaying moves of the boat. Waking up was a revelation, especially when the first thing I saw was the golden sunshine in a steel blue sky. On other days the Sun rose as a dark red disc burning behind a thin mist on an orange vista. The picture that was painted on the horizon each day was always different, different colours, in a million different shades. The dark masts of the boats of all sizes and shapes around us were silhouetted against the sky. I adored those early mornings, especially when I awoke before the wind, and the sea was still as flat and motionless as a pond. In those moments I would remember the word which some Sinhalese used to describe the ocean, *'Ho gaana pokuna'*, roaring pond. The sea may sometimes roar, but at other times it is as quiet as a little pond.

Sleeping on deck had other advantages; the temperature was always very pleasant at night. The heat of the day dissipated slowly and only in the wee hours would I wrap myself up in my sleeping bag. And, I was always glad about not having to share the cabin with Jacques; he snored so loudly that you would think he was sawing his boat in half. Each inch of distance between me and Jacques was something to be grateful for. His snoring must have been heard under-water too, surely – perhaps Jacques is one of the reasons why the whales have begun to migrate from these waters.

With every new day that I began on deck, I looked forward to my adventure more and more.

My delight in life on the sea diminished at least once a day however or, maybe twice. First on the way to the quay, and then secondly on the way home. The morning wind, which wasn't always there every day, whipped the waves into a wild frenzy. I had to row from Jacques' boat to the coast, in an old dingy, for about half a mile. I was already accustomed to the strength of the waves and the water, but now I learnt what it meant to fight against them. In the mornings the current at least pushed me in the right direction. In the evening, however, when coming home after a long working day, exhausted from the workshop, I had to row against the current, in the dark and choppy waters.

Every day when I returned after leaving the boat in the morning the surroundings would have changed utterly. The large blue sailboat which had lain further to the right seemed to have been replaced by a trawler; three yachts that had not been there earlier were swaying before me, while four smaller boats had disappeared completely. I re-orientated myself on the silhouettes of vessels I did not know.

As soon as I paused for a few seconds to get my breath back and find my bearings, the waves pushed me back towards the coast. The water was so choppy that it spilled into the boat and I was sitting in the wet. It always seemed to me, as if the waves were testing the strength of my will.

"What, you still plan to take that little raft of yours out on the open sea?" they taunted me. I got angry.

"Yes! I do!" I shouted at them. "I'm not discouraged that easily! You got the wrong man!"

Their answer was prompt. The next wave hit the boat all the more fiercely. Groaning, the little old dinghy held against it, as it had done all its life. Mischievously, the waves kept rolling and pushed the dinghy this way and that. Through gritted teeth I told them what I thought of them. My words chased after the waves but did not touch them in the slightest.

On the Tuesday morning of the second week in the workshop, a customer came in with the fuel tank of an old car with a fuel leak. Antonio accepted the job and passed it on to Carlos, the head mechanic, who put down the work he had just started on my raft and reached for the welding machine. He fussed around with it a bit and asked his younger helper to hold the tank in the right position. I watched in disbelief. Were they really going to weld that thing, as it was? I foresaw the entire workshop going up in flames and tried to stop them:

"Wait! That's dangerous! You have to let out the fuel first! Have you washed the tank?"

Carlos looked at me as if I had gone crazy.

"No, we haven't washed it, but we emptied it," he said.

I was shocked.

"What?! You just emptied it and now you're going to weld it?" I shouted. I no longer cared if I hurt their feelings or not. What they were doing could have horrific consequences! I tried to explain, "Even though there is no fuel in there, the tank can still explode! If anything, it'll explode all the more easily when it is filled with lots of oxygen and a little fuel, like now!"

Everyone just looked at me blankly. A customer translated my words, but there was still no reaction from the five workers. I tried again to warn them, as best as I could in Spanish, *"Muy peligroso!"* Very dangerous. With a movement of his hand, Carlos brushed my words aside, then he seemed to consider them for a moment and moved the tank beneath a metal table so it would serve as a shield of sorts, in the case of an explosion. It felt to me as if he only did this to appease me. He went back to working on the tank. I dropped everything and ran out onto the street, while everyone else glanced briefly my way and then went back to work. I expected an explosion at any moment, all the time remembering what Jacques and Lionel had told me, "At least they know what a welding plant is" … I was no longer sure that this was a good thing.

When I stuck my head through the gate, half an hour later, everything was as it always was; the tank seemed to have been fixed. The men laughed when they saw me – No explosion!

They were lucky this time, and whilst I was glad that nothing had happened to Antonio and my colleagues, I seriously began to question the situation.

Maybe an explosion was the reason why that drainage pipe now lay in a corner … Once upon a time it must have done its duty transporting waste-water from the flats above, the dirty waste-water that would occasionally spurt down all over us from a hole in the ceiling. Whenever someone took a shower on the floors above us, the dirty water ended up down here; it rained from the ceiling and became a rivulet that found its way into the drain in the middle of the workshop. Most of the sudsy water seeped into the many cracks in the floor, leaving behind a faint soapy scent. My soon-to-be-raft was – of course – propped up in just that exact spot. I had to be constantly on guard to avoid getting a complimentary shower with someone else's used water.

However, the longer I worked there the more convinced I became that 'watering' the place now and then, could only be a good thing. For instance on the next occasion that Carlos welded something, when the gas tube detached from the torch and hissed through the air like an angry dragon on a rampage, throwing out its flames. This time it was not just me who took to his heels: we all fled out into the street. While we watched from a safe distance, the tube lashed all over the place. Everywhere there were plenty of easily flammable things: fuel, oil, gas bottles, spray cans. We held our breath. The situation was dangerous and I already saw half the building going up in flames. *¡Santa Madre de Dios!"* The workers asked for help from above and I saw Carlos make the sign of the cross. Finally Cristiano, one of the helpers, made a determined face – someone had to turn the gas off. He, the eldest, took a deep breath, covered his face with his arm, ran inside and turned the gas tap off. Straight away the dragon lay down with a subdued hiss, as if he had never meant any harm. We all started breathing again.

It never occurred to anyone, even after that incident to repair the damaged gas hose properly. It was simply stuck back into its old place and fixed with tape. After all everything had ended well, so why change anything?

That same afternoon everyone was pretty excited and no one could focus on their work. There was singing and laughing, Cristiano gave a drum solo on some cans and metal parts and even the customers joined in and clapped along to his rhythm. Carlos, who was normally quite sluggish, did a little dance in the middle of the workshop, while we whistled and applauded. "Today we were lucky! We need to celebrate! The work we'll do tomorrow." the workers said, and sent the youngest to pick up beer.

By the end of the second week, my ten barrels were welded together, and I had reached the end of my patience.

We had attached two angle irons, of equal length, to each row, in order to join them later. I had also asked the workers to cut a hole into each of the ten barrels. This sounds like a rather silly thing to do if you plan sailing on these barrels, but since I would be travelling in a region infested with drug smugglers, I thought it would be best if the inside of the barrels could be checked easily. Should the police suspect me of drug smuggling, they could simply open a plastic cap and make sure that my barrels did not serve as a hiding place for cocaine or anything similar. I was being extra careful to avoid having the barrels cut open by suspicious policemen.

After two weeks with Antonio's men, the slow work tempo, on top of the unsafe work environment and the endless waiting, it all finally became too much for me. At the rate we were going my permitted 180 days in Panama would be over before the raft was ready. Something had to change, I thought, and looked expectantly at Lionel. We were sitting in the *Kiosko* enjoying the cooler air of the evening. I had just told him about the incident with the faulty welding plant.

"How much room does your raft need?" he asked.

"About sixteen by nine feet."

"And how many days will you need to finish it?"

"If I can work without interruptions, maybe three days. Four days tops."

Another four days – with Antonio's way of working, would mean another two weeks. I was in a hurry, not just because of my impatience but also because the rainy season would begin in a couple of weeks. I bit my lip and hoped that Lionel would have a solution.

"Well, that should work. You can finish off the rest of the work in the yard, next to my workshop. There'll definitely be enough room – but you have to leave it outside. I don't think my boss will be happy to have it outside either, but he hardly ever turns up. It'll be alright for a few days."

"Are you sure?" I was more than relieved to hear that. "I don't want you to get into any trouble."

"Nah ... it'll be fine. You can use our tools and the welding plant." I could have kissed him! "I can't tell you how grateful ..." Before I could deliver a lengthy speech, Lionel interrupted me.

"I can't be held responsible if anything gets stolen though and, you have to be okay with leaving the thing outside at night, also, to have to work all day, in the hot Sun."

"No problem!" I was so relieved that I would be able to work somewhere else, that I could not care less if I would have a roof over my head or not. If I could, I would have moved the raft straight away and got back to work!

Maiden Voyage: Jacques and I getting busy with the final preparations.

CHAPTER SIX

"If you're taking a risk, rely solely on yourself."

〜

The next morning it was not the wind, nor the rising Sun that woke me up, but my impatience. As soon as I opened my eyes I remembered that today was the day that László and I would move the raft to my new work space. I made a cup of tea and packed my things as quietly as possible. Jacques had returned late last night and I did not want to wake him.

I still had plenty of time before László would pick me up, so I sat down with the little outboard motor that Jacques had given me. The motor was one of many spare parts that had accumulated on Jacques' boat. The place was a bit of a mess, canvas, ropes, hooks, eyelets, needles, flares and life vests were everywhere. He could have set up a floating flea market with all that stuff. The outboard motor was broken – but, if I was able to fix it, I would take it with me, as a backup motor. It probably wouldn't hurt to have a substitute out in the ocean.

There were many other vessels at anchor around us. At some point Jacques emerged, stumbling and smelling of booze. Sleepily he padded to the stern, climbed over the railing, yawned, pulled down his shorts and held on to the rope, his naked butt hovering over the water, as he did his business. When he was done he climbed down the ladder and washed himself with seawater. He did this without any hint of embarrassment. I, on the other hand, was very embarrassed and silently apologised to my neighbours. They must have been used to it however, as nobody looked up from their breakfast, flinched or even frowned at him. I remembered Lionel's equanimity, "It is what it is." I guess people on a boat live in their own little world and do as they please. Later when I asked Jacques if he had ever thought about installing a toilet in his boat, he said, "What for? Whales shit into the ocean too." He preferred to use the extra space as storage for his books, rather than for a toilet bowl, which would only be, he said, "another thing I would have to clean."

Jacques had only just pulled up his trousers when László showed up in his dinghy to pick me up. The bags under his eyes looked just like Jacques', so I surmised that the two of them had spent half the night drinking at the *Kiosko*. His innate cheerfulness was already shining through though, and he greeted me with a wide grin that trumped his bleary eyes.

Once we arrived onshore we rode on Bruce to Antonio's workshop. In the *Calle Ramón Valdes*, we rented a car and a driver. Together with Antonio's men we loaded the rows of barrels onto the car's roof. I paid Antonio 300 dollars for the work and recommended that he use the money to buy a new welding machine. He laughed. He did not like to see me go and he couldn't understand what was driving me away.

Even though I had had a good time with the guys, I was glad to build the raft myself. It was a big relief that I would no longer have to bite my tongue when someone did shoddy work. Now, I could rely exclusively on myself, on my knowledge and skills – and, another advantage was that I no longer ran the risk of being wiped out in a massive explosion!

We drove to the edge of the Panama Canal, in the dockland called *Diablo*, which was mainly industrial sheds and garages, with lots of trees and a few houses squashed in between them. Near Lionel's workshop, a one-way street looped itself around a row of houses and towards the canal bank. There we met Lionel who directed us to a shed right next to the canal. His boss's boat was waiting in a hangar, ready to go back onto the water. The yard was just big enough to accommodate my raft. My new workplace was hemmed in by the narrow road, which ran along the edge of the Panama Canal in front, and the metal sliding door of the garage in the back. But, it was all I needed.

As soon as we had unloaded the barrels, Lionel showed me the tools. Everything was new and carefully stored – the exact opposite to Antonio's mess. I was keen to redo the sloppy welding seams as soon as possible, but I had promised László to help him with his work that day. The three guys had been tremendously helpful, so I was always glad when I got the chance to return the favour. I put my impatience and my raft aside, to help László. Since we had already rented a car, it made sense to use it to return a repaired ship engine to the client.

"You got your passport with you?" asked László and I answered in the affirmative, without paying much attention.

"What do I need my passport for? Aren't we just returning an engine?"

"Do you have it, or not?"

"Yeah, I do. But what for?"

"Well, the engine belongs to a CIA agent. We're taking it to his boat but then we're going to the US Embassy to get paid."

"You're repairing things for a CIA agent? But weren't you arrested in the States? Doesn't that worry you?"

"Nah, my arrest was a long time ago, and they had to let me go in the end – no evidence. The agent doesn't seem to have a problem with me."

He turned his head in the way that was typical for him. Then he shrugged and looked a little embarrassed. I had not seen him like this before. I felt I would be overstepping the boundaries of our recent friendship if I asked for more details.

The longer I knew László, Jacques and Lionel, the more I liked them. But it also struck me that it was no coincidence that they were living in Panama – a country that is not particular about laws and regulations.

After a few minutes László returned to the conversation, "The thing with the stolen computers wasn't me. It was a setup. They couldn't prove anything. Without any evidence they just had to let me go."

Once I had finished helping László, I drove back to *Diablo* to work on connecting the two rows of barrels with five thick gage steel tubes. I was able to work quickly and enjoyed doing it by myself. Despite the heat I was truly content. The next three days I focused on my work and made steady progress – the thing actually began to look like a raft. The narrow road, at the edge of the canal, was a one way street and whoever drove into the industrial estate had to drive past my raft. People often stopped for a little chat and then went on their way. It almost felt as if I were still travelling, fixing Bruce by the side of the road, as I had done millions of times over the last couple of years. The difference was that just across the narrow road, there was the Panama Canal, the most important navigation route in the world. The canal was about 450 yards wide here. Whenever one of the large cargo ships went past, I would look up. I had crossed the canal a few times over the bridge, but it was only now that I grasped the true magnitude of its greatness as an engineering masterpiece.

About 480 years before I planned my own little adventure, the Spanish King Carlos V, had made plans for a waterway. It wasn't completed during his lifetime, but the dream of linking the Pacific with the Atlantic burnt in the hearts of industrialists. In 1880, France began building it under the supervision of Ferdinand Lesseps, a diplomat and entrepreneur, who had previously worked on the Suez Canal. The plan was to dig a trench across Panama at sea level, as they had previously done for the Suez Canal. It was to cut across the jungle and the hilly landscape – Craziness, especially at a time when the car hadn't even been invented! Soon the French found themselves confronted with the Culebra Range, a mighty obstacle, which made the construction of the Panama Canal much more difficult than the Suez Canal. The dream ended in disaster: continuous rainfall and landslides wiped out thousands of workers. Hundreds more were killed by yellow fever. Like a king who sends his soldiers to fend off a foe, so the Culebra Mountains, under siege, sent mosquitoes to the workers, to keep them from sinking their spades and pickaxes into its flanks.

Eight years later, the French gave up on their dream and left. The mountain had been stronger than they. It was decided that the canal could not be built because of the difficult geological conditions. The company that had been commissioned with the undertaking went bankrupt; the largest bankruptcy in history, and Lesseps died shortly after. The canal must have destroyed him physically and psychologically.

Still, the dream of connecting the two oceans did not vanish from the power of human imagination. This time the Americans got involved. President Theodore Roosevelt hoped to gain an advantage for his Navy: US warships were to rule the seas thanks to the Panama Canal. In 1904 the United States won the bid and the work resumed.

This time around, industrialisation did its part. Alongside the building site tracks were lain down, in order to remove the rubble and avoid a landslide. Things looked promising; the work progressed in leaps and bounds. What had taken the French one month could now be accomplished in a single day. But soon the Americans had to fight the same setbacks as the French. Yellow fever brought deaths and panic. Thousands of workers quit and left. Not even higher wages could convince them to stay. John Frank Stevens, the American head engineer, understood that they were not just facing an architectonical challenge, but a medical one as well. Something had to be done about the mosquitoes. He had mosquito nets installed on each window in the workers' settlements and fumigated entire towns. Things improved considerably and optimism returned. But then further landslides occurred. Finally, the incessant rain brought everything to a standstill. The Chagres River alongside the canal had turned into a wild, dangerous torrent and took the very idea of a waterway with it. The Americans conceded that the Culebra Range could not be overcome, but still they would not give up.

This time, Stevens decided that three locks were needed, in order to level out the difference in height of 85 feet. Resistance to this plan was strong: never had anything this large been constructed with concrete. It seemed impossible. It took Stevens all his persuasive power and even when Theodore Roosevelt finally agreed, dissenting voices remained.

Today, we know that it is only thanks to these locks, that the canal could be completed. In August 1914 the first ship traversed the canal. By then Europe was a few weeks into the First World War – the inauguration celebrations were, accordingly, rather restrained. Nonetheless, it was clear to one and all, that something extraordinary had been accomplished. The Pacific and the Atlantic were finally linked!

I could hear the roaring of the ships before I saw them. Large white letters decorated their blue, green and red hulls. A ship marked Mitsubishi went past me, perhaps with new cars on their way from Japan to Europe? The Cyrillic letters on the next ship gave away its country of provenance ... Russia. Did the Chinese containers on the third ship contain cheaply made shoes? Their sheer size and scale made me (and the raft) feel meaningless in comparison. That's how a goldfish must feel next to a blue whale. Those mighty cargo ships were behemoths of the ocean, but compared to the vastness of the ocean, even these giants were nothing more than goldfish.

The Sun was beating down on me without mercy, and it took sweat dripping down my forearm to remind me to stay hydrated. Around noon Lionel would show up and force me to take a break. Without him, I would only have realised in the evenings that I had not eaten all day.

During one of these lunch breaks I asked Lionel what material he would recommend for the rudders and how to get hold of it. He considered for a moment and said, "The best thing to use would be marine plywood – that should last a good while longer than normal plywood. But it's too expensive."

"How expensive?" I asked.

Lionel was looking out of the window towards where two young women were arguing with an older man.

"The size you need will cost you more than 200 dollars. Tell you what, I don't have much of it left, but I'll cut out two rudders from the sheets I've got."

Without Lionel's generosity, it would have been practically impossible to find better material here in Panama City. I had spent the previous days racking my brain over those rudders and now Lionel had offered me a solution, lavishly.

Outside the two women went on bickering. We finished our lunch quickly: work was waiting.

Back in the day *Diablo* was used to house the people who were working on the Panama Canal. Today it is an industrial area. Every single one of the businesses here is related to the sea, the canal, or boats.

People knew each other there, and I stood out like a sore thumb. Most of the people that stopped for a chat were, American Panamanians. I assumed that their parents had moved here when the Panama Canal was still managed by the United States. Their descendants seemed to me, as laid back as any Panamanian, but as soon as they opened their mouths, their accent gave them away. A friendly lot, there always seemed to be a few of them sitting on the bench across the road right on the Canal bank, sometimes even in the mornings, sometimes during the siesta, and always in the evenings. They would drink cold beer and beckon for me to join them. In the heat, bottles beaded with moisture but no matter how inviting they looked, I was not interested in breaks – I had had far too many of those in the last couple of weeks – but we chatted sometimes and one of them even offered me the chance to cut large bamboo trees on his property, which I could use for the deck. I accepted gladly but had no means of transporting it, as his estate was some 30 miles away. So, the generous man promised me that the bamboo delivery for my raft would be sponsored by the American Panamanians.

Another evening, a Dutch family who lived in the area, invited me to dinner. Night was falling and made it impossible for me to keep on working, so I accepted the invitation and spent another evening with strangers, listening to the stories of their lives.

Eventually, I rode Bruce to *Diablo* for the last time. The frame of the raft was completed and I would be able to mount Bruce onto it. I could not wait to launch the raft into the water but, I also felt tense about the raft's reaction once it was in the water – how would Bruce react to suddenly being turned into a raft?
The last few hours of work were the most demanding from a technical point of view, luckily Lionel's workshop had a small crane and, with this, I managed to haul Bruce onto the raft, manoeuvre him into the right position and secure him to the frame with steel bolts, all by myself.
The preparations took all afternoon; I told Jacques and László that the maiden voyage would take place the next day. László looked up the times of the tides and decided that they would come over around noon to help me launch the raft and experience this important moment with me. I decided to spend the night with Bruce and the raft. At night *Diablo* is pretty deserted and I didn't want to leave Bruce by himself, even though he was now securely attached to the raft. I did not want to take any risks at the end stage of things. At dusk, Lionel and I packed up the tools, and then I went home with him for a shower and some food.
It was very late when I unrolled my sleeping bag next to the raft on the hard cement floor. It felt a little surreal. Ever since I was a little boy I had dreamed of sailing the seas on a bamboo raft, and here I was, right next to the famous Panama Canal, with my little

raft ready to be launched the next day. But who could have ever imagined that the stars that hung in the sky above me would ever grant my wish?

Thoughts were playing hide and seek in my head that night. They came and went, too many to hold on to, but I was happy and fulfilled. My body was aching from the hard work of the last few days. My legs and arms felt heavy, the muscles stiff, but the excitement was like a salve and soothed my tense muscles and took away the pain of the blisters on my hands. I felt alive with every fibre of my being. I was unable to sleep for a long time. It was not until the Sun prepared itself to rise, that my eyes finally closed.

The alarm on my mobile phone woke me up. Bleary-eyed I rose, packed the sleeping bag and splashed my face with water. There was already plenty of traffic on the canal and the birds were singing from the trees along the embankment. There would be no breakfast today.

I still had plenty to do and it would not be long before László and Jacques turned up. Today, I would need to stick to a tight schedule. The tides influenced the water level of the canal so dramatically that during low tide, a part of the stony canal bed emerged. The plan was to carry the raft down the steep embankment and leave it on the dry canal bed and then wait for the incoming tide to bring the raft afloat. I was convinced that any other way of launching the raft would be too risky, due to waves and choppy waters. There was a difference of about 16 feet between low and high tide on the Panamanian coast. That day, the lowest water level would be reached at twenty minutes to two in the afternoon. By that time the raft had to be waiting on the canal bed. From that moment on, the water would begin to rise slowly, until it reached its highest point, six hours later. The easiest way would have been a ramp. There actually was one about 300 feet from the workshop, but it belonged to the local police station. Bad luck! Asking the police to help me launch an illegal raft would have been brave indeed. But the odds were high that it could turn out to be a very dumb idea.

We could still be seen from the police station, but unless policemen were standing around outside, they would not be able to see over the embankment.

Around noon László, his girlfriend Isabella and Jacques showed up. I was really glad that they had come. There was a lot to do and I could use every additional hand. The empty raft with Bruce, weighs about 1300 pounds and we had to carry it for about 50 yards: an impossible task, for just the four of us. I had to find a few more people to help us. I could not ask Lionel and his workers as today of all days, they were working elsewhere.

We were all standing around the raft, putting on the finishing touches, when a car stopped. The long-haired driver had his elbow hanging out of the window and I could not help but notice his muscular arms.

"What the devil are you guys building there? I already noticed this thing yesterday," he inquired.

"It's a boater-cycle! A motorcycle that's been transformed into a boat," I explained. He rolled his eyes and laughed.

"I've never seen something like this before! Incredible! And does it work?"

"Yes, of course. I mean … I hope so. We are launching it today for the first time and then we'll find out." His muscular arm drew my attention once again. "We could use a few strong men to help us carry it down to the canal bed. Would you have time?"

His answer was prompt, "Sure. I'll bring my workers, if that helps?"

"Oh, if it helps? You are an angel!" I said, showing my gratitude before he had even done anything.

The man hailed from Norway, and had a business a few blocks down the road that specialised in the underwater maintenance work of ships and boats. His employees were professional divers. Being able to utilise these 'volunteers' was a godsend. It was one o'clock in the afternoon already and we had to get going. The Norwegian promised to be right back with reinforcements and drove off.

Shortly afterwards, five men came towards us. They looked as if they had come straight from the gym. Silhouetted by the Sun, it seemed to me that there should be a soundtrack to this moment, something dramatic and triumphant. Horns, violins, drum beats! I saw them coming towards me in slow motion. I shook my head and was once more amazed at my good fortune. Those five men were just what we needed.

The news about the launch had spread in the neighbourhood and more and more faces appeared on the embankment. I recognised the Dutch family who had invited me to dinner. They did not want to miss this significant moment. The atmosphere was happy and excited. Even though some of them did not believe in my dream, they all wished me the best and were impressed by my determination to travel over the water on what was unanimously agreed to be, "The strangest looking boat that they had ever seen." Now there were nine of us and I made the sign to get ready. The large rocks that secured the embankment made the way uneven and treacherous. We carried the raft towards the water, step by step. Like a king in his sedan, Bruce stood motionless on the raft. The nervousness I felt was like 1000 ants marching through my veins, but I managed to hide it behind a mask of cheerfulness and joked around and played the clown to everyone, which also silenced the critics.

"A little higher!"
"Yes, just like that."
"Go on!"
"Watch out for that stone guys."
"Slow down!"
"Any further?"
"Ouch!"
"Here?"
"Shit!"
"Almost there..."
"Stop!"

We communicated in short calls and inched towards the water. Finally, we put the raft down. Almost noiselessly, a cargo ship threw its shadow over us. László and I looked at it and then we looked at each other; we were both in awe, but there was still a lot more work to be done. The water was rising, we had to hurry. László and Jacques helped me to mount the propeller. At the last moment the bamboo poles turned up. We lay them down next to each other, to create a makeshift deck. Someone from the crowd handed me a Panamanian flag. It gave my raft an official air. Then we tethered the raft to two trees so it would not take off without the captain.

As soon as Bruce had enough buoyancy we were going to travel to Amador on the canal – László, Isabella, Jacques and I. There we would moor the raft to Jacques' boat until everything was ready for the trip. But for now, we waited for the water to rise. Every once in a while a police car drove past and I had the feeling that the policemen were watching us critically. Restlessly, I walked around the raft, checked something here, and adjusted something there.

Finally, after an hour of waiting the water began lapping at the rocks, reclaiming the stony canal bed. At first it was only in the hollows between the stones, moving slowly and shyly, almost hesitantly. For the two children of the Dutch family it all took too long and they needed to eat something.

"Dylan," called their father Peer, "we'll be back in a little while, we just need to get the kids some food. Will you still be here then?"

"Yeah, looks like it. It's not moving very fast."

"Should we bring something back for you? You hungry?"

Only then did I realise that I had not eaten all day.

"A sandwich would be amazing. And would you mind bringing back a gallon of fuel too? I have no idea how far I'll get with what I have."

Stupidly I had forgotten that Bruce's tank was almost empty. This had been partly on purpose, so that the full tank would not add any weight to the raft when carrying it to the canal. But now I was in doubt as to whether the fuel was enough for the maiden voyage. Peer promised to return with food and fuel and off they went.

We kept watch over the water level as it increased inch by inch. And suddenly it was the moment, the moment that I had been waiting for, not just today, but for the last few weeks; the water began to wash around the barrels. Then again, nothing seemed to happen for a while, even though the water reached up to our ankles. Minutes passed, and then the raft gave a jerk. It was lifted by the water, as gently as if angels were pulling it up by silk ribbons. The raft swayed left and right and then it was no longer stranded on the ground. My raft was floating!

My audience applauded and cheered. I joined them, shouting my joy and wiping away a clandestine tear before anyone could see it. We hugged.

László and Jacques had become part of my adventure and it was wonderful to experience this moment together. I was relieved and elated. I loved seeing Bruce swaying on the water. What a feeling! The long working hours were forgotten. All that counted now was this moment. Soon I would set off on my journey. I saw the small boy on the beach with eyes as big as saucers, running this way and that, unable to contain his excitement. I could have run along the canal shouting my joy to all and sundry. The adventure had begun!

In reality however, things were not moving quite that quickly. Before we could set off on our maiden voyage the water had to rise higher. Only once it was deep enough would we be able to mount the two rudders. When the time had come Jacques jumped in and held up one rudder from below, while László and I tried to manoeuvre it into the right position. The waves rolled towards the embankment and got in the way. Finally we managed to insert the heavy steel bolt and fix the first rudder. After that we mounted the second. Once Jacques emerged from the water, I moved the tiller to see how well the rudders moved.

"It works perfectly! Start the motor!"

Jacques and László waded back on land, while I turned the ignition key. The motor started, I engaged the first gear and accelerated carefully. The propeller rotated without a hitch and moved the raft across the water. Everything was working as it should. Those ants that had been marching nervously inside of me were now partying, dancing salsa and going completely wild. I could have danced along with them!

László untied one of the ropes and I went for a little spin, keeping within the range of the second rope. The raft could be steered without a problem and I had become a captain!

"Come on, on board, all of you! I'm your captain for a journey into the sunset!" I joked, and everyone got on board.

"Are Peer and his family back?" I called towards the embankment, as I remembered that I had ordered food and fuel.

"No, not yet," said one of the divers. "But they're bound to show up any minute. Wait for the fuel!"

I was tired of waiting. I was ready to go and find out how the raft held up to the ocean, also, it got dark here at half past six. It would be best to arrive at Jacques' boat before dusk.

The first excitement had passed and the tension returned. We were close to a police station, in the Panama Canal – the PANAMA CANAL – on a raft without official documentation and with a captain without a sailing certificate. My passengers were an alleged computer thief and a pirate who had stolen several yachts. It was time to get the hell out of here. So we untied the second rope and drove out towards the sea, waving at the cheering crowd on the bank of the canal.

The GPS showed me how fast we were going – or rather how slowly, I should say. We moved at about three mph. Plenty of time to look around and keep a watchful eye on each boat we went past. I am an optimist, but at that point each boat coming towards us, or overtaking us, made me nervous. I straddled Bruce, got off again, went from one side of the raft to the other, and used every inch of the shaky deck to escape my nerves. Without success.

After what seemed like an eternity, the port cranes of Balboa appeared on our left. Cargo ships were lying at anchor there. Some were being relieved of their heavy load, while other barges were being loaded up. Little tug boats were busily driving to and from amongst these giants. We were too far away to see the people working the machines, so it seemed as if they had lives of their own.

As we were about to pass under the iconic bridge, the Bridge of the Americas, a small speed boat came towards us. Only when it came close to the raft was I able to sigh with relief: there was an Asiatic babble of voices and then I saw that the passengers were not the Panamanian authorities, but Japanese tourists.

"Ooooh! Aaaah!" Their cameras clicked. We laughed; relieved that they were only tourists and nothing else. We continued on our way, while the tourists followed us for a couple of minutes asking us about the story behind the strange looking vessel.

When we finally relaxed somewhat, we heard the police sirens behind us. I turned around and saw what I did not want to see, a police boat with flashing blue lights was approaching us.

"Shit!" I immediately stopped the engine, since at our speed we would not stand a chance of escaping, and prepared myself mentally for a whole lot of trouble. Would I get arrested? Would they confiscate the raft?

The police boat braked and came as close to us as possible. My friends made themselves invisible as best as they could. When the siren stopped, all I could hear was my heart thumping against my chest, heavy and fast. I looked the enemy straight in the eye and greeted them as if they were my best friends. One of the policemen had a plastic bag in his hands and by the way he held the bag I could tell that there was something heavy inside. The policeman came and stood by the railing and I expected him to jump onto the raft. Instead he signalled for me to come closer. I stepped forward and he threw the plastic bag at me. Instinctively

I caught it. Then the policeman nodded and said something to his colleague at the controls. The boat went backwards, turned away and disappeared as quickly as it had arrived.

"What was that? What's in the bag?" asked Isabella, who was the first to find her voice again. I looked in the bag and couldn't stop myself from laughing. Triumphantly I pulled out two sandwiches, a small bottle of coke and a gallon sized mineral water bottle, the content of which had a dull colour.

"That's the fuel!"

We all breathed a sigh of relief and I began to feel less afraid of the police.

"You see that? I told you no one cares about this little raft of yours!" László was pleased but he admitted that he too had been nervous.

Hungrily we shared the food and toasted to the success of the maiden voyage with a coke. The fuel went to Bruce. Now we would definitely make it to Jacques' *Red Princess*.

We passed the mighty bridge whose wings spanned and held both shores together. The setting Sun and the reflecting red colour of the structure shone brilliantly into the distance. But the enjoyment of the surroundings didn't last long when we heard the police sirens for the second time. Another police boat raced towards us, slowed down and stopped next to the raft. The officers looked at us sceptically, and then one of them asked in perfect English with a friendly voice, "Do you have a license for this ... thing?"

My heart missed a beat. "No," I said, while my friends again did their best to become invisible.

"Do you have life vests?"

I shook my head innocently and smiled.

"And what are you doing with this funny thing on the water?"

"Oh, this is just an experiment. I wanted to find out if my motorcycle could power a raft. We went for a little trip and then I'll take it apart again."

The policeman laughed, "Seriously?"

"Yes, seriously," I joined in with his laughter disingenuously.

"In that case, be careful and don't forget the life vests next time! Good luck! *¡Adiós!* "

They waved and drove off. We looked at each other for a moment and then we just hooted with relief.

I thought the two police boats were a good omen. Everything was going to work out, and now I was sure of it!

"Let's drive out into the ocean, into the waves! Yeehaw!"

All was going well until a red light flared up on the motorcycle dashboard. "Oh no!" It was the warning light for the oil pressure. I had been on the road with Bruce for over two and a half years and I had never had this problem, but now, NOW, during the first hour out on the water, this had to happen. And the oil pressure of all things! The warning light meant that the motor was not being lubricated properly. It would only take a short time to cause major damage. Even if it held up till we reached Jacques' boat, repairing the oil pump meant some major repairs which I wouldn't be able to perform on the water.

"Jacques, how far are we until we're home?"

"About a mile or so."

"A mile!" At this speed we would need another twenty minutes. If there really was a problem with the oil pump, all it would take for the engine to be damaged very seriously, was less than ten seconds. I hoped the lamp would go on flickering as it was rather than begin to glare continuously.

"Keep to the left as much as possible, that way we'll arrive quicker," advised Jacques, when I explained the problem. By now we had left the canal and were out on the open ocean, beyond the ships that were lying at anchor in Amador.

"I have to say, I love how this raft-thing, or whatever it is, glides over the waves. You did well, man!" Jacques slapped my back with approval.

László and Isabella were sitting at the front, their feet dipping into the water. László turned his head in the way that was so characteristic of him and said, "Yeah, it's brilliant. I would never have thought that it would work so well. That thing is more stable than my boat!" he laughed.

"Seriously, I'm proud of you. You adventurer! Really proud!" Jacques nodded in agreement and laid his arm around my shoulder.

"Captain Dylan!" he called theatrically, "The bravest of them all! Because he doesn't know what he's doing!"

I grinned. I was pleased by their praise and proud of myself as the captain of a 'boater-cycle'. I would have relaxed and enjoyed the trip, if it had not been for that little red light. At least I knew what I had to do the next day. It was annoying to go back to fixing stuff, but I was starting to see the positive side. I was happy that it had happened now, rather than later on, when I was out on the ocean. Luckily we reached Jacques' boat without the motor acting up. We moored the raft to the *Princess*. The light kept flickering at irregular intervals. I turned the motor off – no more work today. It would have to wait until the morning – *mañana*. Now I just wanted to celebrate the successful maiden voyage, without living in fear.

At that moment, the mobile in my pocket rang. It was Lionel.

"How did it go? I just got to the workshop and saw that you had already left."

"It was great. It all worked out. The raft glides over the waves like you wouldn't believe, like a dream. And it's super stable."

"Glad to hear it. That's really good news!"

"We're all going to the *Kiosko*, to celebrate," I said. "Are you coming?" The question was rhetorical. Lionel always came when there was a reason to celebrate, or even when there was nothing to celebrate.

"Yeah, sure. I'll be there in half an hour."

We all got on Jacques' motorised dinghy and whizzed off to the marina – or at least it seemed that way after travelling on my slow raft. The regular crowd at the *Kiosko* knew about my plan and somehow word of my successful maiden voyage had gotten around. More than once I had to tell tales about the trip and my encounters with the police. The more often I told the story, the more pleased about my success I was. Putting it into words so many times, seemed to make it more tangible. I really had built a raft! Today, I finally had a beer and enjoyed the attention.

Then Lionel arrived and toasted to our success. What would I have done without him, László and Jacques? I could not have hoped for more enthusiastic, supportive friends and I could not have built the raft so easily without them. I thought of Ron and Christina, who introduced me to László and I sent some positive energy to Rio Sereno. I recounted my story for Lionel, while he added to the few beers he'd already had that evening. Then he put his arm around me and said in a tone of voice reminiscent of a eulogy delivered at my funeral, "Dylan, I'm worried about you. I don't think it's a good idea for you to take your raft out there." I gave him a bemused look.

"You don't know the sea! You don't know how bad it can be in the middle of a storm! My god! I got caught up in two horrendous storms. The forces out there are tremendous!"

He pressed a kiss on my cheek.

"Don't go! You're too young to die!"

"Lionel! You helped me so much to build a raft all these days and all of a sudden you're afraid?" I was disgruntled and pushed him away.

"It's because I know what it's like out there, in bad weather. You have no idea! Once I spent 48 hours in a storm! I couldn't even leave the cabin. My boat was three times – no, ten times as big as yours, and it turned around on its own axis twice! It was terrible! It's a miracle that I am still alive today!"

"If it was that bad, and you were stuck inside, how can you have known that your boat had capsized, with its keel upwards? Weren't you disoriented?"

"Because I was sitting on the ceiling, next to the lamp, for a while. That's how I know my boat was upside down," he said with a serious face, but winking at me.

"Didn't you hear it in the news? Just today a storm blew six cargo ships ashore in Colón. Just like that." His lips shaped an O and he blew in my face, "It blew them ashore like dandelion spores." He got up to get a refill and then with a look back towards me he said, "Dylan, you are a bloody mule."

László had caught the last few sentences of our conversation. He sat down on Lionel's empty chair, lit a cigarette and told me, "Don't listen to him. Ever since that storm he's a wimp. Of course it can be rather wild out there. And yes, there was a storm in Colón today. But I know you can make it. You believe in yourself and that's the main thing. When I took off for Antarctica by myself, there were lots of people who wanted to discourage me. I went anyway."

"You've never told me about that. What was it like, to be out there by yourself?" I was glad to turn the focus of attention on to someone else. László looked at the ground between his feet, and then a smile stole across his face.

"It's amazing. It might frighten you to death sometimes. But it's amazing."

A few years ago László had decided to sail, solo, to Antarctica. Down south, near the white continent, the sea is rough. Storms happen frequently. László wanted to do it by himself and was undeterred by his critics and sceptics.

"Well, I left, and everything went well. I was slap bang in the middle of the Pacific, a thousand sea miles away from the mainland. I was fishing and the damn hook got stuck in my eye. The pain was unbearable. But I couldn't afford to feel sorry for myself. I had to fight for survival. I bandaged the eye and sailed to Chile – one-eyed. On the way I used up my painkillers. I had trouble seeing clearly with the other eye, from the hideous pain I felt."

"That's unbelievable. I can't imagine how painful that must have been."

He nodded. The thought alone made me cover my eye with one hand.

"And what happened to your eye?"

He turned his head and pointed to the left eye.

"That's what happened."

When he got to Chile the doctors told him that his eye could be saved but that the operation would cost 16,000 dollars – money that László, who had been living hand to mouth, simply did not have. He decided to sail to Panama, where he hoped medical treatment would be cheaper. The 4000 miles from Chile to Panama he managed with gritted teeth, in terrible pain. When he finally arrived, weeks later, it was too late. The Panamanian doctors could not save his eye. Today, the glass eye that always watches but never sees bears witness to that accident and explains László's idiosyncratic turn of the head.

"But I would do it all again. If I feel the itch to sail to Antarctica by myself I will and won't be held back by my fear, like Lionel. I know what I'm capable of and you know what you're capable of. Go and find out what it's like out there! My words don't do it justice."

The first lesson at sea: At Jacques' command, I am hoisting the sail for the first tlme.

CHAPTER SEVEN

"A door can be built into any wall, if only you try hard enough."

"Dylan, you got any rope?" Jacques was sitting at the back end of my raft tying the bamboo together, using skilled knots to secure the deck, while I tried to find the fault that had made the red light flicker the day before. I learnt very quickly what it was like to do repair work out on the water: I was loosening a few screws when one of my screwdrivers fell into the ocean and disappeared. "Damn!"

Jacques laughed and knocked on the deck. "Good thing I'm building you a stable deck here. This will, hopefully, make it a little harder for you to lose stuff."

"I have to get used to this. I can't just have my nuts and bolts and tools lying around the way I usually do."

I worked more carefully from then on. After a few minutes I was relieved to see that there were no problems with the oil pressure – it was just the switch that was broken. I removed it. I did not have a spare switch and would not bother trying to find one. I was certain that the engine would run without a hitch over the coming weeks. It had to. And, should the oil pressure sink, then there was nothing I could do about it out there anyway – whether the light was flickering or not.

Once I had put it all back together again, I watched Jacques tying the bamboo deck extra tightly to the frame of the raft, and I was convinced they would last through any storm.

"When you have some time, can you teach me the major sailor's knots?"

"Sure. But let's finish the deck first. Look, that's how you do it."

He showed me how to bind with the ropes. His rough hands were working quickly – they clearly had done this many times before, whereas I found it hard to memorise the individual steps.

We kept working; the radio on Jacques' boat providing a backing track, to the seagulls screeching above us, before they took themselves off towards the city.

"Someone told me, the other day, that you once sent someone a letter bomb ... is that true?"

I was being very forthright, but such a question cannot be phrased in any other way. So I just went for the most direct approach.

"My reputation precedes me, eh?" Jacques wiped the sweat off his forehead and sat on the edge of the raft. "You know me; I'm not a bad person. But when someone takes advantage of me, I get pissed off."

In short, but intense sentences, Jacques told me another story from his past.

"When our son was born, we thought we should settle down for a bit. We decided to stay on an island in the South Pacific for a few months. I did some odd jobs here and there, you know, to keep the wolf from the door. I did some work for someone on a contract basis. But when the job was done, I was simply let down. At first he didn't answer his phone. I went to his office a few times, but his secretary told me that he wasn't there. I was sure he was hiding behind the door. He avoided me for a few weeks. Then I went to his house. He would have to show up, sooner or later. I waited all day and then he came, in his fancy car. I stood before him and asked for my money. He just laughed at me. He said he wouldn't pay me; I was illegal and there was nothing I could do! He told me it was my own fault for putting myself into such a situation. He was taunting me – and that was a big mistake."

"Well, so I sent him a bottle of whiskey. Boom!" His hands mimicked an explosion in the air. "And that was that."

I was silent. I wondered if his reaction was perhaps exaggerated. He guessed my thoughts and answered, "He was in a pretty bad way. They tell me his face still has scars. But no one fucks with me and gets away with it." Even though it had happened so long ago,

Jacques still felt the same sense of anger when he thought about it. "And then?"

"Well, he quickly realised that I was the one who had sent the bottle and reported me to the police. I had to disappear. My wife stayed there with our son. I didn't want them to get involved."

I was not sure what to make of that. Jacques was a good guy and I had never taken his wild stories all that seriously, but there was a big difference between stealing something and sending someone a bomb, I thought.

Jacques continued, "When I was on my own, I realised how much I missed my son, but also, that I had missed travelling. At that point, things didn't go so well with my wife. But now I wonder if I should have been a better father to my son. Nicolas is a bright young man. He studies architecture. I was not there for him at so many important moments in his life. I'm sure he'll be a great architect one day."

Jacques beamed when he spoke about his son, "He is super engaged. There is not a committee at his university he's not a member of. Just like me, when I was young." You could hear the pride in his voice. "The next time I skype with him, I have to introduce you guys."

"Is he still in French Polynesia?"

"He studies in Paris. His mother is French. At some point they went back to Europe, which is good. He has more opportunities there."

"You miss him, don't you?"

"Yeah, I do. Maybe I'll sail across the Atlantic to visit him. It's been too long. I've missed too much." Jacques sighed deeply and then smiled at me.

The Jacques I knew and trusted had returned.

Later that day, Jacques had an idea, "A sail, Dylan! You need a sail! I will build one for your raft. There is no way you can take enough fuel for the trip. And who knows if you'll get the chance to buy some on the way. With a sail you can keep going, even when you're out of fuel."

"Surely I'll be able to get hold of some? The people along the coast must have boats too. There have to be villages, right?"

"Well, if there are people, sure they'll have boats, but who knows if they're motor boats? A sail is a good idea. You might have to wait for wind to come up, but it will come eventually."

"But a sail is too expensive for me."

"No! I'll make you one and it won't cost you a cent!"

"Are you sure?"

He nodded.

"You've helped me so much already!"

"So what? Do you want a sail or not?"

"Well, yes, I guess so. Thank you! But it needs to be easy to manage. As you know, I'm a beginner." I laughed and Jacques rolled his eyes.

"Yes, I know. I already have a plan."

He found a piece of paper and a pencil somewhere and drew a little sketch.

"You still have a few of those long bamboo poles, right?

The pencil flitted over the piece of paper.

"The sail is in the shape of a triangle. We'll rig a four legged mast and attach the boom at the middle of it. There we'll fix the sail. Like this." He held the paper under my nose and kept sketching, even though the paper was now upside down for him.

"At the top we'll attach a rope, so you can hoist the sail with a pulley. And, we'll mount the sail in such a way that theoretically, you can fix it in all directions. Sound good?"

He looked at me for approval.

"That sounds perfect!"

I was as excited as Jacques himself. I had never even thought of a sail before – I had been too preoccupied with the transmission and technology.

The next morning it was already hot and windy, as László, Jacques and I began building the four legged mast for the sail. I could not shake off the feeling that the wind was playing tricks on me. When I ran errands in the city, the sea was flat and still. But, the moment I returned to work on my raft, mischievous winds stirred up the ocean, tossing up the raft this way and that which made even the easiest jobs difficult. Murphy's Law! Today was no different. No sooner had László come over and we'd began to erect the mast then the first gusts of wind started taunting us.

Each of the four bamboo poles had a diameter of about four inches and a length of ten feet. The difficulty lay in tying the poles at the top, in such a way they would not come undone over the coming weeks. Should they come undone, I would not be able to tie them again by myself, all alone, in the middle of the ocean. It took a few hours and plenty of swearing, but then finally, it was ready: my raft had a mast!

Jacques told me that he would organise a sail the next day, and we made a list of things I needed to buy. Having a sail also meant, in addition to the rudders that I would need a centreboard, to help steer the raft. I thought about how best to build it and added more things to the list.

Going by the progress we were making I thought I would be able to launch in two or three days.

That afternoon, László and I paid a visit to the Maritime Office, something we had been putting off until the last minute. László knew a former clerk who could organize the necessary papers, 'without a problem' he told me. His man was working as a private agent for seafaring matters and had 'good connections'.

In order to sail in and out of South American countries I would need three things; an Exit and Arrival document, which is called a *zarpe*, a registration for my raft and an exit stamp for my passport. A *zarpe* is a clearance document that is required; it lists the characteristics of the boat, dates of arrival and departure, as well as the number and identity of the passengers and goods on board. I would only be issued with a *zarpe* if my raft was officially registered. To obtain an exit stamp, I had to show that I planned to leave on a 'legal' boat – which had to have a completed *zarpe* as a matter of course. So, before I did anything else, I needed to register the raft as a seafaring vessel.

I had asked many people about this, and they all had the same answer:
"No way would you be able to register that raft."
"Not a chance in hell!"
"Impossible!"
All but László.
He had been convinced from the start that it would be a cake-walk because he had the right connections. So off we went to the *Autoridad Marítima de Panamá*, a building a few stories high, with a glass front.

While we were waiting in the reception for our man, people came and went, doors opened and closed one car after another stopped outside and people got out of them and entered the building with an air of importance and purposefulness. In the building itself however, everyone fell back into Panamanian lethargy. László's ac-quaintance, a man around fifty, heavy, and with flashy gold chains around his neck, led us through a labyrinth of corridors lit by neon tube lights. Plastic chairs stood in front of closed doors, occupied by people who looked as if they had been waiting there for days. Some slept, some stared at the floor. We were grateful for having been collected at the reception; otherwise we would have never arrived at our destination. Finally our man opened one of the doors, which is to say, he pushed it open with effort and then squeezed his bulk, his stomach sucked hard in, into the tiny office. László and I followed. His office was really just a cell and the lack of space meant that even the area behind the door accommodated untidy stacks of files. There was just enough room for a small desk, with an old computer, a chair and three shelves that covered the windowless walls from floor to ceiling.
The agent was now sitting behind his desk, laughing loudly. He

laughed at me, without trying to hide his amusement. When he had regained his composure, he said, "There is no way you can register a raft like that, not even with my help. A thing like that is not a boat! You can't leave the country on it. You are serious about this? You really want to travel on that thing?"

Again, he began to laugh, annoyingly.

I was not amused by his reaction, but I hadn't given up yet. László spoke with him in Spanish. The man kept shaking his head and answered in English, "No, not even I can help. Absolutely not! It's too risky."

László looked worried. This was not the answer he had expected.

"Can I at least get an exit stamp for my passport?" I asked.

"Yes, that I can do," the agent said, more serious now, and 'calculated' a price based on the situation I was in.

"I can get your passport stamped for 1500 dollars."

Now it was my turn to laugh.

That kind of money was out of the question. I did not even have to think about it. I would rather take off without documents than spend 1500 dollars. And that was it. I did not even feel like haggling. No papers, no stamp, I did not care. I would leave illegally.

"Damn it!" said László. He had been so certain that this would work out.

"What options do I have?" I asked him.

"You can leave without papers. But you'll probably run into trouble in Colombia. I don't know how strict they are down there."

The agent nodded in agreement. "It is dangerous to leave without documents. If I were you, I would reconsider."

Of course he would say that!

I shook my head. I did not have that kind of money, and even if I did, I would not hand it to this 'agent'. 1500 dollars is five months' wages for a mechanic in Antonio's workshop. There and then I made my decision. I would take off without the papers. End of story.

It was a decision that I had taken previously. Before I ventured out on my around the world journey I vowed never to pay any bribes to anyone. If I had to pay, then it would only be official taxes, fines, or whatever charges. I had decided that I would not help this already corrupt world, to become even more corrupt. After two and half years on the road I had crossed so many boundaries, states and borders, dealing with so much red tape and so many difficult situations, but I had never paid any bribes to anyone. I was very proud of that!

While we tried to find our way back out through the corridors, László's can-do attitude had evaporated.
"Fuck! I really thought this would work. What are you going to do now?"
"I'll take off, hiding behind the fog." I replied.
"Are you sure? I mean, sure you can leave without an exit stamp, but it's a risk. I wouldn't do it if I were you."
"What are they going to do? Throw me in jail?" My words sounded harsher than I intended them to. I was disappointed.
"Well, yeah, maybe. Shit. I don't know. It's your decision," László said sheepishly. He felt responsible. I sighed and tried to leave my anger and bad mood behind me.
"Yeah, of course, it's my responsibility. The whole raft is my responsibility. If they want to arrest me in Colombia, then that's what they'll do. Never mind. There will be a solution for this."
I am an optimist after all – and an adventurer.

That evening I cooked a curry for Jacques, while he was working on a job. After dinner he went off in his dinghy without taking a shower first, or even putting on clean clothes. He told me to wait for him, and, that he would be back soon. I watched him, but his silhouette soon disappeared into the darkness. Where the devil was he going? When he went to the *Kiosko* he would always shower first and put on a fresh shirt, and, he had not headed towards the marina but further out, where the other boats lay at anchor.

About an hour must have passed by when I heard the stutter of the dinghy's motor. It was turned off and I could hear Jacques fiddling with oars and ropes.

"Dylan, are you there? Can you give me a hand?"

I looked over the railing and saw that the dinghy was filled with stuff that we needed for the sail.

"Wow. Where did that come from?" I was surprised, and even more so when I realised how late it was and that all the shops had long ago closed up for the night.

"Help me to unload it. Then we'll talk."

Jacques was in a hurry. Hastily he handed me one thing after the other; a wind turbine, a solar cell, a bucket full of flare rockets, a life vest, several headlights, fishing gear. And lastly as he was handing me the sail, he said, "This is for you. We can set it up tomorrow."

"Oh, thank you!"

"And do you still want to know where I got all of this?"

"Not really," I wanted to say, but Jacques went on before I could answer.

"Out there is an abandoned ship. It's been there for months, or even years. The boat and the material are exposed to the elements, and will just rot eventually. So I 'saved' a few things."

That was one way of putting it. My sail was stolen goods. I mean, I knew the man by now, so I am not entirely sure why he could still surprise me with his shenanigans.

The next morning straight after breakfast, we got to work on the sail. The sail seemed to be keen to show me that it had really come from an abandoned boat; the formerly white fabric was now yellow, and its texture felt brittle. If you looked closely, you could see tiny lacerations everywhere. When we unfolded it, it seemed to rip along the lines where it had been folded. We cut it to size, in the shape of a triangle. When Jacques pressed an eyelet into the fabric along the edge, the sail ripped. We tried it along the other edge, but the same happened.

"Darn it. That's too old." Jacques scratched his beard.

"If it can't stand up to the eyelets, then the first breeze will turn it to dust," I said, and Jacques agreed.

"Do you have anything else?"

He was silent for a while, then he mumbled something like, "Yes, but," and went down into the cabin where he began to rummage around. I could hear him banging about and cursing for a few minutes, and then he came back on deck.

He threw a new sailcloth in front of me.

"Here. Let's use this one."

It was obvious that he had not planned on giving me this new cloth. When we unfolded it I knew why. It was in an excellent condition and enormous. If we resized it to my requirement, the whole thing would be ruined.

"I can do without a sail, you know," I said.

"No. I promised you a sail, and that's what I'll give you. It's okay." I could tell that it was not okay, but he lifted a corner, measured the side length expertly with his lower arm, six yards on each side, and then reached for his big shears. He sighed and began to resize. The shears cut through the cloth with a rasping sound. Once the triangle was done, he went to his sewing machine that stood on the deck and hemmed the edges. This time the eyelets could be fitted without any problems. Ten of them made a clean line at regular intervals. Into each, Jacques threaded a short rope, which we then knotted fast to a long bamboo pole, one by one. That was the boom for my sail. It stretched the sail and held it up to the wind. To the middle of the boom, we attached a long rope to hoist the sail, and then tighten or loosen it.

Next I mounted the keel underwater. I had built it the day before, from three pieces of thick planks. It was about five feet long and three feet in height. The waves made it a difficult job. It took a long time to push the unwieldy wooden thing underwater and then attach it to the right place. I swallowed plenty of seawater and felt my head bang against the bottom of the raft more than once.

Once everything was completed, we took the raft for a little spin to test the sail, and so that Jacques could show me how to handle it. This time we were ready for the wind – and once again the wind played with us; there wasn't even a gentle breeze. We waited and waited, until eventually, the white sail began to billow and flutter. I pulled it taut. Then, we suddenly gained speed. The raft was ready!

Bruce the amphibian: a motorcycle becomes part of a sailing adventure.

CHAPTER EIGHT

*"Some say the edge is a dangerous place to be.
I say the edge is the best place to see what's on the other side."*

What should you pack for an adventure on the open sea? I had no idea how long I would be out at sea, or how often I would encounter other people. What quantities of provisions, water and fuel should I take? In the end I decided on 32 gallons each of fuel and fresh water. If that was not enough, I would find a solution for it. I bought plenty of staple foods: bread, potatoes, eggs, flour, oil, pasta, rice, salt and cans of tuna, tomatoes and fruit. I hoped to catch some fish on the way – Jacques had even given me a fishing rod as a gift.

When word got around that I would be leaving the next day, the people from the *Kiosko* and the nearby boats brought me many things that would come in handy on my trip. Just like that, gifts from people I hardly knew. I was deeply touched.

I received a life vest, a manual on sailing in Panamanian waters and coils of thick strong rope. A group of young Swedes, who were sailing around the world, gave me a walkie-talkie and more bamboo poles that I could use to close any gaps in my deck. The walkie-talkie was given to me in exchange for fixing their broken air compressor a few days earlier. Edward, the guy who had to flee from Colombia, uploaded an electronic sea map onto my laptop and gave me an anchor that would have been big enough for the Titanic. An American Panamanian gave me emergency provisions from the US Army, food without any taste whatsoever but with plenty of calories. Jacques and László, who had helped me so much already, gave me light flares for emergencies and a small lifeboat, that would also double up as a dinghy – although, to call this nutshell of a boat a lifeboat, is an exaggeration. The thing was so old that it would sink long before the raft did. Unfortunately the spare engine that Jacques had given me, which I had carefully repaired, had fallen off the dinghy and disappeared into the water a couple of days earlier, when the strong wind stirred up the ocean. But, apart from the second engine, I had everything that I needed, more or less. The only things left to buy were a large lamp, or a spot light and a machete.

My raft also needed a name before I left. I had turned the matter over in my head and decided to name it in honour of my Mother, who had fought so hard for us boys. I was afraid of what lay ahead of me, but deep inside I knew that all would go well. I had learnt this from my Mother, who may not always have had enough money to feed her four children, but who always trusted that everything would be well in the end. And she had been right. She is a fighter to this day and made me what I am – and so I called the raft the *Courage of Bridget*. A friend of Jacques' daubed the words on a piece of wood, which I affixed to the raft.

I was full of beans and felt great. That night, at midnight, I would take off using the darkness as a cover to protect me from the authorities. I did not want my illegal raft to be confiscated before the trip had even begun. Now that the time of my departure had been decided, I would just take it easy and enjoy the remaining few hours, get some rest and enjoy myself. That was when my mobile rang.

"Hey! It's me. How are you getting along?"

It was Martina.

Two years previously when Bruce and I were travelling around India, we had visited Hampi, a village in the south that people had recommended to me as, 'a magical place'. They did not know how right they would turn out to be.

Hampi lies about 150 miles east of Goa. To reach Hampi one

must drive along narrow roads, snaking over a flat countryside. A few miles before the village the picture changes dramatically, to hills with granite boulders scattered among them, as if the devil has been playing marbles. Thousands, if not millions, of rounded rocks, in all sizes, studded the region. Some of them were piled up, with a slow river meandering between the stone heaps.

Compared to other parts of India, the region around Hampi is sparsely inhabited. Sugar cane and banana plantations dominate the landscape, and, if it were not impressive enough already, ancient temples project into the sky among the rock formations. There are dozens of temple complexes scattered around the region: it requires days to explore them all.

I had to stay in Hampi longer than I had originally planned – Bruce had a fault that needed fixing and I had to wait for spare-parts to be sent from Europe. I spent my time photographing the temples and feeding the scores of monkey clans that lived here and, once in a while, getting myself lost amongst the rocks and temples. I really enjoyed being in Hampi and the peacefulness of rural India: watching the sunsets and sunrises from the roof tops of temples, or sitting on granite boulders in the surrounding hills.

One morning I went to visit the ancient temple complex, in the centre of the village. At the entrance I noticed a tall and slender European woman. She looked like a typical backpacker who has been travelling around Asia for a while. She wore wide cotton trousers and an Indian top with long sleeves. I noticed that she was carrying a reflex camera. It was not just her deep blue eyes, or her long black hair that made me speak to her; it was also because I felt quite lonely. Since I had arrived in Hampi, I had mostly been by myself. Apart from a few chats with some shopkeepers and the women who sold me bananas for feeding the monkeys, there weren't many opportunities for a decent conversation.

At the entrance of the temple there was a small wooden shed, it looked like a pay booth. "Do I need to buy a ticket before visiting the temple?" I asked the woman in English. "I don't know," she answered brusquely. I was annoyed by her snub and left her to it. I wandered around the temple for a long time, taking pictures of the ornate decorations that had been chiselled into the stone, hundreds of years earlier. In the inner courtyard, stood the sacred temple elephant. If you held a coin in your open palm and showed it to the animal, it would gingerly take it with its trunk and put it in the lap of the mahout, who sat on a stool beside the beast. The mahout was preoccupied with reading a newspaper, whilst the elephant touched the head of the donors with its trunk and blessed them.

Now the European woman stood before the elephant and offered up a coin. The elephant took the money and did nothing. Someone explained to her that, 'foreigners have to pay at least ten rupees for a blessing'. She found her purse, fished out a ten rupee bill and offered it to the elephant. It took the bill, laid it onto the lap of his mahout and blessed the woman by resting his trunk on her head for a few seconds.

I was amazed to learn that you could teach animals to treat people differently according to the colour of their skin. Now I, who look like an Indian on the outside but was a tourist by rights, wanted to see how the elephant would treat me – and certainly, the sacred animal didn't recognise that I had a Swiss passport and therefore qualified as a foreigner by any standard: and so it blessed me for a single rupee. To be honest, I was secretly pleased that the unfriendly white woman had had to pay ten times as much as me. I went on my way but met her again later, when I was at the top of a narrow staircase and she was at the bottom. I stepped back and let her go up. She rewarded me with a smile and a, "Thanks!" This one word changed the situation completely. I detected a Swiss accent.

"You're from Switzerland!" I said, without thinking. She was surprised that I had guessed her nationality and we began to talk. Indeed, we never stopped talking, right until she had to catch her flight back home, a week later.

Martina is a journalist. She had spent part of her studies in India and spent the last few weeks of her stay travelling. She is also the co-founder of a charity for underprivileged children in Mongolia called Bayasgalant, and, just like me, is a passionate traveller and photographer. In magical Hampi I had found a wonderful friendship. It keeps its strength, regardless of how far away we are from each other. Over the next two years, she sometimes came to visit me on my trip around the world. We had an amazing time on each encounter, but sometimes our meetings ended in arguments. "I can't get involved just now, I'm travelling and I need to focus on that." I told her this often and it hurt her. One night she even threw me out of the hotel room, she could no longer bear my lack of commitment but, we always knew that there was something special between us. No matter how often we fought, we always found our way back to each other. We were similar in many respects, but there was one thing we could never agree on in terms of adventure ... Martina was dead against my journey on the raft!

"Hi Martina! I'm all set, tonight I'm leaving!" I answered her question, full of excitement. These words did not make her happy but she lied for my benefit, "That's good. I'm happy for you. I hope it all goes well."
We spoke for an hour or two, then we said goodbye, which was always hard for both of us. That afternoon, it was harder than usual.
"Don't forget to charge your SIM card so you can get in touch, if you have signal somewhere."
"Yeah, if someone has kindly built a mobile phone antenna for me, out in the ocean." I joked, but still promised that I would call her whenever I could, and charged up my prepaid SIM card that very day in preparation.
She had asked me, days before, to get a satellite phone, so I could call for help in an emergency. I considered it, but decided that they were much too expensive. I told her what I kept telling myself, "Everything will be fine. Don't worry!"
It felt good knowing that somebody, at the other end of the world, was waiting for my safe return.

Then it was time for my leaving party, at the *Kiosko*. Just when Jacques and I were about to leave on the dinghy, László called.

"I told a journalist about you. He wants to interview you tonight and publish an article about you in *La Prensa*. Can you meet with him?"

I was taken aback. I wanted to leave without attracting attention and now I should speak to a journalist of all people? I thanked László for the offer but said that it would probably be best to leave without the media being made aware of it. I asked him to tell the journalist to not publish a word about my trip in his paper.

At the *Kiosko* I met all the people with whom I had spent my evenings over the last month. They had become a family, Lionel, László and Jacques especially, but all the members of the sailing community here in Amador. Over the last three years, I had never spent more than a few days with the same people. For a globe-trotter, saying 'goodbye' and moving on, was part of everyday life. And truth be told, I enjoyed the independence I regained after saying my goodbyes.

However, here in the harbour of Amador, I met the same people every evening and spent many enjoyable hours with them. Almost everyone had contributed something to my adventure. I had grown accustomed to this way of life, yet now the day had come to take my leave. I was excited and looking forward to the trip, but saying 'goodbye' was harder than usual.

I felt conflicted that evening. It was as if each part of me was feeling something different. In my heart there was joy; in my gut, fear; in my brain, common sense and a longing for freedom. My arms and hands wanted to hold on to civilisation and my friends, and my legs wanted to run off, headlong into the adventure that awaited me. Here everything felt so familiar, but where I was going, everything would be foreign.

The longer I sat with these people, who had become my friends, the more painful the expectant loneliness became. The longer we enjoyed each other's company, under the neon lights, the deeper and scarier the darkness of the ocean seemed to become.

Amid the chaos of hugs and good advice I suddenly noticed that Lionel was missing.

"Do you think he took offence when I said I no longer wanted to hear his negative stories?" I asked László.

"Didn't you hear? He had an accident on his way home yesterday."

"Oh no! I didn't know. What happened?" I was shocked and hoped that he had not been injured.

Apparently, Lionel had drunk far too much the day before, as he did on most days – he got in his car and drove home, in a rather spirited fashion. On the way, his boozed-up red blood cells began to dance about wilder and wilder, until there was a loud crash. A short silence, then voices and faces peering into the windows of his car. Lionel was still in a party mood, until he realised that the faces belonged to men in uniform. Policemen? So many? So quick? Maybe he was seeing double. Or had he been unconscious for longer than he thought? The car door was opened, someone pulled him out, and now Lionel realised what had happened. He had crashed into the wall of a building. On the building there was an illuminated sign. It was so bright that it hurt his eyes. He could only read it when he narrowed his eyes. It took a while for the message to get through the alcoholic fog in his brain, but then he understood ... *Policia*. Police!

"Anybody else who tries to drive home drunk would do this as inconspicuously as possible. And Lionel? Lionel crashes into a police station!" László was laughing.

"Ha! That's Lionel for you! And then, what happened?"

"They sorted it out, Panamanian style. Lionel has been here long enough to not fly into a panic. A few bills changed hands and in the end the policemen towed his car to his house and drove him home too. They would find an explanation for the hole in the wall, they said. That's how it's done down here."

I just shook my head.

"And how is Lionel today?"

"Well, he woke up with a pain in his head and neck. He only remembered what had happened when he looked out the window and saw his banged-up car outside! And then he just took some Aspirin and stayed in bed. The car must have got the worst of it."

That story reminded me once more that things are done differently here in Panama – I was hoping that this would work in my favour too.

"Here, give him a call," said László and gave me his phone. "He'll be happy to be able to tell you once more, that you shouldn't leave." Which Lionel did, of course, but this time I had the right answer for him, "At least I won't crash into a police station out in the ocean, eh?"

He mumbled something in response that I could not make out. Then we both said, "See you soon," even though we knew that we might not see each other ever again.

"See you soon," were words I used often that night, but even if I ever did return to Panama City, most of these people would have been gone by then. They led an unsettled life, just like me, here today and gone tomorrow.

A tall Israeli, who I knew only by sight, stepped before me.

"Dylan, my friend. As an experienced sailor I just have to tell you something. We're all celebrating and putting on a brave face, but what's the use. Truth be told, I don't think you'll come out of this alive. Sorry, but you are putting your life on the line if you leave on that little thing there."

I swallowed. This was not something I wanted to hear.

"What are the chances, do you think, that I will not survive this trip?"

"One hundred percent."

I tried to not let this sink in.

"That's your opinion, but I know I can rely on my raft. I don't want to die. I feel as much energy and zest for life in me, as ever before. Maybe I just have a more positive attitude than you," I told him, hiding my anger.

I might have come off as arrogant but I did not want to deal with this, two hours before my departure. This was not the time for doubts. The fear was there, despite my confidence and optimism, but the adrenaline made me wide awake and fully focussed. I had a task ahead of me and I had to concentrate on it with all that I had. I would reach Colombia.

My fear was an indispensable companion. It protected me. A person without fear might act carelessly and run straight into the open arms of danger. To be afraid is a good thing. It sharpened all my senses, but adventure is all about rising above the fears that you carry within you. However, had I listened to those critical voices, I would never have gone on a journey around the world, let alone built a raft.

It was shortly after ten and I was looking for Jacques. It was time to go. I just wanted to focus on myself, my raft and the night ahead. No more discouraging conversations.

Of course I understood then, and I still do now, why so many people just couldn't comprehend why I wanted to venture out on such a perilous journey.

What makes me sail across the ocean on a self-built raft?

It's because it has been a lifelong dream and it has been there ever since I was a little boy. Because that little boy from Sri Lanka, barefoot and with an empty belly, is still inside of me and has never stopped dreaming. And, here in Panama, where the road ends, I was handed this opportunity on a silver platter, or rather, on ten oil drums and some bamboo poles.

That evening at the *Kiosko*, I took advantage of the internet connection. I left messages for friends on Facebook, looked up the latest weather forecasts and charged my SIM card, as I had promised. Then I raised a toast to, 'The adventure' with everybody, they with beer in their glasses and me with coke, for I had to keep a clear head.

I began my round of farewells with a heavy heart and took my leave. I received the last hugs, tips and encouragement. László reminded me to keep my distance from the land. Further south, the waves and rocks would be unpredictable. "Land is your enemy, not your friend. If you don't forget this, you will be fine."

"Thank you. Thank you for everything, my friend! Without your help I would never have got this far. I'm a very lucky man to have met all of you."

"No worries mate," said László "We were all over that crazy idea of yours from the start."

"Now that I know you, I know why!"

He grinned and looked at me in that way of his, and then we hugged each other, as close as brothers, one last time. It was a strange feeling.

Silently, Jacques and I drove back to his boat. For a while, I indulged in the sadness of my leaving here. The waves were beating against the hull as wildly as ever.

The further we were away from the coast, the weaker the city noise became. Jacques steered us straight towards his boat. No matter how dark it was, he knew the harbour like the back of his hand and he always knew instinctively where his boat was. The *Courage of Bridget* sashayed on the waves like a racehorse before the starting shot. As soon as I saw my raft, my emotions were all over the place. Instead of sadness, I now felt excitement.

Jacques went down to the kitchen. He wanted to prepare one last proper meal for me. In the meantime, I stowed all my things away on the raft and loaded up the rest of the material that Jacques had laid out for me, like an anxious father. Then, that last meal was ready; a plateful of pasta carbonara and an enormous fried fillet of fish.

We enjoyed our dinner and Jacques gave me more advice on sails and the wind, which was blowing exactly the way I needed it to tonight, towards the south. A good omen.

We took our time, but then the plates were empty and everything had been said. The wind seemed to increase in strength, as if to tell me that it was 'time to go'. I agreed.

"It's time," I said to Jacques, with a huge lump in my throat. I said goodbye with a warm embrace. When I let go, he pulled me in once more. "Look out for yourself, my friend! And let us hear from you, when you can."

I promised I would, thanked him for all his help and jumped onto my raft.

Life as Robinson: The many white sandy beaches of Isla del Rey lured me into coconut harvesting.

CHAPTER NINE

*"The unknown is the only demon I fear.
And now it's time to befriend him."*

~

March 15th, 2013 was one minute old when I started Bruce's motor and Jacques released the rope that secured my raft to his *Princess*.

"Bon voyage, amigo! Take good care of yourself!" he called, as he threw the rope into my raft and thus severed my last connection to the safety of the harbour.

And so it began – the greatest adventure of my life!

After months of preparation I was sailing out into the vastness of the Pacific, with a motorcycle and ten oil barrels. I kept turning around to see Jacques, with a flashlight, waving at me from the deck of his boat. Soon, all I could see was the light flitting over the water. And then it was gone, the last light, the last familiar thing. I was alone.

Since it was too dark to see where the waves were coming from, I could not anticipate their impact against the raft. An unpleasant situation, not least because I found it hard to keep my balance. In those first hours the water hitting the barrels sounded incredibly loud. My senses were alert as never before: I tried to understand every sound that my raft, the motor, or the sea made. Was there something unusual going on? Where did that creaking come from? Could I hear the wailing of sirens? But the sounds were carried off by the wind before I could identify them. Once it blew into my face and then into my back, which confused me incredibly. It was quite clear from the beginning who was master here. Although the wind stirred up the waves so unpredictably against the raft, that same wind was responsible for pushing my raft onwards once I had set sail. The north wind was my friend, it would carry me south.

Bruce's headlight showed only the first few yards of water. It took a great amount of effort to try and make out anything in the darkness around me, but there was nothing. Only the moonless, starry sky indicated where ships might lie at anchor. To be precise, it was not the stars that told me, but their absence. Where the sparkling sky disappeared behind a shadow that was where a ship must be. Carefully I picked my way between the ferries, yachts, tugboats and cargo ships. Most of them had not turned on their requisite safety lights. Like spiders and their webs, the boats had spread their buoys and anchor ropes around them, as if they were trying to catch me before I disappeared into the Pacific. Their hulls were towering above me. I felt tiny and suddenly I was seized by an irrational fear that I might be sucked below them. Well, to be frank, the fear wasn't that irrational. The banging of the waves against the enormous iron hulls of the cargo ships reverberated loudly. But nothing stirred, apart from the waves and the darkness, and Bruce and I made our way unnoticed.

When I turned around, I could just about make out the glimmer of the city lights far behind me, but when I stood at the front of the raft with Bruce, I could not even see my lifeboat. The rope that tied it to the raft, for better or worse disappeared into the night. After a few hundred yards, I decided to switch off Bruce's headlight: it was not helpful and if anything, it might attract the attention of the authorities. Better to disappear into the darkness and escape unseen.

From the very first minutes, my journey seemed like a test to me. I took the qualification exam of the sea. I could not say whether I was cold from the wind, or hot from all the excitement. A roaring audience surrounded me to test my valour. In my imagination I heard an announcement like those you hear before boxing matches, "And, here he iiiiis, the challenger with his home-maaaade raaaaaft!" Waves hitting the barrels, applauded loudly.

"He will demonstrate how to sail, without any sailing skills whatsoever, ladies and gentlemen!" The voice grew louder, the applause swelled. "The brave dimwit without a reverse gear, but he shows courage, ladies and gentlemen! Great courage! He is sailiiiiiiiing blindfolded!"

An appreciative murmur went through the crowd, or was that the sea in motion and the wind in the sails?

"Put your hands together for Dylaaaaan Samaraaawick-ramaaaaaaa!"

The crowd was going wild for me, and somehow I felt a bit better. Why? I could not say. I was miles away from actually feeling good, but a small part of my tension had vanished overboard.

Slowly, at about one mile per hour, Bruce and I chugged across the harbour and out into the darkness beyond. It took an hour before I had safely passed all the ships and reached the open sea. Behind me, the skyline of Panama City glittered. Further to the right, the lights of the cargo ships were swaying as if they were dancing on an invisible trapeze line. The ships were waiting for morning, and their time to enter the Panama Canal.

I turned the motor off. As soon as the now familiar hum died, I felt lonely. I was listening to the silence. Was there anything?

All I could hear was my own breathing and the swishing of the waves against my oil barrels. All other sounds were drowned out by the dull roar of the water. I rummaged around in a box, found my headlamp and put it on. In the weak light of the lamp, I set sail for the first time. It took forever. The wind was so strong that every minute without a sail felt like sacrilege, ingratitude to the weather gods. I placed the rolled-up sail between the four legs of my mast. It was not easy to get it in the right position because the cloth was so heavy. Once I had managed to do so, I hauled on the rope that ran over the pulley in the middle of the mast. Clack, clack. The boom had reached the top end of the mast. Now all I had to do was secure the boom, fix the sail at the right angle and harness the wind. And straight away the wind asked it to dance. The sail was a little bashful at first, but then gave itself completely to the wind. I felt the speed of the raft increase – it was as if an invisible hand was pushing us over the water. I shouted with joy.

On the road Bruce and I have an average speed of about 50 miles per hour. Since our maiden voyage, I knew we would be a lot slower than that at sea, but still, I had hoped that the sail and a decent wind would help propel us with a decent velocity. That night the *Courage of Bridget* reached a top speed of five miles per hour, aided by the brisk wind and the favourable currents. Over the next few days, I would learn that this speed would count as, 'very fast'.

Before departing I had entered into my GPS the coordinates of the northernmost islands of Las Perlas, my destination. A small on-screen arrow indicated the right direction. The islands lay southeast of Panama City. I steered the raft towards Las Perlas as fast as the wind carried me, running parallel to seven anchored cargo ships to my right. They were about a mile away from me, but I still feared that I would suddenly be faced with a hull towering above me. There was a lot of nautical traffic around. I had to trust that the ships were all waiting in line and had their red and green security lights switched on.

Just as my uncertainly lessened, the wind played its first trick on me: it abated, instantly. My sail, which had been billowing just a moment before, was now hanging limp and dead on the mast.

I challenged the sky, "That's not fair! There was wind for two full days! Never letting up! And now that I need you, you leave me in the lurch!" I was not a sailor yet. The unpredictable nature of the wind was not something that I could accept stoically and I was annoyed. I had planned to put as many miles between me and Panama City as possible before dawn, so that I would be out of sight of the authorities at day break. But when I checked the GPS I saw that we were still moving. The current had taken over from the wind. We were being gently pulled southwards – we seemed to be going in the right direction, even without the help of the fickle wind.

As the wind stopped blowing the waves calmed down and I with them, my nervousness yielded to happiness. I was on my way! I relaxed.

The ocean surrounding me seemed as peaceful as I was. Indeed, I was as peaceful as the ocean. The rhythmic sound of the waves had a calming effect on me. I had nothing to do, as long as there was no wind, so I hung up my hammock and curled up in my sleeping bag, not in order to sleep, but to rest. Only now did I notice how cold it had become. I forced myself to keep my eyes open, and occasionally I unwrapped myself, to check if we were still on course.

Around 4 a.m., I lay down in the hammock and watched three little islands go past to my right. I said to myself, "As long as I can see them, from this angle, I'm going the right way." I turned over and saw Panama City, which by now looked like a city of dolls. My eyes wandered back to where I thought the southern horizon was, and that's when I saw him. He was standing at the front of the raft and looking into the darkness that lay ahead of us – the little boy from the beach in Colombo.

I got up and sat next to him on the deck. We hung our naked feet in the water. It was warm, and it was pleasant to feel it wash over our legs. With every little movement the water glowed green for a couple of seconds, and then it died, only to be rekindled by the next movement. The boy pulled his feet from the water in surprise and looked at me with his eyes wide, seeking an explanation. I knew the glow from the harbour – in the bay where Jacques' and László's boats lay, the green light could be seen in irregular streaks, as magical as the Northern Lights. I explained to the boy that the glow was produced by plankton. A bit like the glow worms in Sri Lanka.

"Do you remember ... all those tiny lights flitting among the trees in our front yard at night, which turned the dusty road into a glittering stream? Just like those glow worms, glow in order to attract a partner, so the plankton gives off light as soon as it touches something else. Isn't it magnificent?"

Slowly he stuck his feet back into the water. As soon as his big toe touched the surface, the water lit up. In the light of the plankton, I could see his face beaming.

Towards morning the night cooled down further, so we pulled our hands and feet out of the water, made ourselves comfortable in the sleeping bag and I told the boy all I knew about the ocean. I passed on all the advice that my seafaring friends had given me. It was important, that he too, knew what to do when the sea got rough. The boy nodded and I knew, from his earnest expression, that he would not forget anything. Then we looked up into the starry night sky and tried to find constellations.

"That's Leo, isn't it?"

"And over there, those five stars that look like an upside down slingshot ... that's Cancer."

When we did not know the right name, we invented one.

"Look! That's Pinocchio! And over there, on the other side, you see? That's the fat Chinese Buddha!"

We laughed. To us, the raft was an island of happiness.

I was hot and uncomfortable. I pushed my sleeping bag aside and felt the Sun on my skin.

For a few minutes I had surrendered to the tiredness weighing me down. Then the heat of the Sun beating down on me woke me up... slowly. When I forced myself to open my eyes, I got a shock. The light was so bright! Shit!

I jumped out of my hammock and checked my surroundings, anxiously looking for rocks, ships and for other dangers. I had fallen asleep, even though I had intended to stay wide awake.

It was already ten past nine.

Never had I missed the sunrise in the last few weeks, but today, on my first day on the raft, I had overslept! Unforgivable!

In the distance, the tips of the highest buildings of Panama City could still be seen, but I was much further away than last night.

Apart from that, there was only water. I checked the GPS and was pleasantly surprised: I was still going south, straight towards Las Perlas. I was relieved – my carelessness was without negative consequences. What if a ship had been on a collision course? This should never ever happen again. Never!

I checked the sail and the rudder. Once I'd made sure that all was well, I realised how hungry I was. A cup of tea, boiled on the gasoline stove, a can of tuna and some bread in hand, it was time for a late breakfast!

László had told me that, a normal sailboat, under favourable conditions, can reach Las Perlas in about twelve hours.

After twelve hours, I had, so far, managed less than one third of the distance to my first layover. Actually, I wasn't too unhappy about it. Considering the prevailing windless conditions over the last 10 hours, I could even be happy that I had made it this far. I spent all morning walking between Bruce and the tiller. My GPS device only worked when it was connected to Bruce's battery. So I walked to and fro, scrutinising the arrow on the display of the GPS. I gently corrected our direction whenever necessary and continued edging south.

When the Sun was at its highest, I could no longer see Panama City.

Mist lay over the water. The familiar spikes of the skyscrapers peeked out of the water once or twice, and then the current carried me away and I could no longer see them. Like Atlantis, the city disappeared into the ocean. For the first time, I was surrounded by water, wherever I looked, nothing but water.

I watched the bright sunbeams reflecting off the sea's surface, like a mirror that has been shattered into a thousand pieces, while the raft gently rocked me. It felt good, but I was also a little anxious. Suddenly, when all signs of civilisation had vanished, I began to realize the risks that I would be undertaking during this journey. Did I know what I was doing here?

Well, yes.

Or actually, no.

Did I have a goal?

Is there a purpose to what I am doing?

Adventure engenders these deep ponderings, before, during and after. Soul searching, finding meaning.

I had been full of enthusiasm, joy and zealousness, until that is, I started the journey. But now here in the vastness of this liquid expanse, I begin to question if there was rationality behind this whole exercise.

I tried to distract myself from such thoughts by rearranging the things on my raft, making sure my panniers would not get wet, and tying up everything that had been lying around on the deck. I didn't want to become a philosopher, I am a connoisseur!

It was hot. I used my sail as a canopy to protect myself from the Sun. I found the sailing manual and looked up Las Perlas. Most of the islands were uninhabited. The island of Isla Contadora, apparently, had some infrastructure, a hotel or two, restaurants and a couple of small shops that also sold fuel. I read that Isla del Rey was the largest island of the archipelago. There was only one large village there, San Miguel: its 1,600 inhabitants made it the most populous settlement in the Las Perlas. Its inhabitants were mostly of African descent. As with most islands and coastal regions around Panama, the roots of the population traced back to Africa. Their ancestors were slaves who had escaped from their 'Masters' on the mainland, to the inhospitable environment of the islands, so that they could not easily be found.

Sporadically I dozed-off while reading my book, due to the energy sapping, sweltering and heat. On one occasion, I awoke suddenly to a hissing sound. It sounded like a whale breathing. I jumped up and searched over the flat water surface, but I could see nothing, wherever I looked. A few minutes later, the same sound, this time behind me. I turned around and again, nothing. Thereafter I kept watching the water with intent, but did not find out whether it had been a whale, dolphin, or just my imagination. When I stared into the water, all I could see were grey fish, in all sizes, flitting below me in swarms. They had no intention of telling me what they were seeing – sceptical of me as they were, and my strange little boat; they preferred to clear-off, as quickly as possible.

A few times I saw flying fish. At first, I thought they were small sea birds coming up for air, after a long dive. Only when their glittering bodies flew right by my nose, did I see that they were fish. Some of them landed on my deck. Maybe that was the way forward for me – so far, I had had no success with my angling skills.

Twice I saw motorboats to my right, tearing over the water far away, on towards an unknown destination. Where were they going? There are no islands in that direction I thought, then double checked that I was still headed in the right direction.

The wind had risen again, but this time it came from the wrong direction and I could not take advantage of it.

From now on the wind and the weather determined my fate. Out on the water, I had nothing to set against the forces of nature but a small raft and an even smaller sail. For now I placed myself in the hands of the currents and hoped things would get better sooner rather than later. I could feel how slowly we were moving. After all the hectic preparations of the last few weeks, I welcomed the slowness. I had reached my goal – and yet remained so far away from it all – nevertheless I was enjoying every minute of it.

Late in the afternoon I noticed that I was not getting any closer to Las Perlas, even though the raft was constantly on the move.

I zoomed out from the map on my GPS and froze.

The dots that marked my route were showing that the currents were taking me straight into the deep Pacific and missing the islands of Las Perlas by a long way. I tapped the buttons of the device but the image remained unchanged. Something was wrong somewhere.

It wasn't that my GPS was faulty. My bow had always pointed towards Las Perlas, but unwittingly, I had moved sideways with the currents, rather than moving forward. I had ignored checking my map; instead I had relied on the arrow that pointed towards my destination. A rookie mistake!

On land, that method, where the GPS device indicates the direction of the destination via an arrow, had worked fine. Out on the water however, with currents instead of roads, or other fixed points, it did not. Had I only zoomed out the map for an overall picture earlier!

I had to change my course straight away. Otherwise the ocean current would carry me past Las Perlas into the open Pacific, missing the islands without even getting any glimpse of them. I had to prevent this at all costs!

From here onward, I had no help, not from the wind, nor the ocean currents.

"Bruce, show me what you can do!" I told my companion, as I started the motor and began to correct the mistake. I could always top up on fuel in Contadora. Now was not the time to think of budget sailing.

Carefully I watched the direction we were taking and took to walking up and down between Bruce and the tiller once more, making sure that another mistake did not occur. I also tried out all kinds of programmes and functions on the GPS device and eventually discovered one of the functions that was unknown to me. I had been using this device for three years, every single day. I had taken it apart to fix it and put it back together again. I had travelled through deserts, canyons and mountains with it, and used it in cities and in jungles. I had never got lost with it. I thought I knew it inside out, but now learnt something new. If I chose the 'course' function, a straight line from my location to my destination would be calculated. If I drifted off the set course, the device would alert me with a sound. Basic knowledge for sailors; a completely new experience for a biker. The situation reminded me that this really was unknown territory. I was a rookie. Those first days I learnt a very important lesson, but most importantly, I learnt quickly.

When evening came, the Sun said goodbye with a magnificent spectacle. Orange and golden colours were reflected on the water, a gleaming path stretching from that ball of fire to my raft. In moments such as these, I often wished I wasn't alone. If only I had someone to speak back a few words, sharing my admiration of the beauty of the world. But I had no time for melancholy; or rather I busied myself with various activities to suppress my wishful, wistful thinking and made sure I was still on course.

I knew that I would need another six, or seven hours, to reach the northernmost islands of Las Perlas. When the stars began to appear I sang, to drive away the fear of the darkness, loneliness and exhaustion. My iPod had broken during my earlier journey (or perhaps I had lost it, I could not remember), so I had to entertain myself and stay awake. The wind, the waves and the clanking of the rudders, the thudding of my lifeboat against the water – they all became part of my backing group, and they didn't care very much about how badly their frontman sang:

"Tonight I'm gonna have myself a real good time.
I feel alive... and the World, I'll turn it inside out – yeah,
And floating around in ecstasy
So don't stop me now; don't stop me now.
'Cause I'm having a good time, having a good time yeahh ... "

No one was there to question the accuracy of my lyrics, so I shouted the words out into the night and felt their meaning deeper than ever before. I was having a good time! The time of my life, and nothing could stop me. I drove away the tiredness that kept charging into every cell of my body like a relentless pack of hungry hounds. When I began to feel that I would not be able to keep my eyes open any longer, I slapped my face, shouted and doused myself with sea water. I could not afford to fall asleep again. This time, I was determined to be stronger than the nagging tiredness. If someone would have seen the methods that I employed to keep sleep away, they would have sent me to a shrink. But luckily, the only one around for miles and miles was Bruce, and he was extremely used to my high jinks and my behaviour did not surprise him at all.

The ocean had its own way of keeping me awake too.

I was sitting on a fuel canister at the back of the raft, next to the tiller, when suddenly below me a beam of light, about four or five meters in diameter, shot up and flashed. In fright, I jumped up and banged my ankle against one of the bamboo masts. What was that? It was as if something had exploded without the sound and then disappeared, as quickly as it had appeared in the first place. My heart was beating wildly. It took me a few seconds to understand: the raft must have come up against a thick carpet of plankton, which was glowing in response. Once my heart slowed down I was able to appreciate the spectacle I had just witnessed. I shouted out a, "thank you!" into the night. That shot of adrenalin was certainly enough to drive out the tiredness for a fair amount of time.

Around 1 a.m., the GPS showed me that two islands were right ahead of me. Finally, I had reached the northernmost islands of the Las Perlas archipelago. It was too dark to be able to make out anything. Although I had hoped to see a few lights, or fishing boats at anchor, there was nothing my eyes could register. The ocean was silent and Bruce roared loudly. I even wondered if the engine noise would wake up the inhabitants. Even though there was no wind blowing, I felt very cold, so, I put on my jeans and motorcycle jacket.

I remembered László's warning, "Stay as far away from land as you can. Land is not your friend, it's your enemy!"

It was time to drop anchor and wait for the morning. I did not want to risk running aground onto some rock that I could simply have bypassed in daylight. I threw the anchor into the water and the hundred feet of rope that had been coiled up on deck was pulled into the sea. It did not take me long to realise that the anchor rope was way too short and it was taut, but without the anchor touching the seabed. The raft kept moving with the current.

"Argh! I just want to get some sleep!" I groaned and hauled the anchor back up.

Less than five hours of sleep, in 48 hours, and my legs were almost give way under my own body weight. I was about half a mile away from the island when I measured the distance with the GPS. I refrained from getting any closer to the land, as I could not see anything in the pitch dark and I was not sure whether to trust the GPS maps and their accuracy.

"Should I move a little closer and try to drop anchor once more?" I asked myself a few times. While I deliberated, the raft kept on moving.

The current was pulling me westward, away from the islands. Then I had an idea: I could propel up against the current. If I rode eastward for an hour and let myself be drifted back by the current I would end up here an hour later. That would give me time to rest and maybe even get a little sleep. Once it was light, I would be able to see the obstacles around the islands and navigate around the danger.

I started Bruce and steered the raft for about a mile against the current, which took about three quarters of an hour. Then I turned the motor off, fixed the tiller and let myself drift back towards the islands. I set the alarm on my mobile phone for an hour later, sank into my hammock and was fast asleep the very next moment. An hour later, the alarm woke me from a deep, dreamless sleep. I forced myself to get up and repeated the manoeuvre once more, then again another hour later. When I woke for the third time, the night had begun to fray around the edges and a thin strip of light could be seen on the horizon. I rubbed my eyes, yawned ... and then my jaw dropped at what I saw. All night I had been convinced that the island was to my right. But suddenly it was on my left. I turned my head and saw that a second island was to my right, wrapped in the morning mist it was hard to see. I must have done something wrong during my last manoeuvre – as I now found myself between the two islands.

A day with new challenges awaited me. When it got lighter, I saw that I had worried needlessly about waking the inhabitants – there was nothing but nature. The cliffs were stained with large patches of white birdlime everywhere. Rows and rows of birds that awoke at day-break then flew off, dotting the sky a million times. The pelicans flew closer to the water than the frigate birds, they seemed to be more attracted to the warmth of the rising Sun. I politely greeted everyone and wished them a good day.

Then I went back to the business at hand. I had to find a place to drop anchor if I wanted to sleep for more than an hour.

The *Courage of Bridget* was between two islands that had nothing to offer but rugged cliffs. The waves bounced off them so loudly that I took it as a warning. I decided to travel straight to Contadora, where I knew that civilisation, and hopefully a good spot to drop anchor, were awaiting me.

It was not easy to navigate through the islands to reach Contadora. The currents around the islands were extremely strong and the water ran as swift as rivers: many times I had to look for alternative paths to steer forwards. When, finally, Contadora emerged before me and the water became shallower, the colours reflecting off the white sandy bottom, created a picture of a paradise. It was an utterly beautiful sight, which cast away my tiredness immediately. The green island had white picturesque beaches and was surrounded by turquoise water. I navigated around the island to the south-side, where it seemed to be best for anchoring the raft. There were some fancy properties on the island; most of them were painted white, which added to the charm. Amongst many other boats, there was a blue sailboat lying at anchor in front of the widest part of the sandy beach.

On deck, two men were standing. When I came closer, one of them shouted, "Hey! You made it here already! Here, take the rope, you can moor your raft to our boat."

I looked up, surprised, and caught the rope which he threw down to me. I had never seen these men before and I had never seen their boat either. When they saw my bewildered face one of them explained, "They told us about you, in Amador. You left a day before us and they said we should keep an eye out for you."

The two men were friendly and seemed pleased to see me. We had a little chat and I learnt that they came from Spain and took tourists on diving and snorkelling trips around Panama. They also invited me to eat with them later that day – freshly caught fish. I accepted the offer gladly, since fish had so far spurned my bait, but, first of all, I went ashore to top up my canisters with fuel. First things first, I thought. You never know when the wind would rise again and beckon me for more adventures at sea.

The weather let me stay in Contadora for two nights. I rested well and enjoy the Spaniards' hospitality. Then the north wind rose and it was time to move on.

When I left Contadora, the elements were in my favour. My plan was to navigate from Contadora straight to Garachiné. From Las Perlas (which no longer had any pearls) to the southern mainland of the Gulf of Panama.

I set sail and made good progress. Every day, the raft, the sail and the ocean became more and more familiar. When I left Contadora with the sail billowing in the wind, I enjoyed being a sailor once again. I had grown accustomed to the constant swaying of the raft, the sound of the waves, and the clatter of the hinges of the rudders, and to the noise of the pointed bow ploughing into the waves, cutting through the water: collectively, all this was a familiar background noise. I had wind and Sun – what else could I ask for?

Standing on the deck next to Bruce, I saw something moving out of the corner of my eye. A small creature had scurried from the dashboard and disappeared underneath the tank bag. I looked carefully. With his heart beating fast, making himself as small and invisible as possible, there sat a little gecko, staring at me with his black eyes and his tiny feet holding him firmly to the tank.

I had a passenger!

I was over the moon. It was an incredible feeling to have another 'friend,' this one made of flesh and blood. I hoped that he felt my joy, when I welcomed him on board! Someone else is crazy enough to travel over the water on a makeshift raft and I told him how brave he was. I named him Wilson, showed him where I kept the life vests and wished him a pleasant voyage.

When things were quiet and I was enjoying the slow but steady progress, suddenly, there was a loud splashing noise. It sounded like one of my brothers trying to plunge head first into the river but belly-flopping instead.

Splash!

There it was again. I looked out over the water surface, and then I saw several black objects shooting out of the water. They looked like miniature Batmen. Gleaming bodies shot through the air – splash, splash, splash – so that it took a while before I could see that they were manta rays somersaulting through the air. They flew high, moving their fins like wings, flopped down on the water surface and then disappeared. More and more of them appeared, the water was bubbling with them. What a show!

Manta means blanket in Spanish, and you could see why – when they flew through the air with their wings wide open, they indeed looked like flying blankets. When they swam past underneath the raft, I was awestruck by their size. One of those graceful creatures could have almost covered the entire raft.

There is not all that much that is known about these animals. Nobody knows about their numbers. However, it is a fact that their population has been decreased by human actions in the last years. Slowly, but thankfully initial steps are being taken and two species have been listed as vulnerable by the International Union for Conservation of Nature since 2013, and trading them is now forbidden, which is a little victory for these magnificent creatures.

Soon, dusk reminded me to find a place to drop anchor. I had not travelled as far as I had hoped. We had managed about twenty miles that day and were in line with Isla del Rey, the largest island of the archipelago. Shortly beforehand I had passed San Miguel, the island's only settlement worth mentioning – a collection of houses with red roofs and 'pangas', the local fishing boats, lying at anchor in the bay were only faintly visible. Unlike the other islands of Las Perlas, Isla del Ray was enormous and it looked as if it were a part of mainland Panama. Everywhere you looked; it was overgrown with thick jungle that only allowed for a narrow strip of rocky beach near the water. On the northeastern side, there was supposed to be a long narrow island, where trees and palms grew, called Espirito Santo. From the sailing guide book, I learnt that I would find a safe spot to drop anchor between Espirito Santo and Isla del Ray.

I only reached the anchorage when night had fallen and had to trust that the information from the book was correct. Once I had passed through the estuary, which was about 300 yards wide, the passage tapered, because, behind Espirito Santo there was another, even smaller, island. The current was still strong here, but at least there were no waves. I steered the *Courage of Bridget* between the islands and dropped anchor and waited for my rope to become taut. It disappeared into the darkness with a splash, within a couple of seconds and with a jerk, the raft stood still in the strong current. I was surprised by how deep the water was between the two islands. Too tired to cook, I just dug out a few pieces of bread and opened up another can of tuna; making sure that before I fell asleep I left a few crumbs out for my passenger too. "Good night, Wilson! Good night, Bruce!"

For the next four days, the wind was weak and I had no other choice but to bob up and down around Isla del Rey and a few little islands off its coast. I discovered a few idyllic and lonely beaches and behind them there was plenty of vegetation, fruit and coconut trees. I dropped anchor at a safe distance and went ashore in my dinghy. There wasn't anyone to be seen, not even a fishing boat. I began to feel like Robinson Crusoe – just better – because I had a raft, knew where I was and had chosen to be there.

I harvested bananas and climbed up palm trees to pick ripe coconuts, just as I had done as a boy in Sri Lanka, a skill I had not forgotten. First, I put my arms around the tree as if hugging it, then I pressed the soles of my feet against the trunk and tried to clamber up as far up as possible. When it was too slippery, I put my feet sideways, around the trunk and pushed from the knees, like a frog. Then, I held onto the trunk with my hands and with the support of my belly, until I had pulled up my feet. Arms up, then push the feet. Arms up, push the feet: just like a monkey, but of course, with lot less agility.

As children, we always climbed up the palms trees. I remember that, as an early teenager, I persuaded my brothers to come with me to a nearby coconut plantation. We used the diminishing light as cover and climbed up the trees to steal a few coconuts. We had developed a system so that the sound of the falling coconuts would not draw attention, all four of us climbed up the tree, one after the other. I went first, as the eldest, and my brothers followed according to age. I plucked the coconut and passed it on to the one below me and he to the one below him, and so on, until it had reached the youngest who was only four or five feet from the ground. If he dropped it, then all that could be heard was a dull plop, which would not be loud enough to alert the neighbours.

Once, one of the neighbourhood boys joined the coconut stealing gang. The palm we chose to climb that day was so tall, that we had to leave bigger gaps between us than usual. We could not pass the coconut down to the next person but had to drop it carefully.

Things were going well, until I dropped the fourth coconut. Then I heard a scream, followed by four consecutive plops. When I looked down, I saw that only one of my brothers was still clinging onto to the tree. The other two and the neighbour's boy were lying on the ground among the coconuts, rubbing their limbs and groaning in pain. My brother had dropped his coconut when the neighbour's boy was not yet ready to catch it. The coconut fell on his head; he lost his grip and fell down the tree. Not only that, whilst falling he brought down the other two little ones with him to the ground. From that day on, that boy from our neighbourhood was no longer allowed to play with us, 'four terrors'.

With my arms full of coconuts I ran back to the dinghy, where I opened one of them up with my machete. I had earned it after that climb, because the trees were heavily stained with moss and fungus and it was extremely slippery. Palms, which are regularly harvested, don't build up a slippery coat on the surface of the trunks, and these trees, probably, had never been touched by a human in their entire lives. I was exhausted when I finally stood on the ground, but happy to have plucked so many coconuts. I hacked at the pointed end until the husk gave way. Then I enjoyed its sweet water, which is not only delicious and full of nutrients but also a natural panacea: high in minerals and an isotonic liquid, it promotes quick recovery after diarrhoea. In an emergency, it can even be used intravenously, to replace bodily fluid loss.

When I carried the next batch to the dingy, I saw a large wave hurry to the beach overturn my vessel and leave it upside down. Not only had I had already stored part of my harvest there, but also my machete and my mobile phone, which I had taken with me to keep track of the tides. I dropped everything and sprinted to the dingy. The coconuts were bobbing about in the water, but the machete and the phone were buried in the sand.

I had to find them again!

The machete was large enough for me to find it again quickly, but the mobile phone had disappeared. Its loss was a big blow.

As a telephone it was useless without signals out here, but that wasn't my concern. It contained all the contacts I had made since leaving Switzerland, including the numbers of my sailor friends in Panama. And, I used it as an alarm and a clock. Even though I knew the saltwater must have destroyed it upon first contact, I didn't want to give up the search. Systematically I scoured the beach for the next couple of hours, walked up and down, dug up the sand as soon as each wave retreated and watched every wave intently, to see if it brought my phone back. I was almost ready to give up when I saw it briefly, tumbling about in the water. I ran over and began to dig up the sand, but to no avail. It was gone forever.

Those days on the island were days of leisure, and I had plenty of time to cook proper meals in the evenings. I even added pieces of fresh coconut to my potato curry and rice, to make elaborate meals with very few ingredients. Sometimes I celebrated the day with a hard-boiled egg! – but I was being careful with my provisions, because I did not know for how long I would be travelling and when there would be the next shopping opportunity.

It was still a long way to Buenaventura and I realised that I had left some of the US army emergency provisions on Jacques' boat. So I also tried my luck with fishing. I fished almost every day – I should say, tried to fish every day, but I never caught anything, at all, and lost nearly all my plastic baits. I resigned myself to the fact that I was an even worse fisherman than a sailor.

When I wasn't roaming around the beaches and the dense jungle, I spent my time optimising *Courage of Bridget.* For instance, I readjusted my hammock, so that I would be able to sleep without back pain. At the stern, I set up all ten fuel canisters, in two rows and hung the hammock over them. That way, the canisters supported my back, keeping it straight and as padding, I used a thin insulating mat between the canisters and the hammock.

Whenever the heat of the day was too much, I jumped into the water. Swimming and snorkelling in the turquoise water was fantastic. I had been spoilt by beautiful beaches on my journey: Indonesia, Australia, the Red Sea, Fiji ... but this trumped them all. Maybe it was because I had it all to myself, and the turquoise water and the white beach of Espirito Santo seemed to me, the most perfect thing I had ever seen. All day long, shoals of fish swam past my raft, and, if it wasn't the fish, I watched the birds. Every morning, when they took to the sky and flew in every direction, I felt as if the bird population of the entire planet was at home here. Sometimes they circled over my raft out of sheer curiosity to see what I was up to. No doubt that they thought I was the weirdest thing they'd ever seen. I loved watching them return in the evening to their nests, with much squawking and cawing. And, it seemed that they told each other, nonstop, what they had seen all day, wherever they'd been.

The dense plankton mass, that was invisible during the day, lit up with every movement of the fish at night. When I tapped against the barrels of the raft, it attracted the interest of larger fish. Cheekily, they swam towards me, opened their mouths and recoiled when they sensed my movement. The small, high-spirited fish, flitting through the water, left wild illuminated tracks that resembled small underwater fireworks. That nocturnal magic all around me was awe-inspiring and I sometimes felt as if I were dreaming, so unreal seemed the beauty of the world below my raft.

On the fourth day, a strong north wind arose and it was time to leave my little paradise. I hoped to reach Garachiné in two days – 18 miles to go.

I pulled anchor at dusk and manoeuvred out of the bay with the help of the motor, then I hoisted the sail. By now, I knew what I was doing: it did not take that long until I had the sail in the right position and it opened with a thud. I loved that sound. It proclaimed a great day of sailing.

As the morning sunshine began to warm the raft, even Wilson crept out of his hiding place and made himself comfortable on

Bruce's handlebar. I was always glad to see him but wasn't sure if he found enough food on the raft. I could never quite tell whether he ate the crumbs that I left out for him, or whether some bird pilfered them instead. However, he didn't look as if he was starving, nor did he look concerned to be on my raft.

I sailed for about five hours and made good progress. We had gone about eight miles when the wind decided that it had had enough for the day. The only way forward from that point onwards was to start the engine. I turned the ignition and pushed the starter button. Bruce coughed a few times and then was silent. I pushed the button again and this time I held it for several seconds. Each one of them felt like an eternity and each rattling engine revolution made my heart beat louder. Ever since I had known Bruce, he had never taken more than two seconds to start up. And now this, out on the ocean of all places?

"Oh, Bruce!" I implored him.

"What is it now? Please! Please! Please! I need you!"

He gave me no answer.

I opened the fuel tank to check if there was enough petrol, even though I knew the tank was full. Then I checked the ignition sparks, and that was it: the engine didn't produce any.

All coaxing was useless. This was a major problem and I knew that without repairs, Bruce would not start up.

And, without an engine, without wind and confronted with strong head currents, I would never make it to Colombia.

Breakdown-service on the Pacific: The fishermen are towing the *Courage of Bridget* to San Miguel.

CHAPTER TEN

"A problem is not a problem. It just adds to the adventure."

~

I was drifting, the silhouette of Isla del Rey far away against the horizon; suddenly I realised that the current was carrying me back towards the island – this was a good thing, in fact it was a great thing! I used the opportunity to check why Bruce had stopped producing an ignition spark and began to diagnose the ignition circuit systematically. I knew Bruce inside out, we had been through a lot together and he had always served me well in the past. Sometimes I had had to fix him by the side of the road, usually in rather unconventional ways, but I had never run out of solutions, or I had managed to find the right help at the right moment.

In Nicaragua, for instance, when the drive shaft broke and Bruce was stuck in deep sand, I was almost in despair. Around us, there was nothing but cattle in a semi desert like landscape. After waiting for several hours, a few gauchos and their horses finally came our way. They tried to help us by towing Bruce with their scraggy horses. Firstly, they tied a rope around one of the horses' neck, and then mounting it they spurred the horse into action. Bruce did not give an inch. The man got off, untied the rope and went to the back of the horse. When I realised what his plan was, I hastily dissuaded him, as he was indeed about to tie the rope to the horse's tail in order to bring out more horse-power! That I could not allow – Bruce weighs 660 pounds and I wasn't about to be held responsible for a tailless horse! But still, these were people who had gone out of their way to help a stranger in need and I had a laugh about it in the end. But that was on land.

Out here on the ocean, things were very different. Unsuccessfully I kept on tinkering, all the while wishing for another serendipitous coincidence.

There had been a time, when I was travelling through Syria when Bruce simply stopped working in the middle of nowhere. After a while I realised that I would only be able to fix him if I had the right screwdriver, one with a long enough reach to unscrew a bolt that was at the very back. What to do? I was sitting by the side of the road scratching my head and waiting for enlightenment. Except for a few goats, in the last few hours I had not encountered a living soul, and in the desert, one cannot rely on anyone else for help but themselves. I began to think up solutions and imagined tools that I could try to fashion with the resources that I had at hand. Time passed, and eventually I heard the sound of a small motorcycle engine in the distance, but I paid it no attention because I was so deeply lost in my thoughts. Fifteen minutes later, a young man with a kind face and a small motorcycle stood before me.

"Problem, mister?" he inquired.

I nodded, "Yes, problem."

I was quite curt, rude even, since my brain was preoccupied with finding a solution to my current dilemma. Only when I noticed the wooden box on the back of his motorcycle, with various tools attached to it with a rope, did I awake from my thoughts. I asked if I could take a look inside the wooden box. He nodded and opened the box – and there it was, lying on top of a jumble of tools was exactly the screwdriver that I needed! The one person to have come this way was a tool salesman! Until that moment I had believed that things like this only happen in movies.

But who would cross my path out here, on the ocean?

A few fish jumped out of the water and dived back in, as if to say: we'll help! We're still here, you are not alone. They made me laugh, and newly motivated, I said to myself, "Onwards!" and pulled myself back up on my feet.

Out here on the raft I could not afford to drop a single screw – below me, the water was waiting hungrily to swallow everything that slipped through my hands. Of course, I was not careful enough at first. I realised too late that my hands had grown soft from exposure to the saltwater and I dropped my tools much more easily than I normally would have. I cursed when first the screwdriver, and then a couple of fork wrenches disappeared. If I kept on going like this I might find out what Bruce's problem was, but I wouldn't be able to fix him since all my tools would be at the bottom of the ocean. I found a washing line, cut it into pieces and tied all the screwdrivers and wrenches I was using to my under-pants – which were the only thing that I was wearing due to the heat of the day. The tools kept jangling around my legs, and I had to be careful that their weight did not pull down my pants. After all, I didn't want to shock Wilson.

That afternoon a black helicopter turned up in the distance. When the pilot saw me, he came closer and circled above me for a minute. I tried to look as inconspicuous as possible for a man on a raft in the middle of the ocean in his underpants, and did not indicate that I had a problem. You never knew who these people were and I did not want to attract the wrong kind of person. After all, I was the captain of an illegal raft. Luckily, they soon lost interest and went on their way.

Eventually Isla del Rey came so close that I was able to distinguish the leaves on the trees. The Sun signalled to me with an array of col-ours that it would soon turn in for the night, and I knew that I had to find a place to drop anchor. I didn't have to wait for too long, as an auspicious breeze appeared from nowhere and carried me into a bay where I could spend the night.

Once I had anchored the raft in a suitable corner, I kept on search-ing for the fault until late that night. It was a process of elimination: one by one I excluded everything that was not broken until finally there was only one reason left why the motor wouldn't start. I had

had an awful sense of foreboding, but now it was confirmed. Of course it was something that I could not fix myself – the hall sensor, or pickup sensor as it is sometimes referred to, was faulty. It signals to the system that the electrical spark should be produced in order to ignite the petrol gas mixture. I shook my head, bit my lip and resigned myself to my fate. There was no way I could fix this on my own. I needed a spare part, but I hadn't seen another living soul for five days, not even a fishing boat. I sat on a fuel canister, with my arms on my knees and my head propped up on my hands, brooding in the darkness.

My fighting spirit soon returned. I was facing a challenge that made my adventure just all the more exciting and meaningful, and I gave myself and Bruce a pep talk.

"Bruce, you will be fine. Maybe I don't know how yet, but we will continue! Something will happen. Something always happens."

Later the next day, a gentle south wind arose and I hoped that it would carry me north. I could not afford to miss this opportunity, no matter how weak the wind was. Every yard further north was one yard closer to civilisation.

I got lucky – I was moving, albeit slowly, and a few hours later I was in line with Espirito Santo. However, just when I thought I was leaving that narrow island behind, the current suddenly pulled my raft back into the bay where I had just spent the night, and there was nothing I could do. The current carried the raft right past Espirito Santo and ditched me a mile further south back out in the open sea. From there, the wind took over and pushed me north again. This time, I tried to sail further out to escape the current, but without success, once more the raft was pushed back into the bay. We went south for a second time, a third and a fourth time. Then I had had enough! I decided to drop anchor behind Espirito Santo and spend another night there. I was frustrated. All afternoon I had been the plaything of the wind and the currents and I had gotten nowhere. There was nothing else to do but hope that I would have more luck the next morning.

I was awoken by the screeching of the seagulls. The pelicans followed them, elegantly and calmly. It was still early and the Sun was hiding behind the morning mist. The underside of the clouds that had gathered overnight was dyed golden by the sunlight. My makeshift wind flag – a mere thread that I had tied around one of the bamboo masts – showed me that a south wind was blowing. I decided to take advantage of the wind, and after a few sips of water for breakfast, I hauled the anchor on board. The wind was stronger than the day before and I hoped that I could gain enough speed to hold my own against the current and leave the bay for good. I steered against the current with all the skills that I had acquired in the last couple of weeks and … yes! This time I got lucky! We managed to leave Espirito Santo behind us.

Bruce, Wilson and I sailed north that morning along the coast of Isla del Rey at a good speed. About three hours after my departure I saw a fishing boat. I moved the tiller to the port side and aimed for the other vessel. Reaching it seemed to take me an eternity. I was shouting to get the men's attention but they only registered my presence when I had almost reached them. There were four men on board of Hispanic provenance and they were clearly surprised to see me.

I had 'un problema' I called to them.

They nodded.

"Podemos remolcarte si quieres." We can tow you if you like.

I did not understand all of what they were saying but their gestures made their meaning clear. Of course I liked!

"Sí, sí. ¡Muchas gracias!" I said and they indicated that I should throw them the tow rope. I tied my strongest rope to the bow and threw them the other end. One of them caught it while the other hauled in their net which had so far only ensnared a few fish.

"¡Vamos a San Miguel!" We are going to San Miguel, they told me, and off we went.

I was dumbfounded at their quick reaction. They hadn't made me wait, they'd just pulled in their nets and off we went – it was better than any roadside assistance anywhere. Halfway into our journey they slowed down and handed me a plate of fried fish, rice and beans which they had freshly cooked on their boat. I accepted the food gratefully and opened four coconuts for them as a gesture of gratitude. The fishermen enjoyed the refreshing coconut water whilst we moved towards San Miguel at full speed. I smiled to myself. Something always comes up.

Two hours later we reached San Miguel. I was not exactly charmed by the picture it presented; this was nothing compared to the turquoise and white paradise of the rest of the archipelago. Simple fishing boats lay on its black beach; some of them were swaying in the shallow water whilst others were lying on their sides in the mudflat created by the receding water. It was low tide. There was a stink of rotting fish and dried algae in the air. The water, crystal clear everywhere else, was dull and milky green in San Miguel. Even from afar I could make out plastic bags, bottles, beer cans, and broken canisters littering the beach.

I was being towed closer and closer to the beach and the water was becoming ever shallower. Soon I felt the rudders and then the keel being pulled through soft mud, which offered more and more resistance as we neared the shore. I gritted my teeth and prayed that the wood would hold up to the pressure. Since the fishing boat had an outboard engine and a flat bottom it had no problems navigating through the shallow water, and the fishermen were not aware that the construction of my raft was different. Nevertheless, I was glad to get as close to the beach as possible, it would be hard enough to reach the sand as it was, wading through that sludge.

Elevated just behind where the stony beach ended, there stood a two storey cube shaped, whitewashed building that was surrounded by a barbwire fence. In front of it the Panamanian flag fluttered proudly in the wind. A few uniformed men stepped out and peered in my direction. They had machine guns slung over their shoulders. The police! I sighed. Why was I not surprised? Whenever you do not need them, there they are. Even here, in this godforsaken place!

I looked over towards the fishermen. They were busy dissecting six or seven sharks at the water's edge. It looked pretty terrible, as the dark red blood pooled and began to congeal. Fins and innards were lying all over the place. Welcome to San Miguel, I thought, and wiped the sweat off my face. It was noon, and the heat made the stink of the place even worse. Still, I was glad to be there, even if I did not know how things would progress from here.

The fishermen towed me closer to the beach. The raft scraped over the sea bed, until both the keel and the rudders sank deep into the mud. The *Courage of Bridget* was stuck. The fishermen untied the rope, waved at me and then took off, most probably back to where they had been fishing earlier. The four men had asked me for neither money nor fuel. I waved after them, and feeling a deep sense of gratitude, I bowed slightly with one hand placed over my heart. Then I began to row my dinghy towards the shore. When that got stuck too, I got out, immediately sinking deep into the mud. Every step was a major effort. My feet and the dinghy which I was pulling behind me were grabbed by the mud as if by a thousand hands. It felt as if I were walking on suction cups. I made straight for the police station. There was no way of avoiding them, I thought, so it would be best to be proactive. And besides, if anyone spoke English in this place then it was most likely to be one of the police officers.

San Miguel looks more like a shanty town than a pretty village. Small one-storey houses with roofs of red corrugated iron sheets were huddled close together, covering a small hill that reached to the edge of the jungle. Out on the boats in the water, Afro-Panamanian fishermen were busy bringing in the catch of the day and pulling the nets ashore. They paid me no attention. Unfortunately this was not something that could be said of the policemen.

I was wearing flip-flops and they got stuck in the mud with every step. I was not that unhappy about this as it gave me more time to think about what to say to them. I felt nervous all over but I did everything I could to hide it. When I pulled my feet out of the mud for the very last time and finally stood on solid ground I decided to stick to the truth and hope that they would be excited about my adventure. Or at least I hoped that they just wouldn't care about what I was doing. I dragged my dinghy onto the beach and gained a few more seconds. Then I made an innocent face and went to speak to the policemen waiting behind the barbed wire fence.

The commanding officer stepped forward. He had a friendly face and a belly that strained against his olive coloured T-shirt and hung over the belt of his uniform trousers. Despite the heat his feet were clad in tightly laced boots. As I had hoped he and two of his men spoke English. I told him that I was on my way to Colombia on a motorcycle-raft and had been saved by the fishermen after they found me drifting out at sea because of a faulty engine. The commander looked at me sceptically and then said, harshly, but not too unkindly, "I take it you don't have any papers. There is no way that thing has been registered properly – correct?"

"Correct. I have no papers." I answered with a nervous laugh and then waited for his reaction.

"Alright, well, let's look at the motorcycle. Maybe we can help."

He turned around, translated our conversation for the others and then off we went to inspect the raft. I thought I was prepared for anything, but not this!

By now the water had drawn back completely and near the raft a sandbank had emerged. It led in an almost straight line to an island directly opposite San Miguel. Now that the water had gone my raft was lying aground on an angle, with the bow in the mud and the stern high in the air supported by the two rudders and the keel. The men were rather impressed with Bruce, the motorcycle that had travelled over the ocean atop ten old oil barrels. They asked many questions and I told them about my journey in great detail. I was being deliberately open and enthusiastic because I had to get these men, and especially their commander, on my side if I wanted to continue with this adventure. I was relieved to see the men relax, in fact, we got quite friendly. At some point, their commander, Captain Raúl, gave the sign to head back to the police station and invited me to join them for lunch.

"I will send for the mechanic. He'll be sure to know what to do," Raúl said.

I thought: the island mechanic? He won't be able to make head or tail of Bruce. He has probably never even seen a motorcycle in his life. The island had no roads; just boats. Since I did not want to spurn his well-meant offer, I refrained from objecting to this idea. We went back to the police station and I received a plateful of rice and beans, deep-fried plantain and a fried chicken leg. We ate together in the shade of the building, each of us balancing the plates on our knees and I got to know the ten men and one woman behind the uniforms. The mood was laid-back.

"Are you guys called out often?"

"No, it's quiet here. Sometimes there is a brawl, but compared to Panama City it's not bad at all."

I learnt that they were stationed for fourteen days a month on San Miguel before they returned home for two weeks.

When we had finished eating, the mechanic came; he was a scrawny little man with dark skin and short curly hair. His face looked sad and haggard, and his hands were shaking. So far, I had not told the commander that I was a mechanic myself and that the island mechanic would probably not be able to help. But now that the man was standing before us, I had to say something – I absolutely did not want him to mess with Bruce. I remembered the shoddy work of Antonio's men. To trust one of them with Bruce would be like letting a charlatan operate on your best friend. After all, I knew Bruce inside out and I already knew what the problem was. I hesitated for a second, and then I pulled Raúl aside.

"Look, Raúl, I'm a mechanic myself. I know my bike better than anyone else. I have always fixed it myself. I know that I need a spare part that I probably wouldn't even find in Panama City."

While I was speaking, I had another idea.

"But … maybe you could ask him if he has an outboard motor that I could buy?"

At that moment I did not know what I would do if the mechanic actually had one. Would I go straight to Colombia without fixing Bruce? Or should I use it to get back to Panama City to find the spare part I needed? I was pretty sure that in Panama BMW parts were hard to get hold of; in fact, that might very well be true of all of Central America. Bruce was by now a patchwork construction – Suzuki and Honda parts, even converted Ford, Audi, VW and Hyundai car parts had been built in – but I wanted to replace the broken sensor with an original. All kinds of options were flitting through my head. The only thing that was certain was that without a motor I would get nowhere.

El Mecánico, as they called him, first looked doubtful and glanced anxiously at the commander when asked about the motor, but then he nodded and quietly uttered a few words. Raúl said something back that sounded like an order. *El Mecánico* went off, muttering a few choice words beneath his breath. I was told we should go with him and that he had an outboard motor for me. It sounded promising And Raúl and I followed him through the entire village, along small alleyways, stepping over little stone walls and crossing backyards full of rubbish. We walked past bedroom windows and open kitchen doors where dishes were clanging and the smell of freshly cooked rice drifted through the air. I had by now lost all sense of direction – the houses all looked exactly the same. *El Mecánico* opened the gate to a narrow backyard and we entered, following him as he went to a shabby shed, the door of which was jammed so tight that the little man struggled to open it. I helped him and together we managed to push it open. The door creaked accusingly. Inside, a thick layer of dust lay over everything and it was evident that nobody had been there for a very long time. The mechanic rummaged through the mess, mumbling all the time under his breath, until finally he located a grey and red outboard engine, which he hauled out into the sunlight. It was not new, which is to say that it looked as if it had been used up until it was worn out, and then finally buried in the shed for the rest of eternity. Was it still working? *El Mecánico* nodded, and muttered something that sounded like "*gasolina*".

He hauled it up onto his shoulder, and as we were leaving he handed me a small bag as he needed a free hand to close the gate behind us. The plastic bag contained a few tools that were clanging together nosily. On our way back Raúl asked about the price of the motor and then translated the answer for me, "He'll repair the motor first. If it runs you can have it for 200 dollars."

At the beach, *El Mecánico* took the motor apart. I did not like what I was seeing. There were quite a few things missing and what did exist was either broken or fixed up in such a way that a blacksmith might as well have been responsible for its maintenance, not a mechanic. I sighed, but I gave the frail man a chance.

El Mecánico, who was busying himself with the motor, caught my eye and said merrily, "*Sí, un buen motor*" A good engine.

That statement may have been correct twenty years ago, but now I wasn't so sure, but I nodded anyway. Raúl joined us and told me in English that *El Mecánico* was always fighting for his survival.

"There is only one car on the island. Not enough work for a mechanic. The fishermen usually try and fix their own engines. Only when they can't manage they'll ask him. See how his hands are shaking? He's been drinking since his wife died. He is a good guy but he really shouldn't drink so much." Raúl shook his head and looked at the man with pity in his eyes.

After about an hour, the first awkward stutter of the engine had become a handsome buzzing – the thing was actually working and I liked what I was hearing. When it was all put together again and the butchered insides were hidden from view that 200 dollars seemed like a good investment.

"Great! It looks as if our deal can go through," I said and the policemen translated. The mechanic showed the hint of a smile. He would install the motor straightaway, I was told, and I did not object. When he was done he took the money. This limited my budget for the rest of the trip considerably. I had withdrawn 500 dollars in Panama City. Some of it had been spent on fuel and food, and now I only had 120 dollars left to last me until my arrival in Colombia. That would buy me fifteen gallons of fuel, which was not very much, but at least now I had a proper boat engine and I would be able to leave San Miguel with the next tide. I decided to worry about the money later.

That same evening I took my leave. The high tide was coming in and I intended to take advantage of it to leave the bay. I had decided to head back to Colombia rather than back to Panama City. Everyone wished me the best of luck, and I waved to them as I went aboard my raft and got everything ready for departure. The night rolled in faster than high tide, so that it was already dark when I started my 'new' outboard motor. I pulled the starter rope – and nothing happened. I tried again, and again, eventually there was some rumbling and rattling but the motor wouldn't start. I kept on trying. Finally, it stuttered and stammered and rattled rather promisingly, and then it began to cough and died off. It had been working perfectly on the beach that very afternoon! I kept pulling at the rope, maybe ten or twenty times, but still the motor remained silent. Eventually I gave up, frustrated. What the hell was going on? Why wouldn't it start?

It was very likely that the motor could not be fixed without a spare part, and I had not been impressed with the mechanic's tool bag. It was highly unlikely that he would have a large selection of spare parts at his disposal anyway. Inwardly I sighed, and summed up the experience as the most expensive ten seconds of my life. There was nothing else to do for now but to drop anchor and lie down in my hammock. Tomorrow is another day, I thought. Maybe something will come up.

I got up at sunrise. The tide was high and I was able to row the 600 feet to the shore. When I opened the gate to the police station, one of the men looked out of the door and called for Raúl.

When he saw me, he looked surprised.

"You're still here?"

"Yes, unfortunately. The motor stopped working. It started but after ten seconds it just stopped. Nothing doing."

"Damn! I'll send for *El Mecánico* straight away. He'll need to fix it. How annoying! Sorry about that."

"Thanks. I don't think that motor can be fixed so easily, frankly. But I don't mind if he'll look at it again."

"Let's see what he has to say. If he's sold you a broken motor, he'll give you your money back; I'll make sure of that!" Raúl sounded quite angry.

My anger had dissipated long ago – I just wanted to find a solution to my problem. The other police officers had stepped out into the morning Sun. They seemed embarrassed for having put me in touch with the mechanic. No need for embarrassment, I thought; after all he was the only mechanic on the island.

We had coffee, and then Vito returned. Vito was a young native of San Miguel who the police had employed as an unofficial servant. He held his hands up and said, "*El Mecánico* can't be found anywhere. Nobody has seen him since yesterday evening. Someone said he was on his way to Panama City."

I sighed. I had expected something like that. The money had probably already been spent. The policemen were upset. I remained calm, "Money can be replaced. But how will I get hold of a spare part for Bruce?"

There are no tourists in San Miguel, and therefore there is no internet either. I asked if any of them had a connection on their smartphone.

"Yeah, sure, you can use mine," said Irving, one of the policemen who spoke English. Maria, the only woman there, brought me some more coffee with a kind smile.

When the connection to the internet was strong enough, I logged on to Facebook and described my situation briefly, then asked: Can somebody help me to organise a hall sensor for Bruce?

I was not sure if there was much of a point in doing this, but trying wouldn't do any harm. The number of my Facebook friends had been increasing steadily since my departure from Switzerland. On the road this was the easiest way of staying in touch with people from all over the world and keeping them up-to-date with my journey. Many of them were bikers too. Some of them I had met, others I had not. When I refreshed the page two minutes later I was amazed to find an answer to my post, written by a certain Jim Julien. I had no idea who he was.

He wrote, "Hey Dylan, I can get a hall sensor for you. Just let me know where to send it to."

I had not expected an answer that quickly. Was he serious? I opened a chat window. Jim wrote that he lived in California and that he was a biker too. He had come across one of my YouTube videos and had sent me a friend request on Facebook. I realised that he had sent it on my last day in Panama City, which was when I last had the internet. Life always knows how and why to interweave people's life stories, sometimes we just realise it too late. Often we do not realise it at all.

This stranger, who was somehow not a stranger anymore, was sitting in front of his computer thousands of miles away, and he was a godsend. We exchanged technical details while he was on the phone to his motorcycle dealer. His wife, who spoke Spanish, called a dealer in Panama City. He had a hall sensor but it cost 453 dollars, and he didn't deliver spare parts, and where the hell was Las Perlas anyway? In Panama? Really? No, that couldn't be. Considering his ignorance, regarding a really not that small archipelago a mere 40 miles from the mainland of his country, it was probably for the best that he didn't get involved with delivering anything.

Luckily, Jim found a second-hand sensor on eBay. It was in good condition, cost little more than 100 dollars and the shipping was included. We decided to have it delivered to Panama City. FedEx did at least know where Las Perlas was, but they still wouldn't ship there. My sailor friends in Panama City did not have an official address, so I asked Jim to have it addressed to the Swiss embassy instead. I did not know if embassies accepted mail on behalf of their citizens, but since it was an emergency I hoped to be able to convince them with a phone call.

The next time I checked my Facebook messages, Jim had written that the sensor was already on its way and would arrive within a week, and that the embassy would accept the parcel for me, for he had already called and clarified.

I was overwhelmed and sat for a few minutes behind Irving's phone deep in thought. Then I thanked Jim and told him to send me his details so that I could pay for the sensor via PayPal.

He answered:
- *You're from Switzerland, right?*
- *Yes, right.*
- *And are you going back there anytime soon?*
- *Yes. Once I reach Colombia.*
- *Well, listen; in that case, send me some Swiss chocolate when you're back home. I don't want money, chocolate makes me happier.*

I read his message twice. Then I asked:
- *Are you sure?*
- *Yep :-)*
- *Wow! Thanks, man! Thank you so much! I am speechless. Why do you do this, for someone you've never met?*

It took a while, and then his answer came:
- *It's obvious that you follow your dream and that you're not driven by your ego or by chasing fame. I find that really refreshing in these times of self-promotion. Your authenticity cannot be faked; maybe that's why your adventure struck a chord with me. I'm a biker myself so when I heard about your journey and how you go about it, I was all for it. I think it's your enthusiasm which is really extraordinary. You do what many would like to do if they had the opportunity, the skills, and the courage. That's why I like helping you.*

That evening I had dinner at the police station. Again, we all sat together on plastic chairs outside. This time, the youngest of the group, Javier, was the chef. They all took turns, though Maria cooked more often than the others. The menu did not change that much: plantains, rice, beans, and chicken. Tonight we were in luck: there was fish rather than chicken. It was funny, here we were surrounded by water and I thought eating fish was something special!

I was sitting next to Raúl who was apologising profusely: "We haven't heard anything from *El Mecánico*. I'm sorry. I'm really annoyed that he disappeared with that money of yours. That guy is a ..."

"Raúl, it's okay. Really. Win some, lose some." I was happy about the sensor and did not feel like speaking unkindly about the mechanic. After all, I had chosen to make a deal with him.

"But still! He stole from you!"

"You told me yourself that he struggles for survival. I feel sorry for him and I don't think he planned to take advantage of me. He just couldn't fix the motor. I'm on a trip around the world and have more tools on me than he does."

Raúl looked at me critically. I thought I could detect envy in his voice when he said, "You must be rich if you can afford to lose 200 dollars to such a ... idiot of a mechanic. And this even though you've been travelling for, what, three years?"

"Yes, almost three."

"See, I'm not a rich man. For me, that kind of money is a lot."

"I'm not rich. You can't judge by what I do how much I have. Three years ago I sold my business and decided to spend it all on a trip around the world. By the time I reach Colombia and go back to Switzerland I'll have about 1000 dollars left. That is very little to build a life in Switzerland on. On my journey I learnt that sometimes you give something away and sometimes you receive something. Yesterday I lost 200 dollars. Today, someone gave me the spare part I needed so badly as a gift. Raúl, you can't imagine how often people gave me something even though they had so little themselves. Just like that, without me asking for it."

"Okay, but still, you're from Switzerland. I could never afford to go travelling like you."

"If it were your dream, you could! And you should! Your head and your heart, they are the true gateways to your dreams, not the dollars in your pocket. I wanted to travel for as long as possible and have as many adventures as I could, so I decided to travel on the cheap and keep things simple. Just me, my bike, my tent and my gasoline stove."

"Were you never afraid? Didn't bad things happen to you?" Raúl remained sceptical.

"No, never. I believe in the good in people. And that something good will always come your way. So, yeah, sometimes you lose something or have to swallow something you don't like, or are annoyed or just have a bad day. But when you can remain generous in these moments and are able to let go … I can tell you a good story about that, actually."

Raúl nodded. His facial expression relaxed as he stretched out his legs and folded his hands across his round belly. I told him the story of Jeff and Tina.

Whilst in Eureka in northern California, I was approached by a man in denim dungarees, with a full beard and a bald head. His cheeks were as red and round as apples and he could have convinced any child that he was the Santa Claus. Bruce, dirty and loaded with luggage, had caught his eye. His name was Jeff. We chatted for a while about motorcycles and travelling and then he invited me to spend the night in his tiny little camper trailer – he was a biker himself.

So I rode behind him through the imposing Sequoia woods and out to a village, which consisted of a handful of houses and a petrol station. He stopped before a small wooden house, and we left our bikes in his back yard and walked around the house to the garden. There stood a tiny caravan, maybe about the same size as my tent. A doll house by American standards, but big enough for me. Jeff went inside the house and called for Tina. I followed him. Inside, things were kept just as basic: there was no TV, no stereo, just an old saggy couch, a table, and a few chairs. But the house was cosy and Jeff seemed to be happy with what he had. He introduced me to his partner Tina and his dog, Fester, a short legged white boxer who fell in love with me at first sight and took to following me around like a shadow. Even when I went to have a shower, Fester waited for me outside the door. I think he would have liked to come in, but I did need some privacy. The shower curtain which hung over the bathtub was decorated with a picture of a large world map. Jeff must be a keen traveller, I thought, though he hasn't told me anything about it. As I showered I looked at the world map on the curtain, and the images and encounters of the last two or three years played before my eyes, just as if I were in a movie theatre. While I washed the dirt off of myself, I also washed the dust off my memories.

Meanwhile, Jeff and Tina had cooked dinner and we spent a lovely evening together. They asked me so many questions about my trip that I barely learnt anything at all about their travels. I had hardly finished one story when they encouraged me to start another. Eventually, after a fine evening of socializing, I sank into the bed in Jeff's tiny camper and discovered a round pillow shaped like a Globe. My suspicions of Jeff as an experienced traveller were confirmed. I wondered if he too had ridden his motorcycle around the world. I must not forget to ask him that tomorrow, I repeated to myself.

It was cold in northern California at that time of year, and I woke up a couple of times during the night. I could hear Fester, who was laying on the cold floor outside the front door of the camper, as he shivered and whimpered in the cold. I tried to take him indoors to his cosy bed, but he wouldn't have any of it. The bitter chill did not deter him from waiting faithfully for me until morning, and then he happily rested his muzzle on my shoes.

The sunbeams streaming through the little window woke me up early, and Fester was pleased that I rose so soon. Until Tina and Jeff were up, I passed the time playing with the dog who could hardly believe his luck.

At breakfast, It was finally my turn to ask some questions.

"Now then. Tell me about yourselves. Where have you travelled to?"

Jeff and Tina smiled at one other.

"Oh, nowhere, really, we just went to Canada once."

"But what's with the world maps everywhere?"

They hesitated.

"Yeah, we would like to travel more but we haven't had the courage."

I didn't understand what was holding them back.

"What are you afraid of? If you want to go, then go. You'd have a great time."

"We went around the world with you yesterday, didn't we?"

Tina laughed and Jeff nodded.

After breakfast it was time to go. I packed up my things, hugged my hosts and petted Fester one last time. As I lifted my helmet off the veranda table, a pile of one hundred dollar bills appeared from beneath it. I was a little taken aback, and I was sure that I hadn't seen the money on the table when I left my helmet there the day before. I grabbed the bundle of notes and handed it to them saying, "That was lying underneath my helmet. I wouldn't want you to look for it. I don't want the bills to be blown away by the wind."

"That's your money," said Tina.

Now, I may sometimes be a little forgetful, but I was pretty sure that I had not left a bundle of cash on the table. I did not have that much money with me anyway.

"No, it's not."

"Yes, it is! I mean … we know it's not yours, but now it is. It's a gift."

Of course I refused, as I had counted the money. Ten one hundred dollar bills!

"A thousand dollars? They gave you a thousand dollars? Why?" Raúl interjected, staring at me in disbelief.

"That's what I asked them too. Their answer was simple and beautiful, but also quite sad: 'We want you to travel for us. To go where we haven't been. We will travel through you', said Jeff, and you can imagine that I was speechless. 'You have to use that money to travel yourselves. Go out and see the world.' I told them. They said, 'Maybe one day. But now you travel for us. We will follow you on our shower curtain.'"

"And all they had was that little house?"

"A small house and just really basic furniture. Nothing new. If I remember it right, they only had a transistor radio. I found it hard to accept that kind of generosity. But just as I learnt to let go on my trip so I also learnt to receive. That's what it is all about, isn't it? To give and to take. To lose and to gain. One time you help, another time someone else will help you."

"But a thousand dollars? Would you give a thousand dollars to some random stranger?"

"I know, it's crazy. An incredible act of kindness. I tried to give it back to them for the longest time. They wouldn't take it. A few days later I needed new tires and Bruce's rear wheel-bearings broke, and I had to buy stuff for my raft so it didn't go unused. You see what I mean?"

Raúl nodded thoughtfully. The others had gone back inside a while ago, but we were still sitting out on our plastic chairs. There was a moment of silence; a couple of moths flew into the flickering neon lights and I enjoyed the gentle rustling of the waves.

"Are they Christian? Are you Christian?" Raúl broke the silence. Religion seemed to be a way for him to understand the good in life.

"No, I'm not. Not anymore. To give has nothing to do with religion. I just believe that all the good that you do will come back to you and that if you want something with all your heart, it will happen."

"But how can you be so sure?"

"I just am!" I laughed and tried to explain. "I don't think about the bad things that might happen. I just say to myself: it will work out. Something will happen, something will come up. I mean, look at you! You could have confiscated my raft. I was nervous when I first came through that gate; really nervous. But I just trusted that it would be okay. I trusted you, and everybody else, and that something good would happen."

Raúl grinned and nodded, and then he rubbed his substantial belly and asked me if I wanted another cup of coffee. I did.

Friends in San Miguel: Maria and part of the police force.

CHAPTER ELEVEN

"You own neither the past nor the future.
The present is all you have.
Use it!"

~

I decided to travel on a fishing boat in order to pick up the sensor in Panama City. The police promised to keep an eye on my raft during my absence. I liked the irony of the situation: the police were perfectly entitled to confiscate the raft, but instead they were going to make sure that nothing happened to it.

Until then I had a week to get to know San Miguel. I ignored the pungent air as best as I could and as I spent the long days sitting in front of the police station I slowly began to see the bay in a different light. The last couple of years travelling had taught me to make the best of every situation. I could have spent that week being annoyed by the rubbish on the beach, and the stench, and the food, and would have ended up worn out and ill-humoured by the end of my stay. So instead, I decided to look closer. I looked beyond the piles of rubbish and the smell and saw black birds stalking through the mud on their thin legs, making a dinner of unsuspecting invertebrates. I saw worms drawing ornate patterns unintentionally on the wet ground, and large red and small grey crabs running off and burying themselves in the sand. The dogs of San Miguel loved playing with them, chasing them and throwing them up in the air. Yes the dogs! The longer I was there, the more I became aware of how close the relationship between the people and their dogs was. There seemed to be as many dogs here as there were families. Every morning, when the ferry from Panama City dropped anchor out in the ocean and the passengers were brought ashore in small dinghies, the dogs swam out to greet their masters. Strangely only those dogs whose owners were on the ferry took to the water. How did they know which ferry their owner was coming back on? The dogs paddled beside the dinghies until they were lifted out of the water by their respective owner. Day by day the low tide retracted the water further and further. Whoever arrived or wanted to leave from San Miguel during low tide had to walk at least half a mile to the edge of the water through deep mud. Those who arrived at high tide and left their boats close to the village had even a bigger problem. They had to push their boat through the mud until they had reached the water. One morning, while I was still in my hammock, I watched five young men heave their battered yellow and blue wooden boat over the mudflat and into the water at low tide. They were accompanied by six straggly dogs which sank up to their bellies into the quagmire; soon they only managed to move forward at all by jumping, but their tails were still wagged cheerfully. When they were ready, the young men got into the boat and petted the dogs' goodbye, then they steered the boat out onto the water. The dogs stood there and watched the boat until it was out of sight, then one of them began to howl, and soon the others joined in. For about half an hour they stood there in the water lamenting, their eyes glued to the horizon in the hope that the boat would come back. Finally, they gave up and made their arduous journey back home. This ritual was repeated every day.

There were always a few dogs playing on the beach during the day. They rolled around in the sand, ate the fish that had fallen out of the fishermen's crates, scuffled with one another, took a nap or chased crabs. But no matter what they were doing, as soon as they heard the engine of a fishing boat, they pricked up their ears and any dog whose owner was out on that boat swam out to meet them. When the fishermen lifted them out of the water, the dogs would go wild with happiness, barking, wagging their tails and bouncing around on deck like little whirling dervishes. I was amazed at the intimate relationship between the humans and the dogs on San Miguel. Nobody could tell me why it was this way. It just was.

When the ferry dropped anchor, it was not just the dogs that made life on the island interesting. Little boys arrived at the beach with their brightly painted taxis (or rather their wheelbarrows) to carry the passengers' luggage to their houses. Each of their vehicles had the letters TAXI written on the side in shaky letters. They were an ideal mode of transport for the narrow alleyways of the island. The boys often ran out into the water and haggled with their clients, just like the rickshaw drivers in India or the vendors in Marrakesh. The littler boys, who were still too small to push a wheelbarrow that was piled high with suitcases and boxes, joined forces with one another and shared the coins out after the job was finished.

I often watched the ocean too. During low tide, it seemed to take a break from San Miguel. I would have advised it to stay longer than a few hours to discover the hidden gems of everyday life so that nothing would be missed. The little taxi boys liked the low tide more than anyone else. When the water drew back, at the same time as the ferry arrived or departed, the children got very excited. Noisily they ran with their wheelbarrows over the sand-bank and out to the island long before the boat came in sight – always accompanied by a gaggle of dogs, of course. The ferry had to anchor much further out during low tide and the little boats dropped their passengers on the island off the coast, so that they could walk back home via the sandbank. A longer distance meant more money for the taxi boys!

While the older children were at school, the younger ones played with little makeshift boats on the beach. The water was fairly clean during high tide – and then the children swam and played in the waves until the ocean had had enough and began to recede. Just outside of the police station, facing the beach, there stood a large old mango tree which seemed to watch over San Miguel. Its branches were so heavy with fruit that even the smallest of the little girls could pick a mango or two by standing on their tiptoes. It provided shade to the concrete bench underneath it, and often there were three or four older men sitting there, chatting, and laughing loudly, most likely complaining about their wives. Sometimes they even sang together. I liked the sound of their husky old voices and when I walked past, I sometimes exchanged a few words with them. The bench seemed to serve the function of a village pub for the men – the women did not come down to the beach very often except for when visitors from the mainland were expected or when they were waiting for the ferry to go to Panama City.

I remained a foreigner on San Miguel. The people accepted me as a guest, even though they were perhaps not quite sure what I was doing there. The language barrier was one problem, and the fact that the policemen kept me from engaging more often with them was another. The uniformed men had taken me under their wing from the off and watched over me protectively. Even when I just went to the shops for a can of coke, one of them always accompanied me. Did they do this out of friendship, or to protect me? Maybe it was just because they were bored. I did not ask. I accepted their protection in the same way as they had accepted my wish to travel over the ocean. Every day that I spent there, laughing with them, eating with them, being bored out of my mind with them, the more it meant that I had become one of them. Without the uniform and a gun of course, but I had become an unofficial policeman.

When they were called out on duty on another island, a long-winded process was set in motion. They didn't have a boat of their own, even though they were part of the *Servicio Nacional Aeronaval de Panamá*, the National Air and Navy Service. When it was necessary they had to go and hire a boat, then go and fetch their own fuel from the police station and take it to the rented boat in order to fill it up. Only then could they take off, wearing their life vests and clutching rusty machine guns. During the time that I was there, they were only called out twice to go out and execute their duties into the neighbouring islands. Otherwise they patrolled the streets of San Miguel, every two hours, on foot, and without anything exciting taking place.

On one occasion the men started talking to me about Maria. They pointed out that she was pretty, a good cook and still single. They thought that she liked me because she did my laundry and often made me tea. I laughed. As pretty as she was, Maria was not my type. But who does not like to hear that someone is interested in you? Just for the fun of it, and because there was nothing else to do, I played along and we flirted. Irving acted as our translator and we amused the whole group. But soon I had to withdraw from this game as delicately as possible as Maria was getting serious, "If you can take care of me and my child we can get married. You seem to be a decent guy."

At first, I thought she was joking, but then I saw the look on her face, and on Irving's and I realised that this was for real. To me, this harmless flirting was as far away from marriage as the moon from the earth. But Maria taught me that marriage does not have to be primarily about love. It can also be about survival and security. I had known, of course, that some women marry out of necessity, in the hope of a secure future. However, to read about it is not the same as actually experiencing it. Her straight forwardness surprised me and in fact it scared me a little. But from then on I held back and made it clear to her that we probably had different expectations of life and not that much in common. Throughout Central America, I couldn't help but notice that there were so many unmarried single mothers. In Panama it wasn't any different, Irving told me later. Maria's offer was nothing unusual. I was a nice guy with a sense of humour, and well off in her eyes. Why get to know each other or fall in love first? I wished her all the best and hoped that someday she would find someone to fall in love with and live as a family.

Two days after his disappearance, the mechanic turned up again. Vito, who lived in the village, had seen him and Raúl sent for him immediately. An hour later, the man was standing outside, probably knowing full well what this was all about. Raúl was glad to have something to do and spoke to him like a father would to his child. *El Mecánico* made for a sorry picture, as he stood there with his shaky hands and his tired eyes. He answered Raúl's torrent of words with a nod and said that he would go and fetch his tools. No excuses, no explanations, just the scuffle of his feet as he slowly went back to his shed.

When he returned, we rowed out to *Courage of Bridget*. He carried his rusty spanners, a few old spare parts and two worn down screwdrivers in a plastic bag. When we reached the raft I indicated to him that my tool box was at his disposal. He began working with slow, deliberate movements. I watched him and wondered what might have happened in his life to make him acquire such a melancholy, hopeless air. After he had worked on the motor for a while he fished a few spare ignition coils out of his plastic bag. They looked about as old as the motor. He replaced them one after the other and then tried to start the motor over and over again. Nothing happened. He began working on the carburettor. He removed it, then built it back in again. Still, the motor remained silent and the cigarette breaks grew more frequent. Since my raft carried 32 gallons of fuel in plastic canisters, I sent him to the dinghy for each break and waited patiently for him to finish his cigarette and climb back on board. He removed the next part, built it back in again and then smoked another cigarette. Two hours and three packs of cigarettes later he had pretty much removed and then built back in all of the motor parts. I indicated that it was pointless to keep going, he would need to take the motor back – but he wasn't ready to give up quite yet. He said that he would do further repairs at the beach, and I understood what he was not saying out loud: he was unable to return my money and therefore he had to get the motor working somehow, anyhow. He dismounted the engine and laid it in the dinghy. I gave him a handful of my surplus tools and told him to keep them. I would be on a plane to Switzerland soon – he needed them more than I did. He thanked me and we rowed back to the shore.

I returned to my friends at the police station to kill time while *El Mecánico* got to working on the motor again. Much later I heard the sound of a motor, and when I went outside I saw him propelling across the bay in his boat and with my motor attached, chugging out towards the open sea. Just when I thought the motor was genuinely working again, the noise stopped. I was not sure at first whether the roaring of the waves had drowned out the sound of the motor or if it had broken down again. I waited ten minutes, unsure what to do. Then finally *El Mecánico* stood up on shaky legs. The boat rocked dangerously, and in my mind's eye I saw him falling overboard, but he caught his balance at the last moment. When he finally gained stability, he waved to me with both arms, as if he had been lost at sea for days. I asked one of the fishermen to go out and tow the mechanic back to the beach. Back on land, he went straight back to working on the motor, hammering and sawing. He drove out another four times, but without success. The motor always howled promisingly at first, but then coughed and wheezed and was finally silent.

Whilst all of this was going on, I was sitting inside the police station looking out through the door with a limited field of vision. It was as if I were watching a cartoon, I could see the mechanic steering the boat this way and that, from left to right, from right to left – and then nothing. Eventually the little boat would re-appear, with *El Mecánico* rowing it back towards the beach. At least this time he had thought of taking the oars with him. In the end he had no choice but to give up. To my surprise he showed up that evening at the police station to return 120 dollars. It was all that he had left, he told me, ashamed, saying that he would have to wait for his next pension payment to return the rest. He was very sorry. He told me that he did not want me to leave San Miguel with that motor; it would be far too dangerous. I thanked him for his efforts and for his concern, accepted the 120 dollars and had Raúl translate (which he did grudgingly) that I did not want the rest of the money.

The next night, as I had just began to doze off, a loud droning noise awoke me. A small freighter with a flat bottom was heading straight towards San Miguel at full speed. What the devil was the captain thinking? The water level was so low right then that not even my raft could have left the bay, and now this cargo boat was racing straight for the beach at full throttle. If anything, judging from the racket, the captain was even beginning to accelerate. When I realised that the ship had crossed an invisible line between deep and shallow water, I began to wave and shout. The men on deck neither saw nor heard me; the engine was far too loud. When it finally hit the shore, the engine noise got even angrier and even louder. Toothlessly the vessel ate its way through the mud and I watched in surprise as it fought its way forward closer and closer to the village. Nobody seemed to be bothered by the racket except for me. Finally, the motor stopped. The thing – was it even a ship? – stood 15 feet from the houses, its nose resting on the sand like a beached whale. Planks emerged over the sides and crates were unloaded. As the whole spectacle was only illuminated by the single street lamp of San Miguel, it was too dark to see properly. I went back to sleep.

The following morning I saw that it really was a small freighter. Crates continued to be unloaded and I assumed that this must be the supply vessel that brought provisions from the mainland. Intrigued, I rowed ashore. On the beach there towered a miniature skyline of a few hundred beer crates. Not bad, I thought. San Miguel only has a population of 1,600 people – many of them children, I might add – and here in front of me stood the average yearly production of a brewery. Who would drink all of this?

That afternoon the policemen were all terribly excited; they whispered like teenagers, poked each other with their elbows and stared wistfully through the open door out onto the bay. Only Maria rolled her eyes and continued playing on her mobile phone as the other six crowded around the door frame, pushing and shoving one other.

"Look at the *gringa*! That's a sight for sore eyes!"

"Oh Jesus, have mercy!" Javier made the sign of the cross and they all laughed.

"Dylan, come and look! There is a sexy blonde!" Irving tried to convince me.

I laughed and shook my head. "I leave that to you guys. Where I come from there are plenty of blonde women."

Raúl, who, as the one in charge, felt obliged to show some kind of restraint, finally gave in and pulled the curtain to one side to peer out the window.

"Man, she is really hot!"

I was intrigued by the words of a man who normally kept his head and sat behind his desk like an unflappable fat happy Buddha.

I stood behind him and looked through the curtain towards the woman as she waded through knee deep water towards the beach. Tanned skin, blond wild hair down to her shoulders, flat stomach, muscular arms and legs.

"American," I guessed.

"She has a guy with her! So you can all calm down again," I called to the men.

"So what? We're not looking at him but at the curves of that goddess," said Irving theatrically.

I rolled my eyes and sat back down again. The men went outside, unsure of what they should do next, they were like little school boys looking for an excuse to knock on the door of some pretty teacher. They loitered near the small iron gate, and greeted her coyly when she came near. Considering the spectacle inside, they now behaved quite civilly, and none of them could muster anything more than a tame *"¡Hola, Bonita!"* Hello beautiful.

197

Not much later Irving came inside and said, "Dylan, the blonde is asking for you."

"For me?"

"Yep," he made his eyes wide and pulled a face.

Somewhat triumphantly I got up and grinned at the others. I could feel their envious eyes on my back as I walked through the door. Well why the hell not ...

Her name was Adrienne and she was indeed an American and lived on Contadora. She had heard about me and the *Courage of Bridget* and that I was stranded on San Miguel. Adrienne and her brother were on a fishing excursion and had come to visit San Miguel for a short break and for a cold beer.

I told her all about my problem and that I was waiting until I would pick up the spare part I needed in Panama City the next day or the day after. I just had to find a fishing boat. The ferry cost eighty dollars, which I thought was too expensive, not just for me, but especially for the people who lived here.

Without missing a beat, said, "We're almost done fishing and then we'll head back to Contadora. Come with us and I will find a plane for you to Panama City. You can stay at my place for the night. It shouldn't be a problem to find a pilot who'll take you."

"By plane?" I asked, perplexed.

"Maybe one of my friends flies to Panama City tomorrow, I'm sure you can go along as additional cargo!"

What a nice surprise, I thought, and I didn't hesitate to accept this unique opportunity to see the archipelago and the glittering ocean from a bird's eye view.

"My Guardian Angel must have sent you!"

She smiled at me charmingly and said she would be back in twenty minutes.

So I would go by plane to Panama City! What an offer. Even though I was not looking forward to returning to civilisation, at least the journey there would be another adventure. With a broad smile I went back to the police station. I decided to tease the men a bit.

"The blonde is taking me to Contadora for the night."

I received whistles and applause, and a few jealous looks.

"I will tell you everything when I get back!" I joked.

"Too bad she has a man with her," Irving said.

I played my trump card.

"That's her brother!"

I enjoyed the collective horror of the men. One of them translated for Maria what was going on and she got up and left.

"Oooh, someone's jealous," laughed Raúl and slapped my back.

I got serious. I did not have much time to pack.

"Raúl, can you watch my raft for a couple of days?"

"Sure. But move it closer to the beach, otherwise we won't be able to see it at night."

"But here the water is too low, even at high tide. And at low tide the weight of the raft will strain the rudders that close to the beach. It's better where the raft is now. Over here, the rudders will probably break. Can't I leave it out there?"

"Either you bring it close to the beach or we can't be responsible for the raft. Your choice. We can't see if someone climbs onto the raft at night to steal something. Know what I mean?"

I did know what he meant and I realised that I had no choice. I had the *Courage of Bridget* towed and left her directly in front of the police station. The keel and the rudders buried themselves deep into the sand. Now, at high tide, it didn't look so bad, but I dreaded to think what would happen at low tide. The rudders which were made of plywood were only four feet long; they would not be able to carry the weight of the raft for several days. I had to try and reduce the weight, so I carried all the boxes and canisters into the police station. When I was done, and her brother were waiting for me. I said my goodbyes to the policemen and got onto the boat.

We made our way to Contadora at a leisurely pace, drinking beer and fishing. Suddenly, the engine began to cough – by now an all too familiar sound to me – and then the only thing that was moving the boat was the waves. I am not a superstitious person, but it did make me wonder – what was the universe trying to tell me? Maybe I should have given Ron a call, maybe there's a conspiracy behind all of this.

"One problem is no problem. It just adds to the adventure," I said to myself and began to tinker with the engine. After ten minutes it was working again. I was not quite sure why or how, but the main thing was that it did.

"You have to have that thing checked properly," I said to the two of them. "I'm not sure what was wrong with it."

Adrienne and her brother laughed.

"What would we have done without you? Who was sent by a Guardian Angel now?"

To see Las Perlas from above was a treat. The water glittered in every shade of blue, and told me to come back soon. The pilot had carried a Turkish TV crew to Contadora and now he was re-turning back to Panama City alone. They were shooting a reality show there on a neighbouring island where two teams had to fight for 'survival' on a lonely island.

Twenty minutes later we reached the airport. I had seen Amador below us and László's and Jacques' boats were still in the harbour. It had taken me two days to reach Las Perlas from Panama City, and on my raft, unable to see either Las Perlas or Panama City, the distance had felt enormous. But from the plane I could see them both, and the forty miles between the gorgeous green islands and the mainland did not seem all that far anymore. It's funny how a different perspective changes your outlook of things.

As soon as I stepped off the plane and onto the runway, the heat and the noise of Panama City hit me like a fist in the face. It felt as if I had been away for much longer than two weeks. From the airport I went straight to the Swiss embassy to pick up my FedEx parcel. A friendly Panamanian handed it to me and said that it had arrived the day before. I opened it straight away, as excited as a child at Christmas. I had never been that delighted about a spare part as I was in that moment. Now I just wanted to go back to San Miguel as soon as possible, but the ferry to Las Perlas left in the morning and I had no other choice but to spend the night in Panama City. I mulled it over. Should I go and see my friends in Amador? It would be fun to see their surprised faces – but I had lost my mobile phone with their numbers on it. What if they weren't at the *Kiosko*? It would be too complicated getting back from Amador to the ferry in the morning. For simplicity's sake I decided to find a guest house in the city centre and then take the ferry back to San Miguel in the morning. I was eager to continue my trip southwards as soon as possible.

Along the way I bought a new mobile phone for thirty dollars and withdrew 500 dollars from a cash point. I did not count the money but buried it deep in my trouser pocket – I did not want to risk being mugged in the middle of my sailing adventure for the sake of a few hundred dollars, and my friends had warned me enough about how careful I should be when carrying cash. At that moment I would have welcomed the police escort that I had found so silly on San Miguel. But nobody paid me any attention here anyway, and I went to find myself a room for the night.

That evening I was writing an email to Jim Julien in the lobby of my hostel, when a young American addressed me. We had a small chat and he mentioned that he worked as a botanist for the nature reserve *Punta Patiño,* in the Darién jungle. He was returning there by boat the next day.
"Oh, I'm going along the Darién on my raft. What's it like there on the ocean around the Darién?"
"You're going along the Darién with what?!"
I explained my plan and asked him many questions. I had to admit I did not like his answers. Of course I had already been

told about how strong the waves were along the coast, but most of my sailor friends only knew about them by hearsay and I had relied on the fact that these kinds of stories tend to be somewhat exaggerated, with each story teller surely adding his own salt and pepper to the mix. That had been my theory anyway, but now I had actually met someone who had been there himself.

"Sometimes, boats that travel from *Punta Patiño* to Panama City cannot leave because the breakers near the open sea are too rough. Boat operators prefer to make the two hour journey back from the starting point of Bay of San Miguel (not San Miguel on Las Perlas) to *Punta Patiño* than risk the dangers. I was once on a boat that returned five times. The waves are wild at the best of times, in bad weather impassable. How will you manage with your little raft?"

"Is that what it's like along the entire coast?"

"It's not just the breakers. The open sea can be pretty rough as well. I mean, I only know the Punta Patiño region, but I heard it's like that all the way down to Buenaventura. Not many villages there either. But the waves are a real threat to the people who do live there. Fatal accidents occur nearly every week. Are you really sure that this is where you want to go with your raft?"

"I'm not a kamikaze. But yes … that's what I want." I suppose there could have been more conviction in my voice. "I'm sure it'll be alright. If it's that bad, I simply won't go ashore. There is a solution for everything."

He just shook his head and I was silent.

Stranded in San Miguel: With an engine breakdown, the *Courage of Bridget* stood on the rudders at low tide.

CHAPTER TWELVE

"Sunshine alone never made rainbows."

⁓

Arriving back in San Miguel felt like coming home. The tide was at its lowest point so the ferry stopped far out and the passengers were transported on small fishing boats to the north end of the small island of San Miguel, where the taxi boys and a pack of overexcited dogs were eagerly awaiting us. Today there were many passengers and therefore there was enough work for all the boys.

As I wandered towards the village I made up stories in my mind to tell the guys about my trip with Adrienne. There was nothing between us of course, apart from that she was a really nice woman who had extended a hand of friendship to help me when I was in need. But the opportunity to tease the policemen with some nonsense was irresistible.

When I reached the middle of the sandbank, my good mood evaporated abruptly. The *Courage of Bridget* was lying flat on her belly on dry land. Both rudders and the keel had broken under her weight. When I came closer, I realised that things were even worse than I had first thought. The barrels – normally invisible below the waterline – were pretty badly knocked-about and their lower half was grown over with a thick layer of barnacles. The state of my raft was worrying. The coat of red paint now looked like the bark of a pine tree, cracked and peeling. Maybe the paint had looked like that even before I had left, but I just hadn't noticed it. It is amazing how you see things through new eyes after being away for a day or two. I sighed and went to the police station, hoping to be cheered up by my friends.

"¡Hola, amigos!" I stepped through the door and immediately

noticed that the atmosphere had changed. There were uniformed men inside that I had never seen before. I searched for familiar faces but found I was surrounded by only strangers. They in turn were just as surprised to see a civilian step into their station. And there were twice as many policemen as before. What was going on?

At the back I finally saw Irving, Javier, and Raúl's sergeant. They returned my greeting with a nod. Not a smile though I noticed.

"Where is Raúl?" I asked.

A tall and well-built man with hard facial features stepped before me.

"Raúl is gone. I am Commander Pedro Villarreal. I'm in charge here. You must be that crazy raft guy. Your passport, please!"

He was serious and I pulled my passport out of my shirt pocket. I did not like this at all. Why were Javier and Irving pretending that they did not know me? Why did they not tell the commander that I was their friend?

"What exactly are you doing here, Mr Dylan?"

The commander examined me, peering over the edge of the red cover of my passport.

"I'm on my way to Colombia, with that raft outside."

"No, you're not! That raft is illegal and you will kill yourself trying to get to Colombia on that thing. We cannot allow this."

I was speechless. I watched as he stepped behind the desk and copied the name and number from my passport onto a form.

My brain began working again. During my absence a staff change must have taken place, and because of the chaos surrounding my departure, Raúl had forgotten to tell me about it.

Commander Pedro Villarreal was not a laid-back Buddha like Raúl. He had a brisk walk, was muscular in stature and had a voice of authority. I could tell he enjoyed his position of power and wasn't shy to show it. I had no choice but to accept whatever he threw at me.

What I had always been most afraid of was now happening. Waves, currents, loneliness and unknown dangers, I had always been certain I could master all of these challenges, but the law and its guardians? They were the biggest challenge of them all. What should I do next? Should I repair Bruce on the sly and leave San Miguel in the dead of the night? No, repairing Bruce would take time. The sensor I would be able to replace in thirty minutes, but before I went anywhere I also had to fix the broken rudders and the keel. It would have been reckless to take the raft out in its current condition. A raft with a working motor but without rudders is useless. I just had to be diplomatic and choose my words carefully. If I riled the commander, I could kiss my adventure goodbye. Villarreal was only human after all. I had to find a way of getting him to understand my side –it was my only chance.

For now though I withdrew, and sat on the cement steps at the entrance of the police station outside. I watched the pelicans and seagulls hunting for fish in the shallow water. The birds circled over the dull greenish water like a black cloud. Frequently a few separated from the cloud and made a mad dash for the fish, pelting like hail against the water's surface. Children and dogs were playing on the beach; young men were still busy carrying off beer crates and other goods. They were all piled into the only car on the island. It was practically falling apart but it still drove up the little street past the police station and stopped at the restaurants, bars and shops along it to distribute the goods amongst them.

When Commander Villarreal stepped out for a cigarette break, I saw my chance. I went up to him and apologised.

"You are quite right, Commander Villarreal! What I was doing here on the ocean, is really dangerous. I have to apologise for causing you such inconvenience. I really am sorry. I don't want to cause you any problems."

He nodded and I saw that he relaxed a little.

"So what's your plan with that thing?" he asked, and before I had a chance to answer, he added, "And where are you headed exactly?"

I liked that he was asking questions. It showed that he was

interested and that made it possible for us to have a conversation between two human beings. A conversation between a police commander and the captain of an illegal raft would have been fruitless.

I found his questions easy to answer. I had had a lot of practise over the last three years explaining my adventure, hundreds of times, to children, teenagers, men and women old and young, from all social classes. Bruce and I were a symbol of freedom, adventure and wanderlust for people all over the world and I had begun to think that there is an adventurer, an explorer in all of us.

"Commander Villarreal, I am on a trip around the world. Just me and my motorcycle Bruce. We left Switzerland many months ago and have now ended up here …"

I told him the story, from the beginning to the end.

"… I gave up all I had to live my dream. What is the point of living 99 years but then regretting the things you didn't do on your deathbed?"

He looked at me for a few seconds, and then his eyes wandered towards the ocean.

"Commander Villarreal, I need your help! Do you think you could …?"

"Oiga, amigo, por favour déme su pasaporte," said someone behind me.

I turned around and there standing before me was an older gentleman with glasses and a blue uniform. He wanted my passport, translated Villarreal.

"Who is that?" I asked.

"That's an officer of the Panamanian Port authority. On the water he is in charge. He wants your passport."

I remembered a Sri Lankan saying: after falling from the tree, one gets rammed by a bull. I handed my passport over without a word and Villarreal began to speak with the officer, who eventually called his office in Panama City. While he spoke he leafed through my passport. Finally he hung up and returned the passport to me, together with some bad news.

"You have to go back to Panama City. We will tow your raft. You are strictly forbidden from travelling on that thing. Is that clear?" Villarreal translated. I bit my lip, nodded and stared towards the horizon. The sky was blue; the Sun shone on my face but a thick black cloud covered my heart. Was this the end of my adventure?

Soon the tide came in. Since Villarreal was busy and we could not continue our conversation I rowed out to the *Courage of Bridget* to fix the engine. It was, so to speak, occupational therapy. I was still not ready to give up. Once the engine was working again, I would be one step closer to continuing my trip. It just had to go on somehow!

When I reached for something behind Bruce's handlebar I remembered Wilson. That was where he had always sat. I had not seen him since my arrival in San Miguel. Had he gone ashore? Or perhaps I had inadvertently carried him into the police station in one of the boxes. I just hoped he had not fallen into the water. He was excellent at hiding but I figured that he was probably not that much of a swimmer; perhaps he was still on board and the warmth of the Sun would tempt him out of his hiding place. I worried about my little passenger. Wilson had alleviated the loneliness of my trip considerably, and made the hours go by a little faster. As I worked on the engine, my eyes scanned the deck and every nook and cranny for my little friend, but he remained invisible. I never saw him again.

Half an hour later I was able to start Bruce again. The sound of the running engine was music to my ears, but I didn't feel like celebrating. Somehow, I would still have to convince Villarreal and the man from the port authority to let me continue on my adventure. I distracted myself with work. I relieved the *Courage of Bridget* from her broken rudders and drove further out into the deeper water by steering her with the oars from my dinghy. What should I do? The thought of just taking off in the middle of the night crossed my mind again, but common sense prevailed.

With the condition my little raft was in, I would not get far. Besides, it would have been a careless act and probably a suicide mission.

Night came and I watched San Miguel from afar. As soon as it got dark the people of San Miguel began their nightly nocturnal competition; as there were no cars to show off with in San Miguel, people used their stereos instead. The loudspeakers were so large that I could not imagine how they could possibly fit inside the little houses. Everybody tried to play their music louder than their neighbours – the ensuing noise was deafening and filled the bay until long after midnight. Since each house listened to different music, all the songs mixed together to become a horrible indistinguishable mess. If the sound had had a colour, it would have been brownish grey. The only thing I could make out were the Spanish voices of the singers. They shouted out of the gigantic loudspeakers as if they were being held captive inside. How I envied the fish that had it nice and peaceful under the water.

I lay down in my hammock and returned to my problem. How could I go on? Would I even go on? A thousand questions swirled in my head whilst I stared up into the starry sky until my eyes fell shut. At some point I thought I could hear the voice of the little boy. "Everything will be okay," he said.

To distract me, he told me stories from Sri Lanka, stories that I had not heard for a long time, of kings and princes.

"Do you remember the story that our grandmother always told us?"

"The one about Prince Gemunu?"

"Yeees! That one!" said the boy and continued. "You have to have a strategy to win your war, just like Prince Gemunu."

"I already tried that. But please tell me that story."

"Once upon a time there was a prince called Gemunu. He wanted to defeat the invading king Elara and reunite Sri Lanka under one king. But his father, the ruling king did not approve the war.

So prince Gemunu called him a coward and as a consequence, he had to hide away from his father and build up his own army to fight Elara. But Gemunu was not very successful with his war strategies and lost many battles. One day, as he was retreating after a battle, he found himself detached from his army and was wandering through the country aimlessly. He was hungry and tired. Somewhere in a rural village he met an old woman who pitied the hungry looking young man and invited him to eat a bowl of rice not knowing that he was the prince. Gemunu was not used to eating steaming hot rice with his fingers and burnt them while trying to pick up big chunks out from the middle of the plate, then burnt his mouth too. The old woman watched the prince who was in pain, yet hungry, and said, 'You eat the rice as clumsily as that Prince Gemunu fights. You have to start on the side and eat in small morsels.' Gemunu realised that the woman had revealed to him a fighting strategy and returned to his army with his head held high, knowing the strategy with which to win the war ..."

Every morning at 7 a.m. a loud whistle sounded that stopped everything on the island in its tracks. It didn't matter if someone was carrying an engine on their shoulder and walking to their boat or going for a morning walk – they all stopped and stood still until the policemen, who had sounded the whistle, had hoisted up the national flag, saluted it and sounded the whistle once more. This happened twice a day. That morning it had awoken me from a deep slumber. I had slept surprisingly well and made my way to the police station with renewed energy. I went straight to Villarreal who greeted me with much more warmth than the day before.
"Good morning!"
"Good morning, Commander! How are things this morning? Any news?" I looked at him closely, full of hope. I thought I could detect a friendly glimmer in his eyes that had definitely not been

there the day before.

"Would you like some tea?" he asked.

"Yes, please," I said.

He sent one of the men for tea and said, with a deep sigh, "I've been thinking."

I waited eagerly for his next words.

"I will help you. You seem to know what you're doing. I don't mind if you continue your adventure."

At first, those words sounded unreal. But then I felt such joy and a relief as immense as the Pacific. Bruce and I will travel on!

"Thank you, Commander, thank you! You're the best!"

But suddenly the memory of that phone call with the harbour authority put a damper on my euphoria.

"Yesterday you said that the officer from the harbour authority was in charge. And he has informed his superiors about me, hasn't he?"

"Yes, he has. That's where the problem is. I spoke to him. He is not convinced."

"Can he arrest me if I leave just with your consent?"

"Yes, I suppose he could. On the other hand ..." Not a muscle on his face moved but his eyes were laughing. "I, the police commander, am responsible for your arrest. So he will need to order me to arrest you, you see?" He looked at me and raised an eyebrow. "And I guess, if that happens, your raft will be a bit faster than my boat. So don't worry about being arrested!"

I grinned and began to like Villarreal more and more.

"What can I say? You surprise me! I am very grateful for your support."

He went on, "My men are stationed up to twenty miles before the Colombian border. I will inform them about your plan. I'll write down the coordinates of these checkpoints for you. They will help you, if necessary. But please be aware: there are many dangerous places down there. The water down south is unpredictable. Take Jaqué, for instance. People die there all the time, just trying to get through the breakers. You have to avoid places like these, and be very, very careful. "

One of the men brought us tea. I took a sip and thought I'd never had a better cup of tea than this in my life. It tasted like champagne to me!

"I will be careful. I told you: I don't want to die!"

Villarreal took out a sheet of paper and jotted down a few long numbers. He seemed to remember them by heart.

"Here," he said and gave me the paper. "These are the coordinates of the police posts. And let me know once you've arrived safely. That's my number here."

My luck had returned.

The next thing I needed to do was repair the broken rudders so that the raft was ready for departure with the next tide. I left my cup of tea half-finished and got busy with the preparations straight away. I was dying to resume my trip – right this minute preferably! Still there was a sense of disbelief in my change of fortunes. Commander Villarreal was on my side and I didn't have to worry about being arrested and being transported back to Panama City anymore.

As I hurried back to the raft and returned with the broken rudders, I recalled my arrest in Djibouti two years previously.

I had been sitting in a café in Djibouti with Martin, a German biker who I had met a few weeks previously in Ethiopia. We had a similar route and had met by chance for the second time the day before. We were having breakfast and exchanging our travel experiences from the last few days. I wanted to show him a few pictures, so I got up, crossed the street and took the camera out of Bruce's tank bag. I had already begun searching for those photos on my way back to the table when I heard someone shouting behind me and felt a hand pulling on my shirt. When I turned around there stood a scraggy, unkempt man before me. His white shirt and trousers made for an odd contrast with his messy hair and yellow buck teeth. He was holding a tattered newspaper in one hand, whilst still grabbing at my shirt with the other. He shouted at me in French and I had no idea what he was saying. The only thing that I understood was the alcohol on his breath. I thought he was an alcoholic who was forcefully demanding money for his next bottle of booze. I shouted back at him, told him to take his hands off of me and to leave me alone. Then I twisted out of his grip and walked across the street to Martin. I had just stepped onto the pavement when the man grabbed me again, this time more forcefully. I turned and pushed him away. Drunk as he was, he lost his balance and fell into a puddle, the white linen of his clothing soaking up the brown water. People stopped and stared, pointed at me and started whispering to one other. The man cursed, got up and went after me again, but this time he was furious. After a short tussle, the café owner and a few others came out and sent the drunken man away.

I felt uncomfortable as people continued to stare at Martin and me as if we were insane. I did not understand what had happened, or what that guy had wanted from me and why everybody was staring at us so aghast. Ten minutes later things became even more disturbing.

"Holy shit! Dylan, this does not look good," whispered Martin and nodded towards the end of the street. When I turned around I was speechless. It did not look good at all.

The guy was back, but this time with reinforcements. He marched towards us with a troop of uniformed policemen. The closer they got, the redder Martin's face became. The little man pointed at us and shouted something and the police surrounded our table with grim faces. They seized us and dragged us to the nearest police station. Our bikes remained on the road, keys in the ignition, with our valuables still in the bags.

At the police station I was told to hand over my camera to the commissioner. He looked from me to the camera and then back again. "I have to check your photographs. It is forbidden to photograph security complexes. These photographs must be deleted."

I was eager to cooperate and told him that I had taken no pictures and that in any case Martin was innocent and that they should please let him go. The commissioner ignored me and continued to click through my photos, deliberately taking his time.

"There are no unauthorized photographs, but don't you know who that is?" he pointed at the drunken man.

I shook my head. "No, I don't. He was bothering me, grabbing my shirt."

"That is an agent of the secret police."

"He is what?" Martin and I stared at each other in disbelief, and then we looked back at the commissioner. Maybe we had misunderstood? The commissioner's English was not very good. Seeing our faces he repeated himself, "The gentleman that asked you not to take any photographs is a secret agent. You attacked him and will now have to answer for your behaviour to his superior, the head of the secret police of Djibouti. Your behaviour is unacceptable."

Martin's face was bright red and I could not blame him. One minute we had been having breakfast and the next we were having to explain ourselves to the secret police. The agent was having trouble standing straight, and when he heard that is boss would be getting involved, things changed very quickly. Just as quickly as we had gotten into this unpleasant situation, everything was swiftly resolved. The agent stepped forward and gave me his hand and said that everything seemed to be okay since we had not actually taken any pictures, and that we had better go. He didn't have to tell us twice!

We went back to the café. Our bikes were still there, untouched, as were our valuables. What a relief! We went inside to pay. The waiter added up the bill and then looked at me, shaking his head.

"Why on earth did you have to push the agent into a puddle, of all people? Nobody does something like that. Everybody knows who that is! You don't argue with the secret agent!"

There are definitely more discrete secret agents in the world than the one in Djibouti! I laughed as I remembered that story.

What luck that I had been able to convince Commander Villarreal!

On the beach I set up everything I needed to fix my broken rudders. Vito fetched a borrowed drill and the policemen helped me to find more material. After about an hour I was ready to get started. First, I had to saw along the break of the rudder to get a clean edge. Then I lay the two sawn edges flush so that they overlapped, and secured them with four bolts. Irving was a great help offering up his hands to aid me in getting the repairs done quickly. Ever since Villarreal had changed his tune, Vito, Irving and the sergeant had all gone back to treating me as a friend.

As I was working, I saw from the corner of my eye that the port authority officer was sitting by himself on the bench below the mango tree. He only spoke Spanish, but I wanted to get him onside where my adventure was, nonetheless. I scraped together all the words that I knew in Spanish and went to speak to him, hoping to get him to change his mind. He was friendly and made an effort to understand me. Then he told me to wait. He got out his mobile phone and made a call.

Finally he hung up and looked at me, *"Tienes permiso para partir."* You are allowed to leave.

Had he really just said that? I was not sure if I had understood him correctly.

"Voy con balsa? A Colombia?" I can leave on my raft? To Colombia?

"Sí, sí." Yes.

"Permiso para partir?" I'm allowed to leave?

"Sí, sí. No hay problema. Colombia permiso." Yes, yes. No problem. Colombia okay.

He adapted himself to my poor level of Spanish so that I could understand. I could have kissed that bald head of his, but then wisely I refrained. I would have loved to know what he had told his superiors: "If he wants to go ahead and kill himself, let him. That idiot! I can't wait to see him fail!"

Or maybe he had said, "He is crazy, but a good kind of crazy. He'll manage the ocean no problem – he has seen worse than that."

I would have preferred the second version, obviously, but maybe he had just said, "You didn't hold him up in Panama City so why should we? You had better do your work properly rather than telling me what to do. I'll let him go and that's that."

I could not read his expressionless face, but I hardly cared. I had some kind of official blessing to travel with my illegal raft! My dream would continue!

I danced back to Irving and the rudders. He understood straight away and held out his hand. We high-fived. Yeah!

Later I sent a text to Martina to tell her the good news. I could not wait to continue my journey and I had to spread the joy. She called me back.

"So you're travelling on?"

"Yes! Tonight!" My words meant to her that she would not hear from me again for days or weeks. She could only trust in what I repeatedly told her: everything would be alright! Her fear seemed far away and I was glad that she did not try to stop me. She made an effort to be happy for me – she did not quite manage but I appreciated the gesture.

We moved on to other topics.

"It's Easter this weekend. I'll visit my sister, and my nieces and nephews will hunt for Easter eggs."

"Easter?! Now I understand!"

On my journey I had lost track of the seasons, bank holidays, even the days of the week. It did not matter to me if it was Christmas, New Year's or my birthday, I greeted every day the same way, with gratitude. Now that I knew that it was Easter though, all the excitement on Isla del Rey made sense. Of course! Hence the many visitors, the beer crates and the increased police force. Before we hung up, Martina looked up the latest weather info for me. I scribbled it down and gave her the coordinates of my next destination. I expected to be there in a few days from now – but it might be longer than that, I told her.

"How much longer?"

"I'm not sure. But don't worry about me."

"Take care."

A small sigh, words of comfort and goodbyes, and then a crackle and silence. I was alone again.

The tides determined the time of my departure. I did not want to wait until the next day and so had decided to leave late at night instead. No more waiting! I was itching to get back out there! When I began to carry my luggage and canisters to the raft, the sergeant came and said that he had seen that I had US army emergency rations, could he perhaps have one or two of those? I did not quite believe my ears when I heard his request. I would be out on the ocean in a few hours on a flimsy little raft, not knowing what would befall me. And now this boy who would be having both his feet on dry ground for the rest of his life was asking me to give him some of my emergency provisions? But fine! If it made him happy – I would be okay anyway.

I filled my water and fuel canisters and then walked up the hill to the village to stock up on food as well. San Miguel showed itself in its Sunday best. Everywhere there were fairy lights, before each house stood a stall with food, and music was wafting through the alleys. Windows and doors were decorated with candles and images of Jesus and the Virgin Mary. People strolled along the alleyways that led up from the beach and the place was bustling. I had never seen so many people in San Miguel. Where did they all come from? An older woman stood behind one of the food stalls. When she saw that I was looking at what she had to offer, she asked me in English, "Are you the young man with the raft?"

"Yes, ma'am. That's me."

"Come in and have a seat." She took me inside her house. "I heard about you. I have a son about your age. May God protect you. You need some proper food before you leave."

She would not take no for an answer and soon I was sitting before a plate of chicken and rice. We spoke about the festival and my raft. Then she proudly spoke about her son who had a job on the mainland and did not visit often. When I took my leave, she held my hand.

"You will take good care of yourself, won't you?"

"Yes, certainly! I will."

I pressed her hand against mine, and felt the callouses from years of hard work. I felt as if I were saying goodbye to my own Mother. We both sighed and separated with a smile.

Outside, the Easter procession was in full swing.
Relics, Madonna figures and crosses were carried through the village on colourful beautifully decorated floats, which were fittingly illuminated with electric light bulbs. A band played melancholy music that dictated the rhythm of the men carrying the heavy floats on their shoulders. With swaying steps, the men moved forward together to the rhythm of the music. One step to the left, one to the right, tilting the float to one side and raising it, one step back and two forward. It looked as if the statues were carried by waves rather than men. It was beautiful, graceful and mystic. The air was filled with the smell of fried fish, grilled meat, incense and smoke. The scene before me was so vivid and colourful that it looked like a scene out of a movie. Wonderful moments of a surreal journey. The Catholic Church plays an important role in the everyday life of these people. Each church holiday is celebrated as passionately and intensely as they do everything else here in Latin America. Of course, people drank quite passionately too, keeping the policemen busy. I watched as they took one drunk after another who was riling up the community to the police station, and left them there for a few hours to sober up.

When I finally returned to the beach, I realised that I had spent too long watching the procession. The highest water level had already come and gone and the water was receding quite rapidly. The policemen and I took a few farewell pictures, I thanked them for their help and then said goodbye before rowing out to the raft as quickly as possible. There was no time to lose and I needed to get going while there was enough water in the bay. After spending a week in civilisation the loneliness on the raft, and especially the darkness, would take some getting used to. As soon as I had sailed around the island, a strong wind greeted me. The waves got larger, wilder and hit my raft from all sides. Just as I was leaving the bay into the deeper water, I felt how the raft was being lifted up high and then dropped down again, from a mountain-like wave into a deep valley. I felt panic. I listened to my instincts and moved the tiller frantically to port side until the lights of San Miguel became visible again. I accelerated as much as possible. I had underestimated the situation – it had been stupid trying to take off in the middle of the night when I couldn't asses the threat posed by the waves. I steered back into the sheltered bay where the cheerful lights and the music of the festival welcomed me back from far away.

By now the water level had sunk even further. I was figuring that I could just about manage to return the raft to where the water would be deepest in order to protect my rudders, when suddenly the raft felt as if it were being held back as if by invisible hands. I accelerated and tried to keep going, but to no avail. The *Courage of Bridget* would not move an inch and her rudders and the keel had bored into the mud. The biggest drawback of my raft was that I had no reverse gear. I would have no other choice but to wait for the next high tide. The water level kept sinking from minute to minute and the white sand bank was emerging, providing a stark contrast to the dark mudflat. Now at least I knew why I was stuck. San Miguel did not seem to want to let me go. I would have to marry Maria after all and stay here for the rest of my life. With my flashlight I checked underneath the raft, and indeed, the keel and the four flat steel bars that supported it were crooked again! Unbelievable! I had only just fixed this a few hours earlier and now I found myself in exactly the same situation all over again. There never seemed to be an end to my problems. It was midnight and I was too tired to do anything about it. I would have to wait for the water to come back in about five hours. By then the keel would be even more damaged by the weight of the raft, but there was nothing I could do about it. At least, I hoped, the rudders would survive the night.

I thought I could see Irving standing in the brightly lit doorway of the police station, and he seemed to be peering in my direction – he must have recognised the white sail in the dark. He went inside and came back with a large spotlight with which he signalled something. I took out my flashlight and signalled back. Unfortunately, I do not know the first thing about Morse code, so I did not know what Irving was trying to tell me or what I was telling him. I just hoped that it was nothing offensive.

The island of Galera: Though I would have liked to land on this beautiful island, the waves where against it.

CHAPTER THIRTEEN

"Speed never mattered much to me.
Until the day that I was overtaken by a jellyfish."

~

When dawn came the world was still grey and things only gradually began to come into focus. The gentle sloshing of the waves against the barrels had woken me. The rocking movement of the raft was an indication that we were waterborne. I sat up, and felt the wind blowing in my face. High tide was here and it was time to go. San Miguel would not hold on to me any longer. I got up and checked the rudders. To my relief, they had made it through the night relatively unharmed – it was just the keel that was damaged. I could fix it later, for now I would manage with a crooked keel. Bruce droned contently when I turned on the ignition and we made our way back out onto the open sea. There were no signs of the waves that had seemed to be such an insurmountable obstacle last night. I pulled the boom forward through the four legs of the masts, set sail and began my fourth attempt to reach Garachiné.

The Sun was bright red and it promised to be a beautiful day. The black dots in the sky turned into birds going about their business for the day. Just like me, the pelicans were travelling – only they were driven by hunger, not by a thirst for adventure.

Eventually I was out in the open sea again. The wind was blowing in the right direction, the water was calm and I made good progress. What a pleasure to be on the move again! A perfect day for sailing!

Later, when the wind let up I used the opportunity to fix the keel. I jumped into the water – tools tied to my underpants – and dived under the raft to loosen the rusty bolts. This time they came undone with much more ease, but the job was nonetheless a difficult one. I had to be careful not to let the nuts and bolts slip through my fingers because I had no spares with me. The only thing I could do was to pop them into my mouth, one after the other, to keep them safe. When they were undone, I climbed back onto the raft, pushed the heavy keel through the water towards the bow and tried to heave it on-board. The wood had soaked up seawater and had now become incredibly heavy. The flat steel bars did not make it any easier and it took a long time till I finally managed to heave the keel onto the deck. Had my mouth not been full of nuts and bolts, I would have been cursing like a sailor. Once the keel was safe, I spit out the valuables and found a place to store them. Then I began to hammer the bent steel straight. Things were not as bad as I had first thought, and it only took ten minutes until I threw the keel back into the water. I jumped in after it and then dived under the raft. Occasionally, a few fish would visit, give me a little nudge and disappear again. I ignored them – the job was tricky and it required my full attention. Mounting the keel was a lot more difficult than dismounting it. I had to fight the waves and hold the heavy keel in an upright position, aligning the holes and then pushing the bolts through them; all of this while diving under the raft and holding my breath. When I climbed back on board two hours later, the skin on my hands and feet was soft and wrinkled. I was starving and cold, but pleased with the success of my mission. With perfect timing the wind picked up and I set sail again. The afternoon Sun warmed my chilly bones while I made dinner: Spaghetti a la *Courage of Bridget* – cooked with seawater and seasoned with curry powder. With a full belly I enjoyed the rest of the day, watching Isla del Rey as it became smaller and smaller.

Do sunsets ever get boring? I have watched the Sun go down a thousand times, but each sunset has its own unique charm, each day that ends has its own memories. The orange and red stripes on the horizon were gently painted over by the dark blue of the night, until finally God emptied his ink pot over the picture, and it was dark.

As the stars rose I tried to figure out how to get some rest without having to hold the tiller constantly, I invented a system so that I would be able to control the raft from my hammock. I lay down and chose two prominent stars about 45 degrees over the horizon. From my point of view they were close to one of the masts and between the two masts I tied a piece of rope. Each time I opened my eyes, the two stars ought to be visible above the rope. When one of them or even both of them disappeared I would need to change my course until they reappeared within the markings. So that I would not have to get up to steer the raft, I tied a rope to the tiller and took the other end over to the hammock. That way, I would be able to steer the raft from my bed! The *Courage of Bridget* was now remote controlled.

The ocean was calm and the wind was constant, so I was able to try my system out straight away. Yes! It worked! I even got some sleep. After a few hours, at some point after midnight, my GPS sounded the alarm. I had moved too far off course. The wind had turned and pushed me southwest, rather than southeast. I started Bruce and fought against the wind for a while, until I realised that we were not moving at all. There was a strong current that was carrying the raft away from my desired course. Two hours later I had to admit defeat; there was no point in fighting the current. What options did I have? On my GPS map I noticed that if I gave in to the current I would reach the uninhabited island of Galera seven miles southwest from here. Well – on to Galera then! I turned the motor off and let the ocean carry me. The Spanish sailors had told me about the island, about its gorgeous white beaches, and the abundance of coconut palms and banana trees. There are worse destinations than this!

By the small hours of the night I was less than a mile from the island, and as usual I watched attentively for rocks that might collide with the raft, but the darkness made such a task impossible. Without an exact sea map and electronic depth gauges I had no clue as to what might lie beneath the surface of the water.

The possibility of being carried off by the current and pushed towards the coast was far too much excitement for my taste. Fear took hold of me while the wild waves and the currents played games with my raft. My fear began to overpower my confidence so much, that for the first time on this journey, I decided to wear my life vest.

Just before dawn the full moon appeared over the horizon. Its light reflected on the water and made my imagination run wild. To me, it looked like a path out of the danger zone. If only I could just climb out of the raft and follow that slivery path to safety!

Finally, Galera appeared, bathed in the gentle moonlight and towering like a fortress over the waves. The waves crashed against the steep cliffs. I circled around the island at a safe distance, hoping to find a place to drop anchor, perhaps even a bay. But wherever I went there were enormous roaring waves smashing into each other. On the south side, the waves were at their highest and it gave me a taste of what was in store for me further down south. Eventually, I had had enough. I could hardly keep my eyes open, so I decided to drop anchor about 300 feet southwest of the island. The waves were high here, but the water was deep enough that they did not break. Within a few seconds after dropping the anchor, the raft stood still in the strong current. I must have found a good spot since the rope went taut immediately. Maybe it had caught between two rocks? Or was this the place the Spaniards had told me about, where they had lost their anchor? Would I be able to pull it up again later? I did not have the energy to worry about it anymore – sleep overwhelmed me.

The island of Galera lies between the Gulf of Panama and the open sea. Up until then I had been travelling in relatively sheltered waters and therefore had not seen any big waves, but now things had changed. Even if the *Courage of Bridget* had proved herself to be robust and reliable, seeing the ten foot high swells now gave me goose bumps. Now that it was daylight and my perception was no longer hindered by my tiredness I properly grasped their true dimensions. Despite my apprehension, I could also appreciate the beauty of my surroundings. The waves rolled towards me and lifted the raft like gentle giants. I followed them with my eyes until they crashed against the cliffs of Galera. Such moments give one a taste of how small you are compared to the vastness of the universe. I felt tiny and weak in comparison to the powerful forces of nature.

"What is it that you're doing here?" I asked myself. "What were you thinking? Why on earth did you climb on a little raft to challenge your destiny? Who am I? What is life? God, are you there? And if so, what is it you do up there all day? How big is the universe?"

I was philosophising, but when a shark fin began to circle the raft. I froze. It was not just one, nor two or three, but ten, maybe twenty. Beneath the crystal clear water I could see a swarm of them. The distinctive shape of their heads told me that they were hammerhead sharks: their eyes were situated to the left and right of a flat head that is shaped just like a hammer. I was not particularly reassured by the fact that I had been told that hammerhead sharks were less aggressive than, say, tiger sharks or great whites. How much meaning does 'less aggressive' hold when you are all alone on a raft far away from civilization? Now that I had seen these sharks, even a tuna nibbling on my toe would frighten me to death. Just as in Canada and Alaska, where every rustle of the leaves would make you think of a bear, even though it would normally turn out to be nothing more dangerous than a ground squirrel. While I made myself a cup of tea for breakfast, I thought about Alaska and those bears.

Somewhere near the border between Canada and Alaska I met three Americans: Attila, Jeremy and Robert. They were old friends, travelling from California to Alaska. Their plan was to ride along the Dalton Highway, the northernmost highway in the world, which ends at Prudhoe Bay, at the Arctic Ocean. We liked each other immediately and so I decided to travel with them for a couple of days. On our first evening, I suggested that we partake in some wild camping. Wild camping? They had never heard of it. Initially concerned about bears, they soon agreed to the adventure and it opened up a new world to them. The next morning they were converted and agreed that sleeping somewhere in the wilderness and being surrounded by nature when you woke up was so much better than staring at the camper van on the plot next-door or the wall of a hotel room. There were no prohibition signs to limit your freedom and there is plenty of fresh air! After that first night, there were no more questions about how or where we would spend every night from then on.

It was our third evening – it was late, but still bright since the Sun did not set during those polar summer days. My three travel companions were so tired that they went to sleep as soon as the tents were pitched, but I was starving and decided to make some dinner. Since I was too tired to cook a proper meal, I decided to warm up a can of goulash on my gasoline stove. I did not even bother to open the can, I just held it over the blue flame. Before the can became too warm to touch, I turned off the cooker and pulled off the ring to open the can. There was a loud bang and a warm sticky pulp covered my face. There was goulash all over me. I wiped the mess off my face and before I opened the eyes my three friends had their heads stuck out of their tents.
"What the devil are you doing, Dylan?"
"Cooking!" I said, rather annoyed at the explosion. My dinner was over before it had even started. The can was empty, and therefore everything else was decorated in goulash, all four tents, everything! An open invitation to our wild neighbours – they say grizzly bears can smell one million times better than humans. Great! This time, I really had screwed up!
Attila clearly agreed.
"Not very professional," he said drily, surveying the mess before he went back into his tent. I cleaned everything up and buried the rest of the goulash far away from our camping spot.

Finally, I too went to sleep, albeit with a grumbling stomach.

The next morning the guys were already up when I awoke.
"Oh wow, what happened to all the goulash? A bear must have licked it off while we were sleeping." I said putting on a serious face.
"Didn't you clean it up yesterday?" asked Jeremy, dumbfounded.
"No, I didn't," I said, innocently, enjoying their reaction.
"Wait – there really was a bear here last night?! Wow! Jesus!" Attila was excited.
"A bear licked my tent clean while I was sleeping inside! What a story!" said Robert.
Jeremy just shook his head in disbelief, staring at his tent and mumbling, "Wow. Just … wow."
I couldn't keep a straight face any longer.
"Sorry, guys, but there was no bear. I cleaned it all up before I went to sleep. I didn't want you to turn into a goulash-seasoned dinner for Grizzlies!"
At that, the guys were disappointed. We laughed and goofed around for bit. But we took care to be extra loud to keep any grizzlies from joining us for breakfast. Standing face to face with a bear was not something any of us was particularly keen on after all.

About a week later I was travelling on my own again. I was getting ready to sleep, when I noticed a penetrating smell. I knew even before I could hear it, that there was a bear nearby: the pungent smell gave it away. I kept as still as possible, held my breath and hoped that I had left my toiletries outside the tent. Never have I felt as defenceless as in that moment. Nothing but a thin layer of fabric separated me from a large, stinking predator that was prowling around my tent. My heart was racing. I imagined some rather unpleasant scenes. How the bear would rip open the flimsy material and get me out of my tent and how I would not stand a chance. With one hand I reached for the bear spray that someone had given to me in Canada. It looks like a can of pepper spray but much larger and it is supposed to be far more powerful. Then I waited with bated breath and hoped that the bear could not smell my fear. After what felt like an eternity, the snooping bear moved further away, and then I could hear it scratching at my kitchen box, which was in reality the top box mounted on Bruce. There was a loud crash. Bruce had fallen over, and the scratching continued. Would the bear get angry if it wasn't able to open the box? Would it keep searching for food and then notice me after all? I felt incredibly vulnerable. In my mind, the bear had turned into a man-eater. What could I do? If it entered the tent I would not be able to use the spray, in a closed area, the strong vapour would knock me out much faster than it would the animal. With the bear's scratching and grunting my fear increased. I had to do something, but what? Thoughts were swirling in my head. I began to see that I would need to take advantage of the element of surprise and scare it away. As long as it was still trying to open the box, it was distracted. I knew where Bruce stood, and therefore where the bear was. I clutched the spray can tightly and released the safety lock. In my fear, the grunting and scratching and snooping seemed to have become much louder. With my hands shaking I reached for the tent zipper. I took a deep breath and then everything happened all at once. I jumped out of the tent, shouted, swung my arms, jumped up and down and shouted again as loudly as I have ever shouted before. The bear gave a start, looked at me for two seconds and then turned around and ran off. I shouted after it for quite a while so that it would not occur to the animal to return. I was euphoric but at the same time more anxious than ever before. I fluctuated between "I did it!" and "what if ..." Sleep was impossible; I was too excited, the adrenaline was still pumping. I packed my stuff as quickly as possible and rode off into the polar summer night.

A few days later I encountered the largest bear I had ever seen. I came around a curve and there it stood, unsettled by Bruce's noise. It was standing on its hind legs trying to see where the noise was coming from. It was enormous, about eight feet in height. Its head turned this way and that. When it saw me it dropped back onto all fours and ran down the slope, its hind legs almost faster than the rest of its massive body, then it crossed the river and disappeared amongst the trees. I was glad that it had run away. About a mile further onwards I came across two hikers. They were women, with backpacks, wearing outdoor clothing. I stopped beside them and was surprised by how young they were.

"Hi there! What are you doing out here?"

"We are on a trekking tour, for ten days. Tomorrow our team will come and pick us up."

"You two, all by yourselves?"

"Yes."

"Ten days, you say?"

"Yes, it's the ninth day today."

"And what about the bears? Aren't you afraid?"

"No. We haven't seen any bears yet."

"You haven't… really?"

We soon switched from English to German as their accent gave them away – they were Swiss. We talked for a bit longer and they had to reassure me many times that they were really okay on their own before I rode on. It seemed unbelievable that a trekking tour operator would leave two nineteen year olds by themselves in the wilderness of Alaska and I was surprised that they had never seen a bear during those nine days. There wasn't a single day I spent there without encountering one. I only hoped that the enormous bear I had seen earlier would not return to the road.

If you do not see your enemy you move in his territory quite unconcerned. As unconcerned as the two women travelled in the wilderness, as unconcerned I had been, when I spent two hours in the water fixing the keel of the raft.

Now I scanned the water's surface for sharks and thought about my anchor, which was still in the water. With a knot in my stomach I started the motor and propelled against the current to take the tension out of the rope. It slackened and I pulled five or six feet of it on deck. Then the rope went taut in my hands and my hunch was confirmed. The anchor did not budge, no matter how hard I pulled. It was stuck. I manoeuvred the raft into all possible positions, trying to find a direction where the anchor would come undone and I would be able to haul it up. I tried for twenty minutes. Nothing moved. I pulled and yanked on the rope – nothing. Half an hour later – I was tired and angry – I took the machete, thinking that I had no other choice but to cut the rope and leave the anchor behind. That way, I would get around having to dive into shark-infested waters to retrieve the anchor. But would I just face a bigger problem later on? I did not have a second anchor and would be unable to stop and rest anywhere hereafter. I took a deep breath and gave myself a pep talk.

"Come on, try once more. You can do it. A problem is no problem." My fighting spirit returned and I gave the anchor one more chance to come up. I lay the machete aside and began working on the rope once more.

"All will be well! Anchor, come up! I need you! Come on! I need you!"

This time, I did not give up and kept pulling and pulling, shouting loudly, just like I had shouted at the hungry bear in Alaska. It took another thirty minutes, but then something began to happen. My back and hands were in pain, but I was past the point of no return. I just kept on pulling and finally I felt a jerk and the anchor came free. I had won yet another battle! Once I examined the rope it was clear why it had become stuck. The rope had been caught between two rocks and once the protective mantle around the rope was broken, it had freed itself. What a relief! I shouted my joy at the top of my voice and it echoed out over the water, I jumped up and down and shook my fists. "I did it! Yeah!"

It is moments such as this one that make you strong. I felt like I had conquered the universe. I had vanquished rocks and stood up to the forces of the ocean! Happiness flowed through me, but soon my common sense returned; I had been in a very precarious situation, and I had been very lucky to get out of it.

I navigated around Galera. On the other side was situated the only beach on the island, the same famous beach that had been praised by the Spaniards. The water was crystal clear and not very deep. While I deliberated a massive shoal of big fish showed up from nowhere. They swam so close together that it looked as if a gigantic snake was meandering in the water below me. I had never seen so many fish all at once. I watched them in fascination, but then I realised: this was my chance! Quickly, I cast out my fishing line. As soon as the baited hook landed in the water, a few of them showed interest by swimming towards it, but then they stopped about three feet away from the bait, eyed it curiously and swam away again. This happened every time I cast out the hook. None of them wanted to bite. It took quite a while for the end of the shoal to glide past my raft and then the water was clear again. I figured that the multitude of fish here was the reason why there were so many sharks.

Since the waves that swept the beach looked enormous, I decided to leave the beach alone and started another attempt to reach Garachiné. That would be Attempt Number Five. There was not much wind that day, so I relied on Bruce's motor to carry me northeast over the waves. Soon, however, I noticed that we were not leaving Galera behind us at all. Quite the opposite: the island seemed to overtake us. I switched the motor off and observed on the GPS that the current continued to pull me southwest. I switched the motor back on and tried once more to move southeast, but to no avail. Instead of leaving Galera behind me, I was being dragged by the currents in the opposite direction. With each hour, I was pulled further and further out into the Pacific. At some point, Galera was no longer visible. I began to feel uncomfortable and began to comprehend that I had a little bit more than just a problem. I was surrounded by water, wherever I looked and

I had spent half the day trying to sail towards the mainland, but instead I had moved further and further away from it. As long as I had followed the ocean currents, and had achieved a minimum speed then the GPS should be able to determine my position and give me an accurate indication of my direction of travel.

However, when I headed for mainland Panama the currents were against me and they were fast. Later, as I attempted again to reach the coast of the mainland, I ended up receiving very contradictory readings from my GPS as to what my direction of travel should be. Sometimes, north was to my left, but as soon as I moved a little more to the left, north was suddenly to my right, then before me and then behind me. Rather than being of any help the stupid thing started driving me crazy! The Sun was too high to be of any help either. When I zoomed in closer on the map I realised that I was going in circles. I tried again, but the result was the same: I moved in circles. Without any reference points the ocean had become a maze without an exit; forget about the mainland, I had no idea where north was! Only when I let the raft be carried by the ocean currents was I given any accurate indications as to where everything was, but unfortunately the currents were taking me in the wrong direction – towards the Galapagos Islands.

The root cause of this problem was that the GPS had an accuracy of 30 or 60 feet and required a minimum speed in order to detect my exact location and receive accurate directions. But in the strong ocean currents the raft was too slow, and hence the device had gotten confused.

Hour after hour passed, and gallon after gallon of fuel was used up pointlessly. Finally I admitted defeat. I had a problem.

The day ended with a magnificent sunset, but on that evening I had no interest in any celestial spectacles. I was too worried. I must have been caught up in the current that Villarreal had warned me about, which headed straight towards the Galapagos Islands. He had told me that only a month earlier a fishing boat with five men had gone off course. Their engine had stopped working. They did not have a sufficient amount of food or water with them, and four of them died. The only survivor ended up close to the Galapagos and was rescued, weeks later. At least I still had enough provisions. But how long would it take to reach the Galapagos? The islands were a thousand miles away from here. My average speed of one or two miles per hour meant that it would be a very long journey. The Galapagos were certainly a place I wanted to visit, but this was not how I had imagined it. Damn! I did not want to go that far! I wanted to go to Colombia and not to the Galapagos. I also wanted to survive.

Would I ever be able to escape this treacherous current? My only hope was the south wind or the west wind. But I had learnt from my experiences over the past few weeks that I could hardly expect winds strong enough, that would blow long enough to carry me back to Panama. I was restless that night, but there was nothing I could do, so I decided to eat something and get some rest. I slept fitfully. Nightmares kept jolting me awake and brought me back to a reality that was a nightmare in itself. As soon as I awoke, I wanted to go back to sleep to escape my hopeless situation. As soon as I was asleep, the nightmares came back. Only when the Sun rose did I resign myself to my fate. I had asked for an adventure, and now all I could do was accept the situation and hope for something good to happen. Something would happen! I was certain.

Dum… dudum… dum… dudum….

Normally the constant knocking sound would have driven me crazy, but out here on the stillness of the ocean it had a strangely calming, meditative effect. The rudders moved with the gentle waves and knocked against the raft with a never-ending dull sound. Ever since I had begun this adventure that sound had been my companion, my conversation partner and my alarm. So far away from all civilisation, it distracted me from my problems and gave rhythm to my thoughts.

Dum… dudum… dum… dudum….

I tried to stay positive, and tried not to take my situation too seriously. For two days I had been drifting on this incessant expanse of water, powerless, and unable to steer the raft in the direction I needed to go.

I could not remember the last time I had seen a human face. It felt like a long time ago. The many sailing and fishing boats of Panama did not seem to travel across this part of the Pacific, and I saw no sign of the cargo ships that traversed the Panama Canal. According to my GPS coordinates, I was only 85 miles south of Panama City. Not that far, really, but only now did I begin to grasp the true dimensions of the ocean. Without points of reference, you lose your way out here faster than a blink of an eye. I am not a sailor and am no expert in navigating by the Sun, Moon or stars. My lack of navigation skills however, where not the reason behind my current predicament, that was because of the currents. Before I had launched the raft, I had been unaware of just how strong a current can be. In the ocean, currents pull you in any given direction just as strong as those in rivers on the mainland. I mean, I had known about their existence, of course, but only when they relentlessly pulled me in a direction that I did not want to go in did I truly comprehend their power. When I constructed my raft I had paid no attention to speed. Time was not important to me and a faster speed would have only meant increased fuel consumption. Therefore I had chosen a smaller propeller and a slower raft. But this decision now held me hostage to the ocean currents, and there was nothing I could do about it. I was forced to stick it out and hope for divine intervention, or at least for a fishing boat to rescue me.

I had no idea in which direction the mainland might be, and my compass was of no use whatsoever as it indicated north randomly, according to where I stood on the raft. The magnetic fields emitting from the motor and the metal in the raft had been interfering with the needle – or at least that's the only way I could explain the jumping needle. In Panama City, this compass had been the only one that I could afford. A Chinese man had sold it to me for seven dollars. And now I knew why it had been so cheap. I felt as if I were a contestant on the TV show 'Who wants to be a Millionaire?' and 'Where is the coastline of mainland Panama?' was my million dollar question, only I had no lifelines left and the prize wasn't a million dollars. It was my life.

It is amazing how narrow the horizon becomes when you are drifting out on the flat water. Standing on the raft, I was about seven feet from the water's surface and I could see for about three miles I figured. Anything that went past me outside of that radius was invisible. Even if I had been stood on the highest point of the biggest cargo ship, my horizon would still have been limited to ten miles. If you look at it like that, coming across another boat out there is about as likely as bumping into Nicole Kidman in the corner shop.

As soon as the sky swept away the dark curtains of the night, the Sun made its usual breath-taking entrance. The colours promised another day without wind. I yawned and looked at myself in Bruce's side mirror.

"Man, you look tired!" I said to the face staring back at me. Not particularly flattering, but at least honest words. There were bags under my eyes and the constant exposure to the Sun had made my skin look rather like old leather. My nose was sore when I touched it; the skin had begun to come off in a few places. It was the tiredness though that I suffered from the most. Ever since leaving San Miguel I had been unable to get enough sleep, hardly ever managing more than two hours in a row. I was wary of sleeping longer than that as I wanted to be in control of the raft. Even during those two hours of sleep I did not sleep deeply, instead staying just below the surface of consciousness, always ready to react if something happened. Whenever my hourly alarm sounded, I got up and checked my surroundings. Where there ships or freighters anywhere, or perhaps land or rocks? If it was dark I looked out for lights. But I was all alone and I never saw anything at all.

The morning went by slowly. The current continued to carry me away from the mainland. When the shadows became shorter I set sail, and sometimes it fluttered a little, but mostly it just hung there, like a corpse on the gallows. However even on windless days I was glad to have a sail because it at least gave me some shade to protect me from the scorching heat.

I sometimes jumped into the water to cool off, which was a real treat, but I did not go swimming very often: I kept seeing sharks, cutting the water's surface with their tell-tale fins. When I did feel safe, I swam around the raft and enjoyed the cool water. I also used that swim to inspect the raft. I dived below the raft and checked the underside for any damage. As soon as I ascertained that everything was in order I climbed back on board, to my safe haven, my little island.

I spend the day on the lookout for other boats. Again and again I scan the horizon in all directions...

Nothing!

Nothing but water... water and then sky, converging at the very edge of my vision. Shortly after noon I see dense, white clouds accumulating. My sail, which has been hanging listlessly for days begins to dance in the air, gently at first, then more energetically. The surface of the water begins to change as well. Only moments before it was a benign, mirror-like surface, but now friendly little waves begin to roll towards my raft.

Minute by minute I feel the breeze become a decent wind. Is this my chance?

I get busy setting the sail but at that very moment the fishing line jerks – was that just the waves?

Sceptically I reach for the line that is tied to the bamboo mast that replaced the fishing rod I lost a week earlier in the ocean.

I have never caught a fish before; maybe today is my lucky day? I check the thin line between two fingers and feel an unequivocal twitch. There definitely is a fish there! Carefully I draw in the line and haul in my catch. It is a big one! My first fish tries to free itself with wild jumps and I struggle to subdue it as the wind increases in strength. Typical! For the last 48 hours I have been drifting aimlessly with nothing to do and now everything is happening at once.

I work fast but it still takes a few minutes to free the thrashing fish from the hook and stun its head against the mast. It stops moving. Celebrations must wait – the wind forces me to act immediately.

I set sail and hope that the wind is blowing in the right direction, against the treacherous current and towards the mainland. I feel the motion straight away as the sail catches the wind. Onwards! Finally!

I am elated but apprehensive. I do not know where the wind is taking me. Further out into the ocean perhaps? I hope not and wait with bated breath, staring at the tiny display of my GPS. For a long time nothing happens, just slowly moving through a blue expanse, then finally I see the first dot … I bite my lip and wait for the second … There!

And another one, and another one until a line has formed: my route. I am headed for the mainland! What a relief! The wind is carrying me back towards civilisation.

I can feel the frustration of recent days fall off me, like shedding a rock from my shoulders.

"Yeah! Bruce, all will be well!

We're going back to Las Perlas!

All will be well! Yeehaw!"

The wind gets even stronger and blows into my sail. We are not going particularly fast though: only one mile per hour. I do not switch the motor on yet, hoping to take advantage of the wind to carry us within sight of the coast. All I want is to see a familiar sight, land and hopefully people. I catch myself thinking wistfully of life in Panama City, the harbour, the *Kiosko*. I think of giving up, playing it safe, going back to where I had started. A change of wind distracts me: it increases in strength and so does our speed. Soon we are going at two, even three miles per hour. The more the gusts of wind whip up the water, the higher the waves grow. When I take my eyes off the GPS, I see that something has changed, on the horizon a thick, pitch-black wall of cloud is building up.

My joy disappears and is replaced with fear.

It is not just the clouds that make my hair stand on end but also the lightning that illuminates the squall line. My eyes cannot even register all of it, so frequently does it strike.

The clouds slide over the sky in thick ribbons. The storm is only a few miles away from me. The waves swell and the water's surface becomes choppy. White crests flash up for a moment before the wind tears them apart. The waves by now are about ten feet high. My horizon has shrunk – now all I can see are walls of water.

I freeze with fear for a minute or two, but then spring back into action. I roll the sail away so that we will not capsize. The wind and waves make this task almost impossible as again and again I lose my hold on the canvas and the wind rips it from my hands and blows it into a frenzy of directions. The control line which is attached to a corner of the sail becomes a whip and I have to twist and turn like a boxer to avoid being hit, at the same time I try hard to catch it and bring the sail back under control. The raft is thrown every-which-way and I have to be careful not to lose my balance and get thrown overboard. So I brace against one of the bamboo masts, with my legs wide apart on the deck to gain stability.

Slowly, inch by inch I manage to turn the boom so the sail will wrap around it. It's an enormously difficult job. Everything I touch seems to slip away, as if my hands are smeared with grease. The constant exposure to salt water has made my skin soft and smooth and every grip requires three times as much energy as usual. But I am glad about one thing; that is to see that Bruce holds his position on the raft effortlessly. He stoically absorbs each jerk and jump of the raft without moving. As calm as you like, he defies the waves as if he were born for it. When I finally manage to wrap the sail around the boom I lay it down and tie it to the deck.

I think I can hear Jacques' voice, "Turn the bow against the waves, so you won't capsize."

For that I have to throw out my sea anchor. My version comprised of two old tyres, I had tied one end of a thick rope on to one tyre and the other end tied to the bow of the raft. A sea anchor creates a resistance underwater that acts as a brake. When wind pushes the raft in one direction it automatically turns the bow against both the waves and the wind, stabilizing the raft and keeping it from capsizing.

Slowly, I make my way to the bow of the raft and throw the tyre into the water. The tyre moves away from the raft. Then I see to my dismay that the rope comes undone and the tyre sinks and it slowly disappears into the deep blue water.

"Dylan, you are an idiot! You are such an idiot!"

At this moment I remember that I untied the rope the day before, to use it for something else. I never bothered to tie it properly afterwards but just coiled it around the tyre in a rather slapdash fashion.

"Argh! Idiot!"

There is no time to berate myself any further, the left side of the raft is exposed to the waves – the next big one might cause a calamity. Hurriedly, I tie the rope to the second tyre, and double checking it is properly attached I throw it out into the water.

I begin to breathe easier when the raft begins to turn slowly against the wind and the waves. Now the raft seems to be quite stable, however the worst is yet to come. The black clouds have caught up with us and the lightning strikes in ever shorter intervals. The chances of surviving a lightning strike out here are zero. In my mind's eye, I already see myself being hit by lightning and falling overboard, unconscious. The only comfort is that it would be a painless death.

There is a deafening sound. A lightning bolt strikes the foaming water only a few hundred yards away from the raft. If only I had a metal cabin in which I could hide.

Michael Faraday.

Michael Faraday! In the middle of the storm I remember the name of the scientist who showed that a closed metal cage will protect from lightning … but what is the point of this knowledge when I can't apply it?!

I have never felt so helpless in my life.

The waves are enormous. I try not to look, focussing instead on my hands and my feet and on what I can do to protect myself. I check once more if all my electrical appliances are switched off and secure everything that is loosely stored on the deck with ropes. Then I stretch a tarpaulin over Bruce, fix it tightly to the deck and creep underneath it.

The wind whips the tarp wildly and the sound mixes with the thunder. The noise is deafening. Even from under the tarpaulin and with closed eyes I can still see the bright flashes of lightning. Raindrops and splashing sea water mix with cold sweat. The raft lurches on the water like a roller-coaster. Left, right, up and down, all at breakneck speed. I hold on to Bruce with all my might, push my feet against the deck and hope to make it out alive. I just want it to be over, to go to sleep and wake up when the storm has gone. What the hell am I doing out here anyway? Why am I all alone on a small raft, lost in the Pacific?

My friends: A part of the Dolphin family that escorted me to safety.

CHAPTER FOURTEEN

"See the world through the eyes of a child.
You will be amazed by its wonders."

~

The waves had been playing ball with my raft for hours now, kicking it back and forth. I tried to force myself to imagine that I was in a theme park, on a roller coaster ride that would be over any minute now, but somehow I couldn't quite manage it.

"You just need to switch off your fear," says the little boy, as if we have swapped roles.

"But how?"

"Close your eyes. Think of something else. Think of … I know! Do you remember the day we went to the beach even though we weren't supposed to?"

I closed my eyes and concentrated. My brothers and I had been swimming and playing in the waves and now we were sitting together on the beach. I had an idea and went back into the sea; I dived underwater and swam in a wide circle back to the beach so that no one would see me. I tiptoed across the sand and hid behind a palm tree to see how my little brothers would react to my disappearance. A few minutes later they began to get afraid and started looking for me. They called out my name, but I did not budge. Eventually, the youngest one in the group panicked and ran home. Only then did I come out of my hiding place, calling after him.

"Jayantha! Jayantha! Wait! I'm here!" He didn't hear me and none of us managed to catch up with him in time. In his fear, he had managed to run the three miles home. By the time we made it back to the house my Mother was in a panic, which turned into a fury when she saw me. We all got a good walloping that day, since we were supposed to be in school and the beach was forbidden to us in any case.

That memory makes me laugh. I am grateful to the boy for distracting me for a while, but the wild bouncing of the raft makes it hard to focus on anything else but my fear of the storm. Even though my eyes are shut I can still see the glaring lights. Should I tie myself to the raft to keep myself from going overboard? No. I will just hold on really tight. But what if I am struck by lightning? Then I will fall into the water and drown after all. I end up grabbing a piece of rope and tie it about my waist and around the mast. I am hardly done when another thought occurs to me: if I was struck by lightning I would surely suffer terrible wounds and probably be incapable of sailing back to land. Maybe going overboard and dying straight away would be the better option. I untie the rope and try to concentrate on my conversation with the boy:

"Hey, are you enjoying the roller coaster ride?"

"Yes!" he says his eyes wide with excitement. They do not show a trace of fear.

"You know, the roller coasters in Disneyland are much better. We have to go there sometime."

"I've always wanted to go to Disneyland! I've seen pictures and films. They have so many crazy things there! America must be an amazing country. And England, and Switzerland, and Australia! I want to go to all of these places," says the boy excitedly.

"What do you know about these countries?" I ask him.

"I know that in Switzerland they have the best chocolate. In Australia, they have kangaroos. And in America, Disneyland!"

We keep on chatting until the roller coaster begins to slow down and the sea becomes calmer.

The next morning I awake because it is unusually silent. It is hot underneath the plastic sheet – the Sun must have risen. I crawl out from underneath my shelter and see the surface of the water is smooth and above me is a cloudless sky. The Pacific lies before me like a gigantic piece of silken fabric. The sunrays dance and glitter on the water. This is what paradise must be like, I think, so silvery and calm. I pinch myself to check that I am still alive. It hurts, ergo I am still alive! I have survived the storm. What a feeling!

It does not take long until I bake in the heat of the Sun. That is alright, though – after all, I need to dry my things. My sleeping bag is damp, my hammock is soaked through with water, all my clothes, even the ones stored away in the aluminium boxes, are wet. The water has gone everywhere. When I first set out on my journey two years ago those boxes were watertight, but numerous crashes with Bruce and dozens of treatments with a hammer have caused them to suffer with gaping holes. Now after the storm, everything is soaking wet. I press my tongue against my damp clothes and taste only rain water, thank God. But the hammock and the sleeping bag taste of salt, which will make the fabric hard and scratchy.

I stretch out a washing line and hang everything up. The *Courage of Bridget* now looks like a small laundry. Finally, I plug the GPS into the battery. I need to find out where the storm has taken me. Yesterday the wind had carried me a few miles northeast, towards the coast. It takes a few minutes, and then the device shows me where I am. I sigh and scratch my head. The storm has reclaimed all of yesterday's progress. I am further out than ever before, but luckily only two miles further south. As far as I can tell I am still caught in the current that is pulling me southwest. The raft is un-damaged and I am grateful for how well it stood up to the storm and the waves. Nothing is missing and all four bamboo poles of the mast are still securely fixed to the raft.

Only after there is nothing else left to do, I begin to feel the first pangs of exhaustion, and then a gripping hunger. I have not eaten since yesterday afternoon. The fish that I caught lies wedged between two bamboo poles on the deck. Everything happened so quickly yesterday that I did not have a chance to cook it. Now it has spoilt. With a sigh and an apology I throw it back into the ocean, and I am annoyed that the elements did not let me enjoy my very first catch. My provisions are damp too. I eat the last few pieces of bread that I bought in San Miguel, but they taste like wet cardboard. Then I open a can of fruit. The sweet juice raises my glucose levels and I feel better straight away. I have survived the storm! Now I just need to get my positive attitude back. Surely I did not get through that storm in order to just keep on drifting like this! That would be too ironic. Something will happen, I told myself. I can feel my optimism returning.

Even after the storm I do not manage to break free of the current. A breeze would have been handy – though preferably not as forceful as last night. I talk to Bruce but he has no advice for me. We spend the day drifting, and the calm ocean around me has an equally sedative and oppressive effect on my psyche. Restlessly I walk up and down the raft. I switch my mobile phone on and off, but I can't get a signal out here. I call for help over the radio set, but nothing comes back, just meaningless noise. A few hours later I check my position on my GPS, and by now I am fifty miles southwest of Galera. I wonder if I will end up in the Galapagos Islands after all. In the meantime I sleep, read, write and think of the people I care about; I tinker with the radio set and listen to the noise it emits. Then out of nowhere, seagulls; they come straight for my raft, take a quick rest and then stare at me with their heads cocked to one side. Then they fly on and I envy them their wings. There is no wind, but I decide to set sail nonetheless, mostly to keep myself occupied. You never know, and I want to be prepared if the wind rises up after all. I lie in my hammock, in the shade of the sail, and doze.

A snorting noise wakes me up. I look out over the water, eager for something – anything – to break up the monotony. I hear that noise again, and this time it is more pronounced. There must be whales or dolphins nearby, I think. And indeed, a few minutes later I see a pod of dolphins. The animals look at me and my raft curiously with their round black eyes, as if wanting to know what the hell I am doing here. They are pretty and playful, and their presence makes me happy. The pod swims around the raft, jumping into the air and dancing for me on their fins. There are about twenty animals, but it is hard to count their exact number. When I knock on the barrels the noise attracts them and they come so close to the raft that I can touch them. They whistle and click in their own language and I answer back, telling them all about myself and how happy I am to have them as my friends. How lovely it is to have a conversation partner and not be alone anymore.

At some point, the dolphins leave. I wave after them and call out: "Thank you for your visit! Please come back sometime! I'll look out for you!"

They say goodbye with a few more clicks and whistles and then their shiny bodies disappear. The loneliness returns at once. To distract myself, I speak to Bruce and tell him all about the dolphins. I tell him that whilst I enjoy the freedom and the stillness of the raft, I do find them hard to bear at times, but where else would I have been able to have such an experience? Under what other circumstances and where else in the world would I have ever had such an intense encounter with a pod of dolphins? The experience makes up for the storm and all my problems. I feel more cheerful now and my hopes are renewed.

"We just have to believe, Bruce. All will be well."

Night comes, and the stars twinkle as brightly as they do in the Australian outback. A few hours later I see pale green arrows shooting in my direction at such a speed that they look like mini torpedoes. The dolphins have returned. They jump out of the water, dive back in, slap their fins on the surface and swim this way and that through the darkness. They seem to be enjoying a game that they are playing with the plankton. They stay with me for several hours and entertain me with their activities and chatter. I am exhausted and I can hardly keep my eyes open, but I try to stay awake for as long as possible. I do not want to miss out on the dolphins visit. In the end though, my tiredness prevails, and I fall asleep.

A new day. The ocean is calm, the water smooth. My sleep was restful and I wake up hungry. Most of the coconuts fell overboard during the storm, but there are still a few left. I open one of them with my machete and enjoy the sweet water. Then I scrape at the soft meat with a spoon – delicious. I do not take more than a few bites though, as my Mother's voice comes back to me: too much coconut causes diarrhoea!

The dolphins have not returned. I look out for them across the water and instead see a shark coming straight towards me; it circles the raft once and then disappears again. I greet the shark, but I am not quite as happy to see it as I was the cheerful dolphins.

By now I am resigned to the fact that I am drifting towards the Galapagos Islands. I would be happy to see land again, and the unique flora and fauna of those islands would make a welcome change from the monotony of the ocean. I still have enough water and food; the fate of the fishermen that Villarreal told me about will not be my fate. I do worry about fuel though, and I think about the friends who are waiting to hear from me. I am also afraid of another storm, but I try to ignore that fear as best as I can. My daydreaming about the Galapagos is interrupted by snorting. First I hear just one noise, then another and another, and then one of the dolphins' jumps out of the water and somersaults.

"Good morning! How are you doing, guys?"

They are back! I can hardly believe that they would come a third time. I am certain that this is the same group as yesterday. They splutter and dive, showing me their grey bellies as they spin in the water. Before they jump out of the ocean they dart at full speed underneath the raft and then shoot up like arrows, dancing elegantly in the air. They put on an amazing show and I am their audience. I applaud, and it seems to me that they enjoy my applause as much as I enjoy their presence. I try to answer their clicking with whistling, but my lips are too dry from the salt and the Sun. There is no sound coming out but the sound of my breath.

Today I swim with them. They stay nearby but still keep some distance between us. Underwater I can see white spots on their dark grey skin. It's unbelievable to have them so close to me. However I can't shake the memory of the shark from earlier that morning and soon climb back onto the raft for safety.

The dolphins leave. Fifteen minutes later they are back; they swim around the raft for a bit and then leave again, going off in the same direction. They repeat this game several times over the next hour. The seventh time they leave, I take note. Why are they doing this? This is not how they behaved yesterday. Are they trying to tell me something? Do they want me to come with them? The next time they return, I decide to follow them. I start Bruce, but he only stutters, it sounds as if the battery is dead. The hair on the back of my neck stands on end and the fear nearly overwhelms me. I do not have a spare one. First the GPS and now Bruce!

"Bruce! You can't leave me in the lurch like that! Not now! Now that I finally have a plan!"

I am terrified. Without a motor my chances of ever reaching land decrease dramatically. I will not be able to manoeuvre the raft and will have to depend completely on the wind, and I've already learnt from past experiences that the wind is hardly reliable! Even if I make it as far as the Galapagos by drifting with the current, I could still miss the island by miles and be unable to do anything about it. I bury my head in my hands. What now?

With trembling hands I reach into my tool box, looking for my multimeter.

"Just don't let it be the battery."

I find the multimeter and connect it to the battery and then measure the voltage. The small display shows numbers. I am relieved. The battery seems to be fine; the problem must be somewhere else. I try to start Bruce once more and feel that the starter motor is giving off excessive heat. That must be the problem! I remove the starter motor and quickly realise that the metal retaining plate has loosened itself and caused a short circuit. That, at least, is something I can fix. Meanwhile, the dolphins have disappeared, but I hope that they will return.

I provisionally fix the problem. My hands are restless and my eyes keep looking out towards the water. Where are they? Due to my inattentiveness, a small plastic part, a so-called isolator, falls into the water and disappears. I end up having to work longer on the job as I have to find a way to replace the lost part, before assembling the starter motor again.

Finally, I hear the familiar snorting noise again. The dolphins are back! I call out to them and tell them to wait. With trembling fingers I push the starter button. This time Bruce reacts as he is supposed to. I am unbelievably relieved. I follow the dolphins without knowing where they are heading. They jump beside the raft, diving underneath it and surfing in the wake of the *Courage of Bridget*. Each glimpse of them is a pleasure and their joy is infectious. Even though I do not know where they are leading me, it feels good to be going somewhere and to have a plan, or at least the semblance of one.

An hour later I check my route. We are moving southeast – not exactly my first choice, but at least we are heading parallel to the mainland, and not the Galapagos. Buenaventura, my eventual destination, lies southeast, about 370 miles from here. I only have enough fuel for about 60 miles. I will not even be able to reach the nearest coastline with that, and land here in the Darién does not necessarily equal civilisation. In fact, the likelihood of encountering land with nothing but uninhabited wilderness is a thousand times higher than encountering people.

The jungle, when you are unfamiliar with it, is not a good place to be. The Darién National Park is particularly unwelcoming because, in addition to an abundance of natural predators, one risks crossing paths with FARC rebels and drug smugglers. I have also been warned frequently of the billowing surges along the coast. Trying to make it to the mainland might therefore turn out to be more dangerous than drifting on the ocean. But what options did I have?

I leave my fate to the dolphins. I have heard of people being rescued by these friendly and sociable creatures, and I am certain that they are very clever, much cleverer than me! If I knew what was good for me, I would never have ended up in this situation. Surely clever people do not find themselves drifting on makeshift rafts in the middle of the Pacific, do they?

The dolphins stay with me all day. Sometimes I feel that they are gently correcting my course. Often they all swim from the right across the front of the raft, and do not budge until I point my raft towards the left. Once the raft is going in the direction the dolphins are indicating, they return to swimming in front of the bow. Later on, they steer me from left to right. It does seem like they know exactly where they want to take me.

At dusk the dolphins are still with me. Around me I can hear them whistling and clicking and splashing. Having them with me gives me a feeling of security. I am no longer alone. I almost feel part of their family. When night falls I switch the motor off. I can no longer see them and it is impossible to follow them from their noises alone. There is no plankton here and the animals are not illuminated in the way they were yesterday. The GPS tells me that we have covered twenty miles today without going in circles. I can also see that the *Courage of Bridget* continues to move forward. The display shows my route with a line of dots. I assume that I am still drifting southwest, out into the open sea. I zoom in closer on the map and almost have a heart attack.

"Holy shit!"

I can barely believe it. I check the GPS several times to make sure that it still works properly.

"I … I am going northeast! Towards Garachiné! Bruce, we are going northeast!"

I howl and scream with happiness. The waves continue to roll against the raft, unimpressed. The dolphins have taken me to a current that pulls me in a different direction. Can this be true? Is this really happening?

"You are amazing!" I give them a drum solo on my barrels and hear them clicking and whistling in response.

"Thank you! Thank you so much! I love you guys!"

Tears of joy and of relief are running down my cheeks. Am I dreaming? I shake my head in disbelief. I would like to hug each and every one of them. I sing and dance, with my arms in the air. "I'm back in the game!"

The tension, which has been building up inside me over the last few days, just drops off of me. I feel safe and renewed with energy. Then, exhaustion creeps into my limbs. My arms and legs begin to feel so tired that it hurts to even move them. I put my navigation system in place and lie down for a couple of hours. Meanwhile, Bruce takes us north. This time, I leave the motor on. I want to reach land as quickly as possible.

The dolphins stay with me all night. I can hear them whenever I wake up to check my course and our surroundings. The next morning they play the same game as yesterday: they swim ahead and then come back to me. This time I follow them without hesitating. You never know when or if the current could change direction, so I need to keep going as quickly as possible. I feel a strong urge to see land again. Reach Garachiné. I set the sail and hope to gain additional speed by taking advantage of the gentle wind that is blowing.

The dolphins and I spend all day together. Suddenly, they flit through the water at breakneck speed, much faster than I would have ever thought possible. I watch them and see that the surface of the water is teeming with a wild mess of fins and long noses. A shoal of fish has awakened their hunting instinct. They swim after the fish, sometimes so fast that I lose sight of them, but they always come back to me. It is incredible. They hunt for food and once their hunger is sated they remember the guy on his little raft. This is one of the most beautiful days of my life! I am headed towards Garachiné with my dolphin family!

By noon it is so hot that the needle of Bruce's temperature display climbs into the red. When we are travelling on the road, the temperature is kept down by the airstream, but out here we are going at a speed of only four or five miles per hour. It is thirty degrees. I have no other choice but to fill two PET bottles with sea water and sprinkle water onto the motor, not knowing how much damage the salt will cause. The water hisses and steams. I fill the bottles over and over again until the needle drops back down to normal. A crystalline layer has formed, and I can only hope that it will not eat into the motor. I cannot wash it off; I only have 15 gallons of drinkable water left.

I have been out here for about ten days. If I stay on target I should be near Garachiné tomorrow. This is my sixth attempt, but this time my chances are better than ever. The Sun sets and makes room for the stars. I turn the motor off. Bruce needs to rest, just like me, and I rely on the current to carry us forward during the night.

The shrill alarm of my mobile phone wakes me from a deep sleep. I hear the familiar noises around me, sometimes close, sometimes further away. It is three a.m. To my left, I see a blinking light. That must be a lighthouse, but the GPS says there is no land nearby. Why is there a lighthouse in the middle of nowhere? My guess is that its purpose is to warn of rocks, and I decide to stay awake until I have gone past the invisible danger. It takes me two hours to get close to the lighthouse. I steer past it at a safe distance. I cannot see anything, no rocks, no surf. It takes another two hours for me to feel safe enough to go back to sleep.

I only get up when the Sun starts burning my skin and hunger pains rumble in my stomach. There is a thin strip of land on the horizon! How beautiful it is to see vegetation and a shoreline once again! But when I check the map I freeze. Garachiné is behind me. I have slept too long and missed it by about 10 miles. Disappointment and irritation build inside me. More than anything else, I need fuel! Now I will have to fight the current to reach Garachiné and use up the last bit of fuel in the tank, and then what if they do not have any? That would be another disaster!

I find the sailing guide and look up if there are any other settlements here besides Garachiné. Yes, there is a small village called Brujas, about forty miles north of Garachiné. According to the sailing guide, Brujas has a calm bay and there is fuel to be bought. It sounds good. Brujas it is!

The mainland disappears from view for a short while. I check and recheck the map, as once again I am surrounded by water. The *Courage of Bridget* plunges forward, propelled by motor, sail and current. We should be able to reach Brujas before dark. Since I woke up this morning the dolphins have departed. They must have left me to it when we got close to land. I miss them, but I feel incredibly grateful. The longer I grapple with this experience the more surreal it feels, especially now that they are gone. But the fact remains: the dolphins took me to a place where the ocean currents were in my favour. Whether it was intentional or by coincidence, I do not know. I believe they guided me on purpose. If anybody told me this story, I would have probably discarded it as utter rubbish, but this is yet more remarkable proof of why people believe in miracles. Without those dolphins, who can say what might have become of my life. They saved me and that experience is etched into my heart forever.

Along the rugged coast: Most of my days I saw no one but nature. Occasionally there were fishermen who found my raft fascinating.

CHAPTER FIFTEEN

"The loneliness is not strongest when you are all alone but
when you see people and you can't reach them."

～

Land.

A strip of land becomes visible, the outline of which slowly contrasts with the blue of the water and the sky. I am optimistic. When I come close enough to see the first houses of Brujas I am elated. The small village consists of a dozen simple wooden houses scattered along the beach. They are painted in all the colours of the rainbow and stand on stilts. The scene is idyllic and the water in the bay is calm. I head for the eastern end of the beach where I can see a few fishing boats lying at anchor and men working. I wave to them and make straight for the boats. I am laughing and I can already feel a torrent of words bubbling up inside of me, so strong is my need to communicate.

I am hardly within earshot when I call out to the fishermen, *"¡Hola!"*

I throw sentences at them; half English, half Spanish. The men are clearly surprised by my presence but try to understand me as best as they can. They answer my questions, nod and smile, and when I ask if the water is shallow enough to drop anchor, they answer in the affirmative.

The longer they look at my raft, the wider their grins become. The fishermen, in shorts and T-shirts, are clearly amused by the funny little raft and the chatterbox travelling on it. I join in with their laughter – I do not mind that they are entertained by me. My heart is beating rapidly.

259

"Brujas, you don't know how beautiful you are," I tell the village in my mind as I ask the men for fuel.

The fisherman on the boat next to the *Courage of Bridget* tells me where I can buy it here. He is intrigued by the raft and asks me many questions. His name is Orlando; and we shake hands over the water. He is in his forties, has a moustache and wears a faded violet T-shirt. I absorb every one of his words like a sponge. When I show him my empty canisters he tells me to hand them over. "Give them to me. I will fill them up for you."

I give him all the empty canisters and search for the money in the tank bag. I find two hundred dollars which I give to Orlando. When he leaves I keep on searching. In my wallet, I find the 120 dollars that *El Mecánico* returned to me, but where is the money that I withdrew in Panama City? I did not touch the 500 dollars during my stay in San Miguel and I have not had any opportunity to spend it since. How would I have spent it out on the raft? Perhaps on a round of drinks at the shark bar for my friends the dolphins? I am puzzled to say the least.

It is still a long way to Buenaventura. Bruce will certainly need more fuel than I can buy with that amount of money. Expecting to find an ATM in Brujas or anywhere else on the way down south is like looking for a haircut in a bakery.

While I waited for Orlando to return, I searched the raft and racked my brain for any sign of the missing money. It was nowhere to be found. The only sensible explanation I could come up with was that the ATM only gave me 200 dollars instead of 500. I had put the twenty dollar bills away in a rush, and I remembered that I did not count it then. I wipe the sweat off my face. Just another problem, but no matter: I had stopped being annoyed at some point, out on the ocean. The bigger the problems, the bigger the adventure!

I help Orlando push a wheelbarrow with the full canisters through the sand. Then we haul them into the dinghy. Orlando hands me my change. Now all I have left to reach Buenaventura – my final destination, which is still 600 miles away – is 165 dollars and

45 cents. I row back to the raft, heave the canisters into it and open one of them to check how clean the fuel is. The colour is too dark and it smells of oil. Of course! Here they use a mix of oil and gasoline for their boat engines. It is not what Bruce needs, but I take it as a compliment. The *Courage of Bridget* is indeed turning more and more into a proper boat, with her sail and barnacles clinging to the barrels. Poor Bruce, rusty and encrusted with salt, his days as a motorcycle are behind him it seems.

Orlando is waiting for me; he wants to show me the village. I ask if they have any normal untainted fuel, and he understands straight away that he has made a blunder. He is sorry but I just shrug it off.

"It doesn't matter, really. As long as they sell pure petrol here. I'll exchange it tomorrow; if you can you show me where the shop is?"

He nods and wades in front of me through the knee-deep water. I ask if it is safe to leave my raft here. His dark eyes take in the raft, me and the houses. He looks straight at me and says:

"Sí. It is safe here. Vamos?"

As soon as we set foot on the beach my world starts moving up, down and sideways all at once. I close my eyes and see the ocean swaying before me as if the sight has been burnt into my brain. When I open my eyes again, I see the trees, the houses, the beach, literally everything is moving around. I must be suffering from motion sickness and I feel dizzy. The swaying movement, which my vestibular system is simulating, does not agree with my empty stomach. I hope it will stop soon. Half joking I ask Orlando if there is a restaurant here. To my surprise he nods and points towards one of the houses.

"Won't you come and eat with me?" I ask spontaneously and he agrees.

Half an hour later two plates of beans, plantain and fish are put on the table before us. Brujas is still swaying and the dreary food is the same as everywhere else in Central America, but I enjoy the conversation and the company. After a while the swaying becomes less pronounced.

Brujas does not only boast a restaurant, but a telephone box as well! I throw in some coins and call Martina. When the money is used up she calls me back. Her voice betrays the relief she feels. She is happy to hear that I still exist, and am still in one piece, with my sense of humour intact. I give her a summary of the last few days but skip over the scary parts. Instead I tell her about the dolphins, the manta rays and their somersaults and how calm and peaceful the ocean can be. I tell her about my loneliness too, how I talk to Bruce and that I sometimes forget that he is just a heap of steel.

"You mustn't say that! Bruce is Bruce," she admonishes me. "He went through a lot with you."

"Yes, Bruce really is my best friend, my travel companion. We belong together" I admit, and then ask about her life in Switzerland. I prefer to keep the memories of the fear I have often felt to myself. Martina has more than enough to worry about as it is. But she comes back to the subject again and asks if the journey has been dangerous.

"Well, sometimes it was a little dangerous, but I always find my way back to the shore" I reassure her.

"I was so afraid when I didn't hear from you. You can't just disappear in the Pacific! I need you."

"I won't. I'll just swim to land if there is an emergency," I say, half joking.

"Do you ever wear your life vest?" she presses me.

"Well, sometimes. But you know I'm a good swimmer. And I really do my best to not just disappear. I promise. You will get me back in one piece."

I have to admit that I have missed talking to Martina. It feels good to know that somebody is waiting to hear from you. For the first time, I begin to feel something like anticipation at the thought of going home again. This is a new feeling.

I ask Martina to let a few friends know that I am alive and well. Once more she looks up the forecast for me. It looks like the weather will be stable for the next few days. I promise Martina that I will call her from Garachiné, and then we say our goodbyes. No matter how often we practise them, it never gets any easier.

I wake up at dawn. Brujas is still asleep. It is the same here as in San Miguel: At night the people bring their oversized stereos out of doors and fill the place with a deafening noise. Now finally even the ocean is soundless. Once in a while, I can hear the crowing of a cock and the dull thud of falling coconuts. I had noticed heaps of rotting coconuts on the beach yesterday. In Sri Lanka, each part of the tree is utilised, not to mention the culinary versatility of the nut itself, so it was incomprehensible to me that the people here would disregard this wonderful gift of nature. Their dull food would be much improved upon by adding fresh coconut milk. The thought alone makes my mouth water and I open another coconut from my stash.

When the little shop opens I exchange the oil petrol mix for pure petrol. Then I top up my water canisters, say goodbye to Orlando and Brujas and leave. My destination: Garachiné. My seventh attempt!

As soon as the *Courage of Bridget* leaves the sheltered bay I can feel the wind. It comes from the north, which is good. Maybe I will reach Garachiné after all!

The cliffs jut up into the sky like glass shards, as if they were about to rip it open. How long before the waves throw me against them? An hour, maybe two? About a mile lies between me and them. I have tried to drop anchor but without any success. Every day Bruce has a new problem. Today I was unable to start him, again. He is tired. I look at him, worried, and knock encouragingly against the tank. This time, it is the fuel filter. It is clogged and the fuel will not flow from the tank to the motor. Since buying Bruce ten years ago I have only had to change the filter once – in the US and not that long ago. The original filter before that lasted me 120,000 miles. Now, six months and 6,000 miles later, it is clogged already. It just goes to show the quality of the fuel that I had been using on this the last leg of my trip. There is no wind to help me out and it looks like I will have to hope and pray for a fishing boat from Garachiné to come my way. Another hunt for spare parts lies in store for me.

Garachiné had come into sight two days ago. The tide was low and the bay was half empty then, like a bathtub when you pull the plug out. The bay is framed by tall green mountains. Between the receding water and Garachiné there was a wide mudflat, it was too wide to wade through, so I travelled on without setting foot in the village. At that moment, after reaching Garachiné after so many attempts, I suddenly realised that I had no business there. I had topped up on fuel, water and food in Brujas. Besides, I had very little cash left. I spent a night at anchor, resting in the quiet bay that was about three miles northwest of Garachiné, and then I continued my journey southward.

Now, ten miles further on, I was stuck. Well actually, I wished that I were stuck: I had tried to drop anchor several times, but the water was too deep here. Now I was drifting dangerously towards the coast, and the coast consisted of nothing but rocks and cliffs. Realising the imminent danger, I tried to manoeuvre away from them, steering the raft with all the skill that I had learnt over the last few weeks, and using the oar of the dinghy to hold my ground by rowing.

For four hours I had been watching the cliffs coming closer and closer. Although I tried to use the time to figure out the cause of the engine problem, the waves and the current kept interrupting my work. Instead of repairs I used my limited time to keep a watchful eye on my surroundings, and to carry on rowing hard against the current.

Again and again, I looked to the horizon until finally I spied a little black dot. I was not sure if it was even a boat, but I grabbed my bright orange life vest nonetheless and began to wave. After a few minutes I climbed onto Bruce to be higher up and more easily visible. I waved until my arms nearly fell off; I waved and called for 20 minutes. The boat – and it was a boat! – came closer, I called louder. It took about another 30 minutes before the fishermen could see me and headed in my direction.

"You have a problem?" they called.

"I can't start the motor. Can you guys tow my raft?"

"Yeah, sure. But where is your companion?"

"I am alone."

"Alone?" They sound surprised.

"Yes, alone," I say.

"Where you headed?"

"To Colombia."

"To Colombia?" Did I hear surprise again, or was it dismay?

They told me that they were going to Garachiné. I nodded, that was good. I asked if I would be able to find spare parts there; a fuel filter, to be more specific. I held the filter up and they narrowed their eyes to see across the distance what I was showing them. They spoke briefly amongst themselves and then one of the five men aboard nodded.

"Yes, they have that in Garachiné."

I hoped that was true, but I remained sceptical. I was being towed for the second time on this trip, and unlike the last time these fishermen were asking for ten gallons of fuel in exchange. They had seen the canisters and were taking full advantage of my situation. I handed over two canisters without showing any hesitation, but this time I did not give them away as whole heartedly as I would usually have done. I was certainly glad that they were helping me but my money was dwindling considerably.

I shook off the thought and continued to work on Bruce as I was being towed to Garachiné. Let them have it, they were welcome to it! Somehow I would find enough fuel for the last leg of my journey.

We reached Garachiné within the hour. The water was calm and

I hoped that it would remain so until the next day, so that I could complete my repairs a little easier.

The next day began with a mission: I had to find a new filter and fill the empty canisters with fuel. Before me lay a desert of mud, and in order to make it easier for me to cross the mudflat all I took with me in the dinghy was some cash, the four empty canisters and the old filter. I rowed through the shallow water for half a mile until I got stuck, and then walked for another mile, dragging the dinghy behind me on a rope. I walked for ten minutes and seemed to make no progress whatsoever.

"Don't look at the village," I told myself. "It's all in your head. Just focus on what's right before your feet. Take your time."

Whenever I felt something sharp underneath my feet, I shifted my weight to keep my balance, and tried to avoid the razor-like shells and stones. The walk was tedious, but ever so slowly I began to make progress.

Soon, I began to look like one of those rice farmers in Asia. They stand in the water and the sludge all day, ploughing the fields with their buffaloes, sinking knee-deep into the mud where snakes and crabs hide, dipping their hands into the muddy water without knowing what awaits them there. Nobody would call them adventurers; after all, they are just doing their job. But to me, they are the true adventurers surely, struggling barefoot through the sludge, every day, to feed others. They are the true heroes in life! What I do here is an adventure, just for myself, and a pointless act for the rest of the world.

"Don't complain about this. You're here because you wanted to be," I tell myself off.

"But I was right not to stop here the first time," my inner voice talks back at me, stubbornly, as I step on another shell whose sharp edges slice through the sole of my foot.

Finally on firm ground, I tie the dingy to a tree and look for a shop to buy fuel in. I ask a few fishermen for directions but receive only vague answers. In the alleyways of the village only stray dogs keep me company. A gaggle of children, dressed only in their underpants, scurry past me. Their faces tell me that they are the descendants of a tribe of Native Americans. This is all I see of the 1,200 inhabitants of Garachiné.

A little further on, I finally found a shop that sells a few spare parts, tools, screws and fuel, all squished into about 20 square yards worth of space. While my canisters are being filled up, I scan the dusty shelves for something that looks like a fuel filter, but I find nothing. There are no other shops or workshops here. I will have to clean the clogged filter somehow in order to give it a new lease of life. I have no idea yet how I'm going to manage this. I pay for the fuel. How will I ever make it back to Buenaventura with just twenty dollars in cash and thirty gallons of fuel? It is almost impossible to estimate how much fuel I will need, given the unpredictable nature of the waves, wind and the currents, but I'm almost certain that the fuel I have will not be enough. I try to stay positive regardless, and hope for another miracle.

The shop owner lends me his wheelbarrow in order to transport three canisters, each holding five gallons of fuel, to the beach. I am glad he did, otherwise I would have had to carry the heavy load on my shoulders. Fortune and misfortune are bed fellows, without the one thing, the other cannot exist. I had no spare filter, but I did have fuel and had encountered a very helpful shop owner.

Cleaning the filter took a lot of effort and cautious planning; normally fuel filters are not reusable. In order to repair Bruce I headed back to the sheltered bay northwest of Garachiné. I settled on a place about a mile south off the lighthouse of Punta Garachiné, the point that marked the southern entrance to the bay of San Miguel. Here, I planned to spend a couple of days fixing everything that was broken and doing a thorough check-up. On the third day I would travel on, along the coastline and towards the Colombian border. 80 miles, that's what I hoped to manage within two or three, or maybe five or six days. It was hard to say what was awaiting me out there.

I managed to do a thorough check up and repaired everything in the first two days. On the day prior to my scheduled departure, I cooked some pasta and a fish that was a gift from some fishermen, and then enjoyed a quiet evening. I could feel my sense of adventure returning. I had caught up on sleep and had replenished my provisions. I was full of anticipation. On the other hand, I had still not tried to start Bruce after all the repairs. I was not sure what was holding me back – maybe I didn't want to spoil the evening and the gratifying feeling of having completed my work. I felt content. I loved travelling on the *Courage of Bridget* and having all these incredible experiences!

The waves were raging. The *Courage of Bridget* hit the water hard. I dreamt about the storm, and moved about restlessly.

Another blow, and flashing lights – or was it lightning? Slowly I emerged from a deep sleep. That bright light again. Is it the Sun? My hammock swings wildly. Am I dreaming about the storm still? Confused, I open my eyes and stare straight into the bright beam of light from the lighthouse. Hang on – the lighthouse? But … that cannot be right. Did I not drop anchor far away from the lighthouse? Finally the light illuminates my sleepy brain cells. "Shit! Shit! Shit!"

The anchor must have come undone! I jump up and see the rocks of Punta Garachiné looming dangerously close to the raft, and then the raft itself is thrown up and down by the wild waves before they crash against the cliffs. I pull the anchor up. When I haul it onto the deck I see that part of a fishing net is tangled in it. "Oh no! Oh, for God's sake …"

I pull part of the net out of the water, but I do not have the time to disentangle the anchor or pull the entire net on board. Shit! I leave it as it is and run over to Bruce. I wish I had tried to start him yesterday. I turn the ignition key and push the starter button. Bruce jumps into action straight away, which is an enormous relief! Thank god!

I engage a gear and try to steer us away from the rocks. Just when I think I have almost made it, the motor stops as if it has been jammed or blocked by something in that very instant. Immediately alarm bells start ringing in my head. Instinctively, I know that something has been caught in the propeller and this is choking the engine.

I lie on my belly and reach one hand down between the bamboo canes to the propeller. Yes, something is there. A thick rope has wrapped itself around the drive shaft of the propeller. Hastily, I strap my flashlight to my forehead, grab the machete and jump into the water without a second thought. The rope must belong to the fishing net. I need to get rid of it as quickly as possible. The waves are playing ping-pong with the raft. I hold on to the steel frame of the deck from underneath the raft with one hand, whilst trying to free the tangled driveshaft from the rope, and in the process I swallow plenty of sea water. I cough and spit it out before the next wave comes. I begin to yank on the rope so it will loosen enough for me to cut through it. Something is dragging it down. Why does this rope look so familiar? My anchor rope has the same thickness but I have only just hauled the anchor on deck, so it cannot be back in the water – but Oh God yes, it is my anchor rope! How is this possible?

Then it dawns on me: the net that I did not manage to drag out of the water completely must have pulled the anchor back into the water as I tried to steer the raft away from the cliffs! Thoughts are swirling in my head, but mostly it is just fear! More and more waves and each time they lift the raft and dump it down towards the rocks. I bang against the barrels with my arms and shoulders. I cannot tell how close we are to the hidden rocks that lie beneath the water's surface. I am afraid of being caught between the raft and the rocks. But there is no time to think; I can't cut the rope and lose the anchor, I have to free the rope right now! I throw the machete on deck and dive back into the water and pull on the rope. The next wave bangs my torso against the barrels, my shins against the keel. If I could open my mouth I would shout at the waves, tell them to let me work in peace, but I am forced to struggle on in silence. I only open my mouth to catch my breath. Go! Keep going!

The rope releases slowly. I unwind coil after coil, ignoring my tired legs, I just need to remain on the surface of the water and keep going. The rope holds on to the drive shaft like a Boa constrictor to its prey. I unwind the rope one last time and climb back on deck, the rope in one hand, as I pull up the anchor with the net. This time, I make sure to heave the entire net out of the water. Finally, it is done. As I step over the net, I get my feet stuck in one of its loops, but thankfully I somehow manage to make it to Bruce without falling overboard. I start the motor, run back to the rudders and adjust them so the raft is headed towards the open water. Then I run back to Bruce. I accelerate and try to return to the bay, but soon I notice that the raft isn't moving forward – the receding water of the tide is too fast for the raft. Once again, it is the current that ruins my plans. Finally I realise that it is absurd to try and fight the currents I decide to go with them instead, away from the coastline and away from the danger, and out into the deep water.

When everything is quietening down, I am feeling very cold. Only now can I begin to breathe properly, I cough and spit. I have to dry myself. I wipe the water off my arms and legs and find that it feels strangely viscous and sticky. I look down and see blood, blood everywhere. The sharp mussels that encrust the bottom of the barrels have ripped my skin open. I feel the burning pain only now that I can see the wounds. Exhausted, I sit down on a canister, dabbing at the blood with a towel. This could have ended very badly; I could have gotten seriously hurt. Just like the salt in my wounds begins to burn, so do the thoughts in my mind begin to plague me. What if the raft had been thrown against the rocks while I was still underneath it, its weight would have crushed me instantly. And the blood – has it already attracted the sharks?

Until sunrise I keep a safe distance from Punta Garachiné. As soon as there is enough light to see the water's surface clearly, I leave. Garachiné has not been good to me and I am glad to leave it behind!

I reach *Playa de Muerto*, the Beach of the Dead, it is one of the few coastal Embera villages that can be found here. I can see the traditional round palm houses from my raft; they look beautiful. I cannot wait to go ashore. Commander Villarreal advised me to enjoy the hospitality of the Embera tribe by spending a couple of days with the people here, to get a glimpse of their lives. And it will certainly do me good to recover from the exertions of last night.

I navigate the raft parallel to the white beach, up and down looking for a suitable landing place. But I am unable to get closer than half a mile from the shore. The further south I go, the higher the waves are. There is no bay here, which makes it impossible for me to drop anchor, and even if I could, I would not be able to make it through the breakers in my little dinghy. The beach is completely exposed to the furious waves sweeping the beach with their full power. Slowly I begin to see people coming out of their round houses one by one and they are looking at me. They must be intrigued by the odd looking little vessel going up and down searching for a possible landing place. They seem so close and yet I cannot reach them. I feel the need to tell someone about last night, a need for company and hospitality, but the waves are merciless. They roll underneath the raft and whisper, "There are things you better leave alone." So I listen to the little voice inside of me and decide to keep on pushing my raft further southwards. I am thoroughly disappointed and I feel lonely. The loneliness is not at its worst when you are all alone and cut off from civilisation, but when you can see people, but you cannot figure out how to reach them.

Along the coast, the wind is blowing in my favour and I make good progress. The untouched wilderness that drifts past me is stunning. From my raft I can see mountains, cliffs, dense jungle and even waterfalls. What a treat to see something other than just water. Once more I am reminded of how breath-taking this planet is. I feel grateful for having seen so much of it.

It gets even better later on: a pod of pilot whales shows up. They are black and look a little like dolphins, except that they are bigger and with round faces and no beaked nose. The animals move at a leisurely pace and seem to be less curious than the dolphins. I slow down the raft to watch them but they pay me no heed, they are too occupied with swimming just below the water's surface for a long time, then they hit the water with their tail fins and disappear into the depths of the ocean.

Since early afternoon I have been trailed by two little birds. I do not know what species they are. They are white all over, except for a black head and a red beak. The birds circle playfully around my raft, landing on the water about twenty or thirty yards in front of the raft, then flying up again once I overtake them. They follow me, playing this game for hours. At dusk, pelicans fly over my head towards the south in a V-formation. I greet them but their only response is the steady flapping of their wings, four or five times vigorously to gain height, and then they glide forward until gravity pulls them down, almost touching the water. Then they fly away. The flock moves in a collective wave and it looks as if they are riding an invisible roller coaster.

It is almost dark when a dishevelled brown bird lands on the bow. It looks exhausted with its feathers ruffed up. It is probably look-ing for a cosy place to spend the night. At first it struggles to keep its balance on the rocking raft, but it soon learns to stand com-fortably on one of the bamboo poles on the deck.

"Welcome on board!" I say. "I am Captain Dylan. If you have any wishes, please do not hesitate to speak to me. Enjoy your trip on the *Courage of Bridget.*"

It stares at me, possibly thinking that I seem crazy, but harmless.

It seems that the universe has become aware of my loneliness and sends me friends to keep me company. I am unbelievably grateful. I sing and dance and take the time to appreciate the small things, such as the fact that there are butterflies out here, miles and miles away from the mainland!

Or a swarm of bees that found refuge on the raft. It is just magnificent! I think about the last few days, feel life pulsing in my veins and feel that I am no longer alone, even in the impenetrable darkness surrounding me. If only everyone could experience this happiness! I think of all the people who live in fear, the people who are hungry and in pain and I wish I could share what I am experiencing with them.

I give a piece of my happiness to the little brown bird, the pelicans, the whales and the butterflies, and the dolphins. I hope they will carry it for me and distribute it amongst those who are sad, lonely, distressed and in pain. Then I move the tiller to the port side to spend the night out in deeper water. Good night, you glorious world! I am looking forward to seeing you again tomorrow. The little bird sits at the front and shows me the way.

Adventure at its best: Walking through the jungle and in knee deep mud. Who would think getting a visa stamp is this hard?

CHAPTER SIXTEEN

"The world is full of friends that you haven't yet met."

~

30 hours pass. Night falls again, and once more I am forced to move away from the coast to avoid its nocturnal dangers. The sail is set and I make good progress. I have barely slept since that night in Garachiné. Every slight breeze and each high wave makes me start nervously. I stay alert, like a watchdog.

Shortly after midnight, I see light reflecting in the clouds, but beneath them everything is pitch-black. When I consult the map I understand why: I am outside of the *Bahia Piña*, a deep bay that is concealed almost entirely by a long tongue of land. I decide to go there and get some rest. Once more I realise how slowly I am moving: it takes three hours for me to reach the bay. When I reach the far northern corner of the bay floodlights are glaring ahead of me and nearly blind me. This must be the fishing resort described in the sailing guide, the Tropic Star Lodge, where I might be able to drop anchor.

I navigate closer and see a dozen sport fishing boats. The brightly lit resort makes me feel sceptical. My rusty raft and I do not belong here. After all you don't take a donkey to Ascot. Their security would surely notice me soon, so I turn and head to the other side of the bay; which takes me more than an hour to reach. Here in the darkness I feel more comfortable. Then – finally! – I sleep for a few hours.

At dawn, the rain wakes me. I can make out the outlines of the few houses in Puerto Piñas. I stretch the plastic sheet over the hammock and go back to sleep. At 10 a.m., the rain has let up and my tiredness has dissipated. I make some tea and receive a visitor from the village, as a friendly looking man heads towards me in a dugout canoe. In the canoe, there is a bunch of bananas, a pineapple, and a papaya, which the man hopes to sell me for my breakfast. But none of the fruit is edible and it is far from being ripe. I have to disappoint him not only because the fruit is unready to taste, but also because my wallet is almost empty and I cannot afford fresh fruit.

We still have a nice, friendly chat. He speaks good English for someone who comes from a jungle village. There must be a lot of foreigners coming into the fishing resort, otherwise why would anyone learn English out here in the jungle. Once the villager takes his leave, I decide to head back to the fishing resort after all. Surely they must have internet there. I could look up the weather forecast and get in touch with Martina and my friends.

I navigate straight to the landing pier of the Tropic Star Lodge, but then a security guard comes towards me. He tells me I cannot moor there and that I should drop anchor further out and away from their last mooring.

"Do you have internet that I could use? I need weather info. I'm coming from Panama City, heading towards Colombia" I call back to him.

He lifts his eyebrows and says that he will have to check with his boss. A few minutes later he comes back with another gentleman, who gestures for me to come closer.

"Come, come, you can moor here. Not a problem."

I drive to the pier and the two men help me with the ropes. Then I jump onto the jetty and receive a warm welcome.

Paul is the manager of the resort and invites me to use the internet for as long as I need it. He takes me to a large single storey building where the office is located. Paul finds me a table on the veranda, and then gives me the password and some freshly pressed orange juice.

"Make yourself at home! I'll see you later, I need to go and look after the guests," says Paul, and then off he goes and I am left to myself. Everything here is clean and tidy – not at all what I've become used to since I've been on the road travelling.

Fabio shows up a little later, he is the technical manager of the complex. He informs me that the resort can accommodate 30 guests and has a staff of 150. Fabio and I hit it off right from the start, and time passes without us knowing. At lunchtime, Paul returns and I am invited to eat with the team. After a month of canned tuna, bread, rice, plantains, beans, fish and pasta, my eyes widen when I see the meal. Steaks! Salads and fresh vegetables; chocolate mousse and ice cream for dessert! It's a different world altogether, and proof of how quickly a survival adventure can change!

Fabio gives me a tour of the resort in the afternoon and shows me his own little kingdom – the workshop. My eyes widen for the second time that day. It is gigantic and very well equipped. Whatever needs to be repaired will be handled here, says Fabio, and then he adds, "If you have anything that needs repairing, you are welcome to do it here! You know what, stay at my place, you can stay as long as you want. Be our guest! You can repair your things tomorrow."

He doesn't have to ask me twice!

The next day I finally fix the starter properly, after having already patched it together several times along the way. When Fabio sees the thick crust of salt covering the motorcycle engine he helps me to clean it off with freshwater. We take a hose down to the raft and wash the salt off Bruce. I somehow get the feeling that Bruce is smiling.

Once Bruce is taken care of, Fabio and Al, the fishing master, invite me to go fishing with them. Finally, a chance to learn how to get those fish to bite! I haul in my first ever catch, and it's a whopping sailfish. Though fishing has never been my hobby, I get to learn a trick or two from these men. Though it may look easy, reeling in a fighting fish isn't for unfit people. It needs a lot of muscle power and good technique to haul them in without losing them. Once we were done with sport-fishing, we started fishing for food. There are many mouths to feed at the resort. When they are on duty the staff get their meals at the Tropic Star Lodge, but the workers live in a village close by which can only be reached by boat. It's unbelievable how many fish there are in the waters around Darién! When we cast the hooks it doesn't take more than ten seconds to hook a fish. There is a moment when Al has a fish on the hook, and an enormous Marlin jumps out of the water and takes Al's fish with it. The scene only lasted a couple of seconds, and before we had even had a chance to comprehend what was happening, the ten foot Marlin jumped up triumphantly in front of us with Al's catch in his mouth as if he wanted to show off the plunder that had been ours a few moments ago.

The next day, Al invited me to go fishing again, this time for Red Snappers. They are the tastiest of them all, he said enthusiastically. We spent several uneventful hours on the boat and waited for Red Snappers that resolutely refused to show up. I confess that I began to get bored. The only thing more boring than fishing is watching somebody else fish. I stretched my arms and yawned, and in that moment my eyes caught sight of a shoal of red fish swimming just under the water's surface a little further out. Al continued to fish on the other side of the boat and had not seen them.

I called out, "Al! There are lots of them!"

He looked over briefly, mumbled something under his breath and then went back to focusing on his fishing rod. I meanwhile was fascinated by the spectacle of the jumping and splashing fish and watched them with greedy intent. But I couldn't help but wonder why Al was paying them no attention whatsoever. If he, a seasoned fisherman, was not interested in these beautiful fish, then those Red Snappers must be out of this world, I thought.

However, I couldn't just sit here and ignore this spectacular event and I found myself commenting on the scene before me:

"Wow!"

"Oh, they are jumping! Looks like a fight or something."

Al kept staring straight ahead and held his fishing rod out into the water.

"Oh, Al, look at this! These must be quite big fish, maybe two feet at least. It's all red."

Al remains cool and disinterested.

"I won't be told by someone who does not know how to fish where the fish are."

He doesn't say this out loud but he is probably thinking it to himself and continues to ignore me for another 15 minutes.

I stand up to get a better glimpse. There must be thousands of them – the shoal must be at least 60 feet in diameter and it resembles a red carpet floating on the water. I feel like a child that wants the attention of his preoccupied father. "Daddy! Daddy, look!"

"Al! Al! Look! There are thousands of red fish! Are you sure that these are not Red Snappers?"

Finally my voice penetrates his thoughts and he looks more closely. As soon has he sees the fish, his jaw drops and he yells in excitement,

"Oh my god! Look! Red Snappers! Thousands of them!"

He reels in the line in a hurry, runs across the boat like a headless chicken, stumbling over fishing rods and almost going overboard. Quickly he turns on the engine and heads straight for the fish. There are thousands of them, right on the surface, jumping about, swarming with each other, splashing water as if they were out on dry land. Al casts out the fishing lines but none of them bites. As we stand there watching the teeming mess, I ask him why they are all so close to the surface, but he does not know.

"In all these years I have never seen the like," he declares excitedly. Today you wouldn't have seen it either, I think to myself and grin – if I hadn't told you.

The next morning, Paul holds a newspaper under my nose.

"You are a star!" he says.

The paper shows a picture of me and the *Courage of Bridget*. Only when I read the name of the article's author do I remember.

"Ha! I had forgotten about this! I spoke to her in Contadora. She is Swiss, working in Panama City as a journalist. I asked her not to publish the article until I was gone. I'm travelling illegally and didn't want anyone to know about me."

"What do you mean, you're travelling illegally?" Paul asks immediately.

"I don't have an exit stamp in my passport," I say, and then explain to him that my raft and I are travelling without papers. Now of course I remember the impending crossing of the border, till that moment I had forgotten all about it. Ever since I'd left Panama City so many things had happened and bureaucracy was the last thing on my mind.

As if Paul is reading my thoughts, he says, "You could run into trouble if you show up at the Colombian border without a stamp. You do know this?"

"Yes. But what other option did I have? I was sure that there would be a solution to this."

"Well," he says, and grins at me. "There is. In Jaqué, the neighbouring village, they'll give you an exit stamp. I'm sure that nobody will ask for papers there, either."

I look at him, astounded.

"Really?"

"Yes! Normally, only people from Puerto Piñas and Jaqué have their passports stamped there. Foreigners who want to travel on to Colombia never come here. It's definitely worth a try. I'll send someone to go with you. You have to go there by foot though. It's not easy to get to but you should manage it in half a day."

A few hours later, Brian, the security guard, has taken me under his wing. We go with a third man, who hails from Jaqué.

Before we leave, Paul says, "We have completely stopped taking boats to Jaqué. It's too dangerous. The breakers are so high and wild; it's a threat to the people who live there. To make it through the waves and reach the sandbank behind the estuary is almost impossible though people try it all the time and get injured and even killed on a weekly basis. That's why it is best for you to cross the bay by boat and then continue on foot."

280

The path that we take is too arduous for the inhabitants. They prefer to try their luck with the breakers. Their fate is closely linked to the waves, the ocean here is deep and the waves crash against the coast with full force. For many villages along the coast, the ocean is their only connection to the outside world and it is also their livelihood. Behind the villages there are mountains that are covered with the impenetrable Darién jungle. So the fishermen in their little boats have no other option but to risk their lives daily by fighting against the waves.

We take one of the boats belonging to the resort to the other end of the bay where there is a sentry post for the Panamanian police. When we get there, a modern speed boat lies at anchor. I can see straight away that the policemen here are far better equipped than the ones in San Miguel. Their guns show not a trace of rust, and I do not feel particularly reassured by this. The officers already know about me; I am not sure whether that is because of the inhabitants of the village, or Commander Villarreal …or maybe it was Paul who informed them about my coming.

They greet us warmly; write down our names and my passport number. A man wearing a bulletproof vest writes down in scrawly, awkward letters what kind of clothes we are wearing. He speaks into his walkie-talkie and then waits for an answer that I do not understand. Brian helpfully explains that the officer has just described to the guards and the snipers stationed along the jungle path what we look like. Presumably so that they will not accidentally shoot us.

We are then asked to walk forwards under the watchful eyes of a policeman. He holds his machine gun with both hands, with his finger on the trigger, ready for action. He stands in the middle of the path in a wide stance and watches us until we disappear around the first curve.

Soon, we start walking uphill, and since the ground is muddy and slippery it becomes a very slow process. By the time we reach the next sentry post it has started to rain, and we are forced to seek shelter below the canopy of a small hut. We are greeted by about a dozen policemen and four or five skinny dogs. They ask us to wait, and as we are waiting I see that there are several huts hidden in the jungle around us. There are about a dozen chickens running around the camp, and a large fire with a pot of soup bubbling above it. The sentry post feels like a cosy little village, and it gives me the impression that the soldiers here have to farm for their own food. As cosy as it seems however, the stark reality is that these security personnel are stationed here to protect the two nearby settlements from being attacked by FARC rebels.

Only when the snipers have been warned about us, are we allowed to move on. The overgrown path continues uphill until we reach the highest point. Then we descend on the other side, following the many loops and curves of the path towards the bank of the river Jaqué. Occasionally the path becomes almost unrecognisable as any kind of path at all, and disappears until it is nothing more than a swamp. We sink knee-deep into the mud, making slow and arduous progress, as the sounds of the jungle accompanying our journey. Our walk ends in a maze of mangroves. We have arrived at the low tide and there is no sign of the river Jaqué other than the narrow trenches that disappear through the mangroves. Brian washes his feet and his legs before putting on his white socks and trainers again. He does not enjoy the dirt and has washed his feet about fifteen times already, only to dirty them again a few steps on.

Promptly a dugout canoe appears navigating its way through the narrow trenches. We get in it and the man in the canoe manoeuvres us carefully through the tangle of the mangrove roots. We cross the river and finally reach our destination, Jaqué! I am taken straight to the police station which seems to be reinforced like a small fortress. For a small settlement such as this the number of police personnel seems to be rather extreme. The commander reaches for the phone and calls the immigration officer, who arrives a little later with a stamp that he carries in a scuffed up briefcase. The stamp is the only official thing about him. He wears a T-shirt, shorts and flip-flops, and gives me the impression that being an immigration officer is only his side-line job. He could just as well be one of the fishermen out here.

Brian gives him a quick summary of my situation. The man nods, looks at me, compares the picture in my passport with my face and then slams an exit stamp down onto the passport.

Officially, I have just left Panama.

The ink on the stamp is still wet but Brian is keen to take off quickly as he wants to be back home before dusk. Going back is exactly the same process, but this time in reverse and again we stand in front of the policemen as they note down what we are wearing so that the snipers will not shoot us on the way back.

When the jungle finally clears and the southern end of *Piña Bay* lies before us, we encounter four policemen in very high spirits. Our arrangement was to radio the resort once we were ready to be picked up, but the policemen have decided to take us across the bay in their speed boat which has 750 horse power. We have barely taken our seats when one officer starts all four engines and opens up the throttle. The boat accelerates faster than a Formula One racing car and we hold on to the railing for dear life, with our bodies wobbling in the wind like flags in a storm. The police-men seem to be enjoying the joyride though, and I have to confess that I do too. But I can tell from Brian's pale face that this will be the last time he accompanies anyone for an exit stamp.

And then it is over. It feels like we have made the three mile cross-ing in about twenty seconds flat. The officer behind the steering wheel can barely contain his glee as he moors the boat to the landing pier.

At the Tropic Star Lodge, a few guests have by now heard about me and of my adventure. Paul asks if I would be happy to show some pictures of my travels that evening and I gladly consent. Later, some of the guests want to go for a little spin on the raft, to get a feel for what it is like out on those ten barrels. Most of them are Americans, and with their characteristic enthusiasm they throw superlatives at me. "Man you are a badass genius!," "you must be the bravest person on this planet."

Then they open their wallets and press dollar bills into my hand; this is for the rest of my journey, they say: a hundred, two hundred, and four hundred. I stand on my raft and feel like a clown at a fair. Paul and Fabio give me something as well; and in the end I have seven hundred US dollars in my pocket. They help me to fill all my empty fuel canisters and tell me to take as much food as I need. I am speechless and accept all of their gifts gratefully. I need them now more than ever before.

On the fifth day it is time to go. During my stay in Bahia Piña it has begun to rain every single day. It is a clear sign that the rainy season has begun. The showers are gentle for now, but will soon become stronger. It has been more than five weeks since I left Panama City – I never thought that this journey would take me quite this long. The raft is in a bad shape, and the saltwater has aged the barrels quicker than I would have liked. In many places the paint is peeling away to reveal large rust stains.

Fabio pulls me into a hug and wipes a tear from the corner of his eye. "Goodbye! Take care of yourself!"

We are standing on the jetty, surrounded by other employees. Al gives me a handful of bait for my fishing rod. Then I untie the rope and steer the raft slowly out into the bay. After a while when I turn back I see that a motorboat is heading towards me. When it comes closer I recognise Fabio, and I see that he is trailing a second boat behind his. I hit my forehead with my hand when I see that it is my dinghy – I have actually managed to leave behind my life boat, my dinghy, without which I cannot actually land anywhere!

Fabio shakes his head, amused at my forgetfulness. He hands me the rope of the dinghy.

"Make sure you don't leave your head behind anywhere!" he laughs and then hands me a small canister of motor oil. "You never know. Best to take this with you, you'd never get your hands on motor oil in the Darién!"

Two days later, the weather changed. The sky above became grey and reminded me of a winter's day in Switzerland. It had been a long time since I had experienced one. Despite the overcast sky it was still quite warm. There was no wind and I had to use the motor. Since the changing of the seasons had already begun, I would have no hope now of catching the north wind. I rolled up the sail and took off the keel, after all a motorboat does not need a keel and it would only cause more drag in the water.

The world that drifts past us is impressive. The branches and leaves of the trees along the coast almost touch the water's surface. Often, there is only a narrow strip of white sand between the jungle and the ocean, sometimes there are a few rocks protruding over the water. I push forward through the night without stopping and reach *Punta Guayabo Grande* on my second evening – a bay where robberies of sailboats are frequent, according to the sailing manual. But it is also one of the only places around here where I can drop anchor. In the sailing guide book, there is no mention of any place from here onwards. It is already dark and I hope that nobody has seen me entering the bay. I am not overly concerned though, as nobody could possibly – not even in the dimmest light – confuse my raft with a sailing yacht. I soon fall asleep with the thought of reaching Colombia the next day playing on my mind.

Visiting the Mursi tribe in Ethiopia: You'd think such weapons as spears, bows and arrows would suit their traditional attire. But machine guns are a common sight in the jungle.

CHAPTER SEVENTEEN

"When I had nothing else, I filled my pockets with hope."

~

The GPS shows me that I have crossed the Colombian border.
I have made it! I am in Colombia!
I celebrate my success, but I am still aware that I have a long and arduous journey ahead of me. The next settlement with any kind of recognisable infrastructure is still seventy miles away.
I pass ten, maybe fifteen fishermen on their long, narrow wooden boats, which are locally referred to as 'pangas'. They greet me, are friendly and curious. Most simply carry on with their fishing and study my raft as I pass them by, however two men in a small motor boat pack up their fishing gear and head towards me. The men seem to be intrigued by the sight of me and they ask me many questions. Without slowing down the raft I answer them and exchange a few words as best I can in Spanish. Then they invite me to visit their village and their house. I have never yet rejected an invitation on this journey – but this time my gut instinct tells me that these two men are up to something no good. I cannot put my finger on it but I do not like their behaviour.
I offer my apologies and refuse, indicating that I have no time. The men slow down their boat but keep on following me. They do not speak to me again but trail the *Courage of Bridget* from a distance of about 20 yards.
What do they want? Are they waiting until the other fishermen are out of sight? Will they try to rob me? Abduct me? I try to look confident – but confidence alone will not ward off an attack. I have nothing to hand that I could use to defend myself. Not even a bear spray! Frantically, I think about what I could do before the

situation gets out of control. Finally I have an idea! I reach for my walkie-talkie, making sure that the men can see it, and then I speak into it.

"Hey, Bruce, have you seen those two funny-looking guys? Do you think we can chase them away? Over."

The noise of Bruce's motor, and that of their own boat makes it impossible for them to hear what I am saying, or if I get an answer. I hold the walkie-talkie to my ear and pretend that I am listening intently. Again I talk some kind of nonsense into the walkie-talkie, angling my head towards the two fishermen and trying to make eye contact.

The second time when I pretend to listen to the non-existent answer, the boat following me stops, and the distance between us increases. Finally, they turn around and leave me to it. I knock on Bruce's tank with relief. "We got them!"

This experience shows me that I need to be more careful. It seems to me to be prudent to leave the coast behind and stick to the deep waters. On the one hand this is a shame because of the gorgeous lush landscape, the rocks and the caves and waterfalls, but on the other hand, I am keen to avoid confrontation.

I steer the raft west and exchange the uncertainty of the coast for the safety of the ocean – but what does safety actually mean here? As long as I can still see land, I know that in the case of bad weather or an emergency, I will be able to reach the mainland and find people to help me. Further out, I may be safe from other people but I will also struggle with orientation problems, strong currents and the forces of nature. Still, overall when it comes to risk taking, I will favour nature over other people any day.

I certainly do not want to insinuate that the inhabitants of the Darién region are evil or bad, or even that anyone at all is inherently evil. I believe that every person is good at their core and that we are all the same. After all, we are all born naked and helpless, with a soul containing the seed for goodness. Until now, I have rarely had any problems with people on my journey. Rather, I have met good, helpful people everywhere I have been, and because of this the few negative experiences I have had have been all the more unexpected and frightening; and they have taught me to trust my gut feeling.

I learnt to read body language, and to closely observe my surroundings and react to signs of danger immediately. As a traveller you enter alien environments by default, and you will find that sometimes you are welcomed with open arms, and that sometimes you are not. I remember the time when I visited a village in the Mago National Park in Ethiopia – sometimes you get a feeling of mutual distrust from the off, and this was one of those instances.

My stay in Ethiopia, an especially fascinating country, was a long time ago now, back in the autumn of 2010, at the very beginning of my trip around the world. I had been travelling for a few hundred miles along a dusty track heading to the Omo valley, in order to visit the tribes of that region. I reached the Mago National Park at around noon. The entrance was blocked. As I came closer an armed soldier came out of his little guard house and told me that I would only be allowed to continue on my journey if I was accompanied by a soldier. My motorcycle was fully loaded, including two spare tyres which were traveling on the passenger seat. I told the soldier I would prefer to continue on my own, and that I had no space to carry a second person. Besides, I did not feel comfortable visiting the village with an armed escort at my side, as that way the people there would mistrust me straight away. More soldiers stepped outside and we discussed the situation until finally they gave in, but not without warning me:

"It is dangerous and some of the men are unpredictable and violent. But if you insist, the responsibility is yours."

The bumpy track was riddled with stones and holes, and about forty miles along it the first village of the Mursi appeared. The village was made up of simple straw huts; and the hub of community life took place in a large square. The entire community seemed to be out of doors. The people wore very few clothes; their bodies were painted with colourful patterns and covered with decorative scars. The women, who were naked from waist upward, wore clay plates in their lower lips; a very distinctive tradition; when a young girl becomes a woman, she cuts her lower lip open and begins to stretch it by inserting clay plates into it in increasingly larger sizes. So that the plates will sit without a wobble, women will often also remove their lower incisors.

The people greeted me and showed me the daily routine of life in the village. The women milled grain and cooked while the men were shooting the breeze, sitting in the shade of a large tree. I tried to talk to them as best as I could and was met with cordiality, which was not just friendliness but also a matter of commerce. Tourists were their only source of income. Each picture I took was carefully examined by the men, and the number of heads in it determined the price, at a rate of two *birr* per head.

While I talked to a group of men I noticed three younger men standing further apart from us. One of them was shouldering a rusty machine gun, and the other two held machetes in their hands. I had no idea what they were saying to one other, but I didn't like what I was seeing. I felt keenly that it was time to go. I thanked the villagers for their hospitality and took out my wallet to pay for the pictures. Once the payment was done I got on my motorcycle and started the engine. Suddenly, the three young men came running towards me and held on to the handlebars on both sides. They tried to turn off the motor, but luckily did not know how or where it was. The men threw me and Bruce off balance, and I was unable to ride off without falling. Thankfully the ringleader was still carrying his gun on his back and had not pointed it at me. He clearly did not expect me to put up any resistance – but that was where they were wrong.

As quick as lightning I folded down the side stands, jumped off the motorcycle and reached for my pepper spray, which I carried in an open pouch on my hip. Then I directed the spray can at the three men and shouted at them at the top of my voice. The two that had been holding on to Bruce ran off straight away and became part of the audience that stood further back and watched in silence. The leader stayed where he was. To protect myself from the spray, I pulled down the visor of my helmet. This had an unexpected effect on the rest of the tribesmen and immediately they ran off in all directions looking for cover.

The leader of the group, seemed startled but remained standing in front of me, with his machine gun, mercifully still strapped across his back. Even if he did not understand my words, he could still hear in my voice that I was holding a weapon and that I wasn't impressed by him. I held the spray can towards his face as I removed the AK47 from his shoulder, then I ordered him to march towards the houses. He complied, and as soon as he had turned around and walked a few yards I jumped back up onto Bruce and took off. The AK47 I discarded on the tracks a few hundred yards outside of the village.

The green mountain range shrunk, and soon it was nothing more than a line in the distance. I noticed that there was another advantage to rafting further out in the deeper waters. Near the coastline there is a lot of driftwood in the water, especially towards the evening as the light fades. The pieces of wood that have been in the water for the longest time are the hardest to notice. They lie just beneath the surface without any hint of danger. Often it was hard to evade them and when I did see them, always at the very last second, it was already too late. Each dull bang against the barrels made my heart sink: when would there be a tree that was harder than my rusty barrels? When would a piece of driftwood collide with my propeller and bend its blades?

I was glad to move away from the land and leave behind the driftwood and the handful of people along the coast. I returned to the vastness of the open Pacific as the land behind me disappeared into the fog.

The Sun put on a show-stopping performance that evening. The cloud formations on the horizon were lit up in every colour; red sunrays penetrating the clouds and touching the surface of the water. One beam after the other forced itself through the orange clouds. It was a real spectacle!

When the day exchanges shift with the night, something happens: the fishing line jerks! I get very excited and touch the line to check if it is just the waves causing the movement, but no – I can clearly feel a fish moving and I can even see it! Carefully I haul it in. It's a handsome sized fish, and I am rather proud of my second catch from the raft in more than five weeks.

"Oh, come on," I say to myself while I take the fish off the hook. "There is really no reason for you to be proud of your fishing abilities. This is only the second fish in five weeks of trying!" But then Dylan the advocate takes over and talks in my defence: "Yes, but the perseverance of casting out the line every single day regardless of every unsuccessful attempt, that's something to be proud of."

I often talk to myself out there on the raft, or to Bruce or to the *Courage of Bridget* – or to my video camera to chase away the loneliness.

Unlike on the previous occasion, the weather for my second catch is good and the sea calm. I begin to prepare the fish. I am determined not to let it spoil this time – I want to prepare it with care and savour the meal. Before I have finished cooking my beautiful fish curry, it gets dark completely and I realise that the mainland is not as far away as I had thought. I can see three tiny red lights on the horizon, which are probably lighthouses. I like seeing them – where there is light, there are people, and even if I choose to keep my distance from them today, it still feels good to know that I am not the only human being around.

After dinner I made some tea and continued to watch the three lights as they became smaller and smaller, and I enjoyed the starry sky above me as another wonderful day ended. Presently I corrected our course. I had made good progress today. It was only about fifty miles to Bahia Solano, the first city on the west coast of Colombia.

Slowly, my eyes begin to close. I set up my makeshift autopilot system and set the GPS alarm before I lay down in the hammock. I was not quite asleep when I noticed the sky illuminate faintly. I sat up and stared out into the horizon. It took a while, but then it happened again.

My hair stood on end as I realised what it is. Lightning!

Soon I saw that the clouds were gathering. It was a dreadful sight. I stood up and walked this way and that. There was more lightning, which revealed a solid black wall of clouds in the distance. The gathering storm clouds seemed to be darker than the very night itself. The storm was still far away, but for how long?

I wanted to find out from which direction the wind was blowing, and so I switched off the engine. Once the propeller was no longer pushing the raft forward, I could feel that the wind was coming from the direction of the coast and I was relieved. Let the wind blow that storm away from me!

But my disquiet returned when I saw that the waves were swelling from minute to minute, and that the lightning was becoming more frequent and moving towards me. Once again, I stopped the raft and checked the wind.

It was still blowing from the coast, so how was it possible that the dark clouds were headed my way? What should I do? Should I make for the coast and seek shelter?

I watched the three lights. According to the GPS, I was eight miles from the coast. I would need at least three hours to manage such a distance. Did I have that much time? And even if I did, would I find a sheltered bay where I could drop anchor? Would the breakers turn out to be as dangerous as the storm? Did László not tell me: land is your enemy? Hundreds of questions and thoughts were swirling in my head. I was frightened and hardly able to think straight and I struggled to make a decision. Suddenly, the three lights in the distance began to flicker. They disappeared for a while and then they reappeared. The intervals between their switching on and off were erratic. What was going on there? Soon I realised that the rising waves were obstructing my view of the coast. Without thinking I changed course and headed towards the mainland. I accelerated as much as I could. Again and again, I looked over my shoulder to see how close the storm was.

Suddenly the engine began to stutter, Bruce began to overheat and I began to panic. After that first storm I knew what was in store for me, and now that Bruce was giving up the ghost, I really was terrified.

"I knew it!" I shout into the night. "I shouldn't have caught the fish! The fish brings bad luck! I am sorry, fish! I am sorry I stole from you ocean! I'm sorry, but please don't let the storm come my way."

I am beside myself. Then common sense returns.

"What are you saying? Pull yourself together, fool! You have no time to lose. You need water to cool down the engine so that it will stop stuttering. Quick!"

I take the empty water canister and hold it underwater until it is full up. Then I place the canister on Bruce's saddle and attach the two hoses to either side of the engine so that the water will run down on to the cylinders. I invented this system a few days ago and I am grateful that it seems to be working. Oh God there is lightning ahead of me. I look up and see black clouds ahead of the bow. This cannot be happening! Is there a second storm coming from the coast?

"Shit! Now I am lost!"

I press buttons on the GPS and see that the raft has turned by 180 degrees while I was filling up the canister and installing the cooling system. I am headed towards the storm, and away from the coast, and at full speed! I sprint to the back of the raft and move the tiller to the port side, then wait for the raft to react. I try to orientate myself on the lights of the coast, but where are they? In the darkness, all I can see is the lightning that illuminates the night.

Suddenly, I can see the lights again. They are ahead of me about

30 degrees to the left! Good! I no longer care what those lights actually are, I just want land. The wind is whistling in my ears, the waves are getting higher and higher. Now I can feel that the direction of the wind has changed. It is coming from my back and bringing the storm with it. I no longer dare to look over my shoulder. Over my head, I can still see the stars. But for how much longer?

"I should not have caught that fish! I should not have caught that fish!" I shout into the wind.

"Dylan! Since when are you so superstitious? How does one fish cause a storm? Every day, millions of fish are caught. According to your logic, every fishing boat would be caught in a storm whenever they reel in a catch? Do you really think that you're in trouble because of a fish? Do you think you're so important that storms happen, just because of you? It's coincidence that you caught a fish before a storm! COINCIDENCE!"

I try to calm down but the lightning is close, and the thunder becomes more frequent. The sky is rumbling and the waves too. The dinghy bounces up and down behind the *Courage of Bridget*. My fear increases.

"Dylan! Focus! It's a long way to the coast. Come on, keep going! All will be well."

Soon the clouds overtake me. The stars above me begin to disappear, and then I feel the first drops of rain. At first, they are small and harmless, but soon they pelt hard against the deck. The waves ebb and flow in the darkness. As the rain becomes even stronger and more and more lightning flashes, I decide that it is time to turn off the engine, so as not to attract a lightning strike. I disconnect the battery from Bruce and throw out my sea anchor to stabilise the raft. Soon, the *Courage of Bridget* turns and faces the wind, the waves and the terrifying picture of the storm that is illuminated by the lightning. I put on my life vest and stretch the tarp over me and Bruce. Then I begin to talk to him to assuage his fear. A storm at night turns out to be even more frightening than a storm during daylight. Wind and rain whip the tarp, and my only wish is to switch off my brain. I do not want to think about anything anymore! But I am not in control of my mind. Images drift past me. I did have a beautiful life. It was not always easy, but if I had the chance, I would do it all over again. Many of my dreams have come true and I enjoyed many liberties. I regret nothing. Just one wish remains: to be with the people that I love, just one more time. I see their beautiful smiling faces before me. I want to tell them that I love them, have always loved them. In my mind, I relive the moments of the past, as if I were watching a film in my head. The film of my life. Finally, I see Bruce and myself, and the many places we have visited, the landscapes, the people.

The raft hits the water's surface, hard, and brings me back to reality. I am exhausted; I can barely keep my eyes open and do not even try. I do not want to see the lightning anymore, nor do I want to feel the wild jolts of the raft, nor hear the shrieking wind. I try to calm myself down and switch off my senses, and this time I somehow seem to manage it.

I see the boy from the beach in Colombo. This time, he is not with me on the raft but holding the hand of a man who is walking along a road. It is a beautiful day and the sky is blue. The narrow, unpaved road leads through a tea plantation. I look around and see carefully tended lush green tea bushes everywhere. They cover the rolling hills as far as the eye can see, stretching all the way to the horizon. It's a magnificent view. The road meanders up the hills and becomes a network; an invitation to lose yourself amongst the fields.

"Hey!" I call to the boy. "Hey! Where are you going?" He does not answer, but holds on to the hand of the man and purposefully moves away from me, further and further. I call again, this time louder, "Hey! Don't you want to go to the beach with me? We can build a raft! What do you think?"

Finally, the boy turns around. He looks at me and smiles. "No, I can't. One raft is enough for me," he says. "It was fun. But now I need to go with daddy."

I nod and smile. My eyes follow the tea bushes until I can no longer distinguish them from horizon. The Sun beats down on me and the sky is blue.

I wake up still lying on Bruce with my head resting on the tank. I sit up and rub my eyes, stretch out my aching back and try to find my bearings.

Where am I? Why am I sleeping on top of Bruce? I find that I am still wearing the life vest. Slowly, my memory returns. The storm! I peek out from underneath the sheet and to my great relief I see a clear blue sky. It looks like a beautiful sunny day: the storm is over! I have survived my second storm! As I process this information, I feel life returning to each cell of my body. What a feeling! I am still tired but I have to get up, keep going, and move forward. I am alive!

When I creep out from underneath the tarpaulin, I see land. So far, so good. I wonder where the storm has taken me this time. I connect the battery and connect the GPS to Bruce. It takes a while for the map and our location to show up on the display. We seem to have drifted off towards the north, but only by a couple of miles. I haul the old tyre back on deck and start the engine. I position the rudders in such a way that the *Courage of Bridget* is headed back towards the coast. I feel the wind in my face and the Sun on my skin and I am deeply grateful for having made it through the night.

A little while later, I see blue smoke coming from somewhere in Bruce. What is going on? I inspect the engine and see what has caused the smoke. No! Can this be happening? I look closer and hear a hissing sound, and see more smoke coming up. Another problem! The sight glass of the oil level indicator has ruptured. Black, viscous drops seep through the crack and land with a 'hiss' on the hot exhaust pipe. This is not good! I switch the motor off and seal the glass with some silicone. Then I dip the corner of a cloth into some petrol and begin to clean the oil smeared glass.

As soon as I touch it, it splinters into a thousand pieces.

"Great! Now I've broken it completely!"

After surviving two storms, even this does not fluster me anymore. The sight glass is made of plastic, not glass, as I had thought. The petrol has triggered a chemical reaction and the oil runs out. There is more hissing and smoke from the motor, and more sighs from me. Damn! How can I go on like this? The motor will barely run for thirty seconds without oil, and without a motor and no wind, my chances of continuing my journey are almost zero.

All of a sudden I feel that my raft adventure is over. Bruce is telling me that he cannot go on anymore, and now all of a sudden I also remember last night's dream: the boy had had enough of the raft and left.

However, I could not just stay out here; I needed to move from this point somehow. I was a few miles from the coast. In the distance I could see an antenna; perhaps it was a military base or a village. I seemed to be able to make out a few houses as well. Instinctively I switched on my walkie-talkie and searched for channel 16.

It was time to ask for help.

"Hello, this is the *Courage of Bridget*. Can anyone hear me? Please answer." I try for half an hour. "Mayday, this is the *Courage of Bridget*. My motor is broken and I need help. My position is 7 degrees, 0 minutes, 58 seconds north. 77 degrees, 50 minutes, 20 seconds west. Please answer."

Nothing. No answers. I try over and over, but the walkie-talkie remains silent. All I can hear are the seagulls screeching at each other.

The more time I spend waiting for an answer, the further I drift away from the antenna and the village. I have to help myself, I have to try something. Frantically I go to my tool box and rummage around in it. I look for something in the right size to plug the hole in the engine. There are a lot of bits and pieces in the box. Finally, I find a small round metal disc, which in reality is a valve shim from a car engine. I hold it up in front of the hole. Ah! A perfect fit! I am glad I carried all these seemingly useless parts around with me.

Normally most of these little things that accompanied me on a trip around the world would be useless for fixing a motorcycle, but all it needed was a little creativity. I had been able to mend many things with very few resources, such as my tent, the gasoline stove, zippers, the GPS device, my camera, the board computer and most commonly Bruce. Many times I had also helped other motorists with all kinds of problems. The bits and pieces that I carried around with me as spare parts came in handy dozens and dozens of times. I enjoyed helping people – you could even say I did it purely for selfish reasons. Whenever I help someone, it makes me happy and I always get some positive energy from it.

The metal disc was a good start. I pushed it into the hole and sealed it with silicone. There was no time to wait until it was completely dry, as the ocean kept pulling me further and further away from the settlement. After only twenty minutes, I topped up the motor with the oil that Fabio had given me at the Tropic Star Lodge and started Bruce.

He seemed to be running well, but for how long would my make-shift solution last? I had to get back to land as soon as possible and then decide what to do next. I did not even know what other options I had. After what seemed to be an eternity, I got closer to the coast but soon realised that I would not be able to land there. Once again, the enormous breakers stood in my way. That last mile between me and civilisation was an almost insurmount-able obstacle. I ran my eyes along the coast and spied a little bay further north, with what seemed to be a ship lying at anchor, probably at a distance of about four miles. It looked promising. I steered towards it and kept a close eye on the engine. The slow-ness of the raft was unbearable.

The picture became clearer as we moved closer and I soon saw that what I thought was a ship, was in fact a building. But still, the bay would make for a good shelter. I could see a pretty little village behind a long white beach. There were a handful of wooden houses on stilts, and between them two brick houses. I could also see that there were some soldiers on the beach, but they quickly withdrew behind the thick foliage.

What was expecting me here? I had crossed the border with an illegal raft without any registration papers – after all, where would I have been able to get an entry stamp out on the ocean? But: What will the soldiers make of that? I decided to be proactive, just like I had been in San Miguel, and appeal to them for help. I dropped anchor and rowed ashore in the dinghy. I walked along the beach, meeting a few curious children along the way before I saw the soldiers at the southern end of the village. They had set up a temporary camp there – a few tents, a hut and even a makeshift gym. I counted twelve men in all and they all had very young looking faces.

I started a dialogue with them.

"¡Hola amigos! ¿Como estas?" Hi friends! How are you doing?

The commander, a chubby man of about 30 years old came up and introduced himself as Vladimir. He was friendly and curious and spoke a little English. I told him what I was doing there and stressed that the engine of my raft was damaged. Vladimir and his soldiers were not concerned about my missing papers. Instead, they invited me to eat with them. As we sat at the large communal table, Vladimir told me that about five miles from here there was a larger settlement.

"The town is called Jurado and has a population of 5,000 inhabitants. Bigger than anywhere else around these parts. Once a week, a cargo ship leaves from Jurado to Buenaventura. I think that would be the way for you to go. There is no other infrastructure."

"And where are we here? What is this village called?" I ask.

"Ardita," says Vladimir.

"Ardita. That's a pretty name! Can you drive from here to Jurado?"

Vladimir laughs. "No! There are no roads. This is still the jungle of Darién. The villages here are cut off from the rest of Colombia and from each other. There isn't even a footpath leading from here to Jurado"

Later I rowed back to the raft to spend some time ruminating. What should I do? Was this really the end? I checked my repair work. Already a tiny drop of oil had made its way to the surface through the silicone layer. I had not managed to fix the damage completely. Just like that little drop of oil forced its way out of the engine, the truth forced its way into my consciousness.

My raft adventure was over.

"Enough is enough," Bruce seems to be telling me.

"You are quite right," I answer. "It is time for our adventure on the ocean to end."

I feel that this is the right decision, but the thought of prematurely ending this wonderful journey becomes unbearably painful. I have a lump in my throat and I am fighting against the tears. I close my eyes and feel a pain in my chest. Eventually I cannot hold back any longer and I cry unashamedly. The emotion of the last few weeks is overwhelming me all at once. This has been the most intense period of my life. I have felt terrible fear and immense joy. I cannot imagine what it would be like to travel on without the *Courage of Bridget*. I made her with my own hands, and now I will have to take her apart.

"I will have to leave you behind! I am sorry," I tell her. "How wonderful was our journey! What glorious things we have seen! A once-in-a-lifetime adventure. I thank you for carrying me over the waves! Thank you for protecting me." I talk to her until it gets dark. It feels as if all three of us, Bruce, the *Courage of Bridget* and I, were grieving.

I lie in my hammock, listening to the sound of the waves and enjoying the gentle swaying of the raft. I lay my hand against one of the bamboo masts, and feel the cool smooth wood. With the other hand I hold on to Bruce. Bruce and the *Courage of Bridget*, my two faithful travel companions. I can hear voices in the distance, and the laughter of the children of Ardita. Then the stars appear faintly in the blue sky, and gradually they become brighter. I feel the *Courage of Bridget* pulsing; I feel her heartbeat against my palms. Then, sleep overpowers me.

Some people forget they were mere dreams and follow them until they become reality.

The end of an adventure: With the help of soldiers I bring the *Courage of Bridget* to land.

EPILOGUE

~

The day after my arrival in Ardita, I brought the *Courage of Bridget* ashore. Steering her through the breakers and having her run aground on the beach was the last dangerous task remaining. To my relief, the soldiers were waiting for us in the sand. They helped pull her onto the beach and detached Bruce. Within two hours, he had gone back to being a roadworthy motorcycle. I took him for a spin on the white sandy beach of Ardita; he was the first motorcycle ever to touch that sand.

We carried the *Courage of Bridget* to the upper end of the beach; her deathbed. I hoped the villagers would help themselves to her parts and give them a second life. The anchor, the sail, the lamp, the canisters, all the ropes and any other sailing material I gave to the fishermen of Ardita.
At the beach I burned the bamboo deck – the stage of my entire world for six weeks – and then the mast.

I stayed for another week in Ardita and enjoyed the hospitality of the villagers and the soldiers. I ate more cashew nuts than ever before in my life. The people of Ardita did not know that the nuts hidden inside the fruit that fell from the trees were edible. I love cashews and could not bear to see them rot on the sand, uneaten. I repaired many broken things for the soldiers during my stay and I saw for myself why they were stationed there as one day the village was attacked by rebels. I spoke to the villagers and the soldiers about their lives at the edge of the jungle and heard stories that would fill another book.

Then came the day of my departure. We loaded Bruce onto a small wonky boat and sailed to Jurado. There he and I were loaded onto a small cargo ship along with thousands of coconuts and taken to Buenaventura. From there, we went to Bogotá and I flew back home to Switzerland on my own.

Since my return I have lived and worked in Switzerland, but six months later I went back to Colombia to continue my journey with Bruce all the way down to Argentina. From Buenos Aires, Bruce and I returned to Switzerland where he now enjoys a well-earned retirement.

After such a long journey returning to normal life can be hard. The clocks that I hadn't seen for three years started to set the rhythm for my life once again. I began see my new daily routine as just another challenge. And thanks to the friends all over the world whom I got to know, I always feel as if I am travelling. I have met so many wonderful people in so many different countries! I am always happy to hear from them, or even be able to repay their hospitality.

However, there is also sad news. After a long battle with cancer Thushari died in the spring of 2014 in the arms of my Mother. Before her death, Thushari also had to experience the death of both her parents and her two sisters; an unimaginable tragedy! Once again I am reminded of how fragile life truly is. I find some comfort in the fact that I have been able to go to Alaska for her, to see her dream destination and show her the pictures which made her very happy.

Since the summer of 2014, there has been a regular ferry service between Panama and Colombia; so from now on no biker will have to build a raft in order to overcome the Darién Gap.

I managed to track down László after about two years of silence.

László and Isabella left Panama a couple of months after I had ended my raft adventure, headed in the direction of the South Pacific. One day they were pounced on by a team of French Navy forces assisted by a helicopter and a warship.

László wrote to me that 'there were mean looking soldiers and they grabbed me and chained me to the superstructure of their ship and sailed 125 miles at full throttle to an island'.

On the island they prepared him for extradition to Hungary. But later László was somehow able to convince the French authorities that the Hungarian authorities had unjustly and wrongly accused him, and changed his status from a witness to the accused. Subsequently the French let László go free. Since then he's been enjoying his 'freedom' and is looking forward to becoming a father soon.

Jacques too has left Panama for an unknown destination. But he has also found the love of his life: an opera singer. They both seem to have found a compromise: Their home is still a boat but this time a very spacious yacht which includes two toilets!

Unfortunately there has been no news from Lionel.

One day, I found an email in my inbox from Jeff. I had not heard from him since our meeting 18 months earlier. He wrote:

Hi Dylan,
It's me, Jeff. Do you still remember me? I am the guy with the world map on his shower curtain! How are you doing? I have bought myself a plane ticket to Australia. I'll buy a motorcycle there and will travel around for a few months. Got any tips for me?

I could not hold back my tears.

More information to Dylan's
adventures, updates & photos at:
www.ride2xplore.com
www.facebook.com/ride2xplore/

There is a **live multimedia presentation**
to Dylan's rafting adventure and world travels.
If you are interested either in booking the show or seeing
it, please visit our website for dates or contact us by mail:
info@ride2xplore.com.

ACKNOWLEDGMENTS

My thanks first of all to Jacques, László and Lionel, who have helped me so much with the building of my raft! Even if your names (and a few others) were changed: you know who you are. Thank you to Ron and Christina for putting me in touch with my three pirates.

Thank you, Greg, for telling me about the Darién Gap. My thanks to Commander Pedro Villarreal and Raúl Sanchez (not their real names) for their sense of adventure and for turning a blind eye when I most needed it.

An enormous thank you goes around the world! During three years of travelling the world, I have encountered too many people to mention them all by name. My thanks collectively to all of them, and no less heartfelt because of it. Thank you for your hospitality, your help, your friendship and the support I have received from you. You have shown me that I was right to depend upon the kindness of strangers. Without these encounters, my trip would not have been half as good. You will always be in my heart.

Last but not least, a great shout-out to all those who helped to make this book possible and who lent their skills and time to our project. Thank you, Silvia Lehmann, Sabine Leuba, Claudia Walder, Pia Walder and Fabian Leuenberger.

A special thanks for the English Edition goes to Susanne Wagner, Katherine L Ryan, Casey Cheuvront and the fellow adventurer Stephen Baker. You are all great!